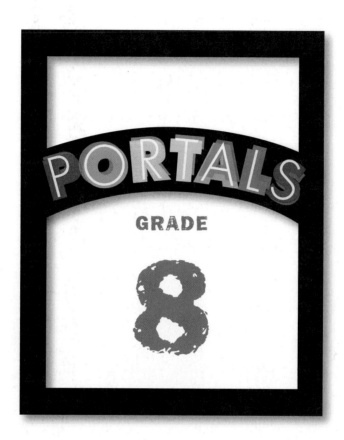

PORTALS

GRADE

8

PORTALS

GRADE

8

HOUGHTON MIFFLIN HARCOURT
School Publishers

Opening Up New Worlds

People ask me,

"Where do you come from?"

But they never bother to ask,

"Where are you going?"

You're about to enter *Portals*. This step will open up many new worlds to you. As you study, you'll have a lot of help, but you'll be the one keeping track of the progress you are making. You'll ask and answer questions. You'll decide how you will respond to opportunties. Those decisions are yours, after all. So, where *are* you going?

Recognizing Words

This is a must. Once your know how to identify and pronounce the words you read, you're well on your way. In *Portals*, the pieces of the word puzzle will start to fit together. For example, you'll learn which sound is most likely for a group of letters that has several possible sounds. You'll also learn how to break up very long words in ways that make it easy to pronounce them.

new Moon   waxing crescent   first-quarter M
                    Moon

Does the
Moon Really
Change Shape?

FOCUS Why does the shape of the Moon
the sky?

hat shape is the Moon? So
a shape like a circle or a b
"D" or "C." Sometimes, it look
epends on the day you look at the
It is the Sun that lights the Moo
ts own light. It **reflects** light from
he Moon when sunlight bounces off
The Moon **revolves** slowly a
th around the Earth
don't colli

What is the Moon?

The Moon is a natural **satellite**. That means it is a body that is in **orbit**. The Moon **revolves**, or moves around, **planet** Earth. Earth's **gravity** pulls the Moon toward our planet. Therefore, the Moon does not float away into space. If gravity
we in
some ti
movem
pull of
Moon
Togeth
Earth's

How does the Moon look up close?

The Moon looks bright and shiny from down here. It does not look like that up close. Up close, it looks rather plain and boring. There is no life on the Moon. Plants and animals cannot survive. It is all a dull, pale brown color. Rocks and dust are everywhere.

Look closely at the Moon. You can see big, dark **patches** on its surface. People used to think these dark patches were big seas or oceans. Later, scientists found that they are areas that used to be covered with **lava**. That lava is now hard rock.

What are craters?

The surface of the Moon is covered with **craters**. These craters were formed long ago. Big and small **asteroids** **collided** with the Moon. This made craters. An asteroid is a rock that orbits the sun. Craters on the Moon can be tiny

Look closely at the Moon. You can see big, dark **patches** on its surface. People used to think these dark patches were big seas or oceans. Later, scientists

The Moon has big rocks.

satellite Any object that revolves around a planet or other larger object.
lava Very hot, melted rock.

asteroid A piece of rock in space.

137

Vocabulary

Learning vocabulary is like so many other things—doing it just once won't make it stick in your mind. When you came to class on the first day of school, you were probably told everyone's name. You didn't remember them all right away, but after a week or so, you did! Learning new words takes a while, too. In *Portals*, you'll have many experiences with each new word. You'll read them, hear them, and work with them in stories, poems, articles, and cartoons. Before you know it, the words—a lot of them—will be yours! You'll own them.

TEKS • 1.A RECOGNIZE WORDS. • 1.B CONFIRM PRONUNCIATIONS AND MEANINGS. • 2.A EXPAND VOCABULARY. • 2.B DETERMINE MEANING THROUGH CONTEXT. • 2.C USE WORD SKILLS TO UNDERSTAND MEANINGS. • 2.D DETERMINE MEANINGS AND PRONUNCIATIONS. • 2.E IDENTIFY WORD RELATIONSHIPS. • 3.A READ SILENTLY. • 3.B ADJUST READING RATE. • 3.C READ ORALLY.

Fluency

You want fluency! It's a reading skill that is important whether you're reading silently or out loud. Fluency is all about reading accurately, getting each word right. It's also about using expression, speaking softly or loudly, sounding excited or sad. Fluency is also rate—how fast or how slowly you read. That will depend on what you're reading. For example, you'll probably read difficult text more slowly, and fun stories more quickly. *Portals* will help you read accurately, with appropriate expression, and at a suitable rate. (You'll also be keeping track of your reading rate as you go through *Portals*.)

Selection **3**

from **Home of** ____
by Katherine Applegate

FOCUS: What would it be like to move somewhere that is different in every way from your homeland?

Kek comes from an African country torn by war. He has lost most of his family. He is brought to the United States to live with his aunt and his cousin Ganwar. Dave, an American man, helps him get settled. Now all Kek has to do is fit in—somehow!

This story is told as a series of poems. As Kek's words show, things that are ordinary to you can seem very strange to a newcomer.

Snow

When the flying boat
returns to earth at last,
I open my eyes
and **gaze** out the round window.
What is all the white? I whisper.
Where is all the world?

The helping man greets me
and there are many lines and questions
and pieces of paper.

At last I follow him outside.
We call that snow, he says.
Isn't it beautiful?
Do you like the cold?

I want to say
No, this cold is like claws on my skin!
I look around me.
Dead grass pokes through
the unkind blanket of white.

176 ▸ DAY 8

I like the way the <u>surface</u> of the water <u>reflects</u> the <u>patches</u> of light.

ELPS • 2.C LEARN NEW EXPRESSIONS AND VOCABULARY THROUGH LISTENING. • 2.D MONITOR UNDERSTANDING OF SPOKEN LANGUAGE. • 2.G UNDERSTAND SPOKEN LANGUAGE. • 2.H UNDERSTAND IMPLICIT IDEAS IN SPOKEN LANGUAGE. • 2.I DEMONSTRATE LISTENING COMPREHENSION. • 3.D INTERNALIZE VOCABULARY THROUGH SPEAKING. • 3.E SHARE INFORMATION IN COOPERATIVE LEARNING INTERACTIONS. • 4.C DEVELOP BASIC SIGHT VOCABULARY.

Purposes for Reading

There are countless things to read and many reasons to read them. Suppose you're looking for information. You might read a nonfiction book or a newspaper. If you're reading for entertainment, you might pick a novel or short story. If you want to solve a problem, you might first try using a search engine on the Internet. Knowing what you want to get from your reading will help you choose what to read and how to read it.

TEKS • 6.A READ FOR VARIOUS PURPOSES. • 6.B READ SOURCES. • 6.C USE VISUAL REPRESENTATIONS. • 4.A USE PRIOR KNOWLEDGE AND EXPERIENCE. • 4.B DETERMINE PURPOSE FOR READING. • 4.C SELF-MONITOR READING AND ADJUST. • 4.D SUMMARIZE TEXTS. • 4.E MAKE INFERENCES. • 4.F ANALYZE AND USE TEXT STRUCTURES. • 4.G MAKE CONNECTIONS ACROSS TEXTS. • 4.H CONSTRUCT VISUAL IMAGES. • 4.I DETERMINE IMPORTANT IDEAS. • 4.J MANAGE TEXT. • 4.K USE QUESTIONING TO ENHANCE COMPREHENSION.

Comprehension

There are a lot of reading skills to learn, but don't be put off. You probably know most of these skills already, even if you don't know their names.

- You turn the door handle, open the door, and walk outside. The order in which things happen is called *sequence*. First you turn the door handle, then you open the door. . . well, you get the idea.

- It starts to rain. The street gets wet. That's called *cause and effect*. The rain is the cause. The wet street is the effect.

- While you wait for the school bus, you tell your friend the story of the movie you saw yesterday. Maybe you didn't know that you just gave a *summary*, but you did.

You'll apply your comprehension skills throughout *Portals*. You'll find out that authors don't always present things the way you might find them in real life. Events may not be written in order, or an effect may be described before you know its cause. *Portals* will help you put all the pieces of the comprehension puzzle together. Comprehension means understanding, and that's the big idea when you read!

ELPS • 3.G EXPRESS OPINIONS, IDEAS, AND FEELINGS. • 3.H NARRATE, DESCRIBE, AND EXPLAIN. • 4.G DEMONSTRATE COMPREHENSION OF TEXT. • 4.I. EMPLOY BASIC READING SKILLS. • 4.J EMPLOY INFERENTIAL SKILLS. • 4.K EMPLOY ANALYTICAL SKILLS.

RELATIVE SIZE OF THE SUN AND PLANETS

JUPITER   SATURN   URANUS   NEPTUNE

Finding Information

It's the twenty-first century, and finding information is easier than ever. Even so, you need to ask the right questions to get the right answers. *Portals* will help you come up with the right questions and find the right sources for the information you want. You'll use diagrams and charts to understand complicated ideas easily. You'll even be asked to watch television programs and videos as parts of your research! You'll also have plenty of practice presenting the information you find to other people.

Evaluating Credibility

As you research various topics, you'll want to know whether you can trust your sources. *Portals* will help you figure out how trustworthy a source is, especially on the Internet. You'll also learn how writers can try to persuade you. (Sometimes they do it for a good cause, but not always!)

You'll also discover when an argument that sounds reasonable shouldn't convince you. Here's an example:

My cat catches mice.
Squeaky is a mouse.
So, my cat will catch Squeaky.

It sounds right, but it isn't.
We'll tell you why it isn't right.

Responding to Text

After you've read something, then what? Often you'll be asked whether or not you liked what you read, but you'll also be asked why. *Portals* will help you discuss and write about what you've read. You'll use your own knowledge and experience to support your responses, and you'll also quote and give details from texts.

Connections

The reading selections in *Portals* cover a lot of different topics and styles. In many of them, you'll find events that relate to your own experiences or those of your friends. You'll see how many different cultures have the same kinds of stories. As you learn about other cultures, you'll see what they have in common with your own culture. You'll understand the world better, and you'll understand your place in it better, too.

- 7.B RESPOND TO TEXT. • 7.C SUPPORT RESPONSES. •
- 9.A COMPARE TEXT EVENTS WITH EXPERIENCES. •
- 9.B RECOGNIZE THEMES AND CONNECTIONS THAT CROSS CULTURES.

Selection 1

THE CROW AND THE WATER JUG

a fable adapted by Eve Rice

FOCUS: How can starting small help y

Crow has a **task** *that may be too big! So she will s will get done.*

One day thirsty Crow came upon a wate
"Now I will have a drink," she the
She put her beak in the jug, but
could not get a drink.
So she reached farther in. She flap
her neck.
But still she could not get a single drop to drink.
"I know," she thought. "I'll turn the jug over on its side." And
then she pushed with all her might.
But no matter how she tried, the jug still stood upright.

from the Plains Indian Museum
r settled hers
ny years a
nerat

The lessons and the selections in *Portals* go together in a way that makes sense. The pieces have all been put together.

Portals will help you get to where you're going.

TABLE OF CONTENTS

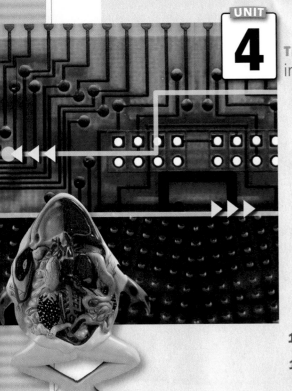

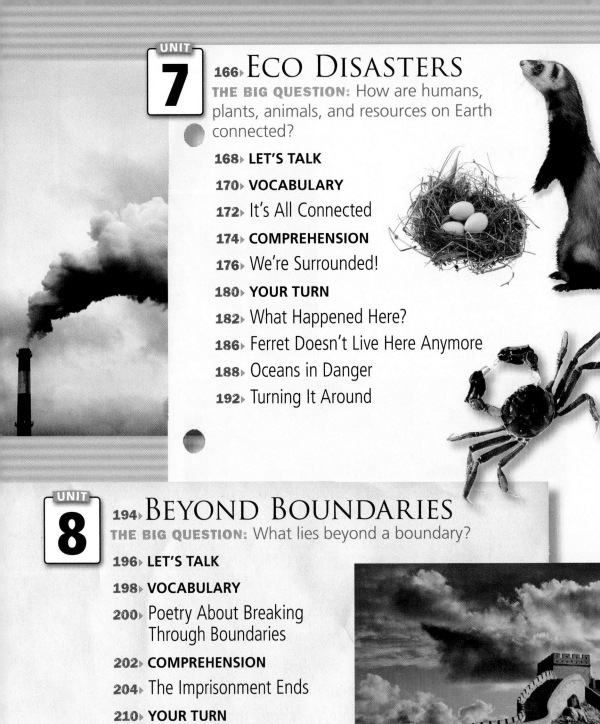

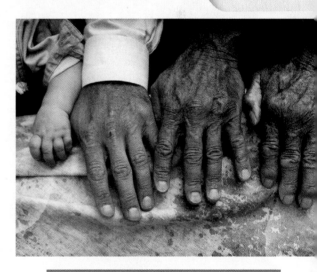

HORIZONS

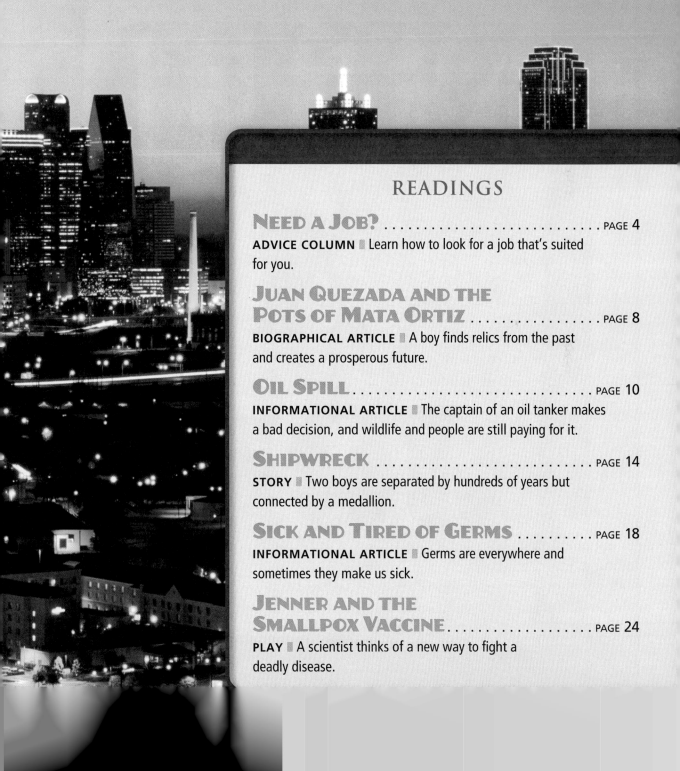

READINGS

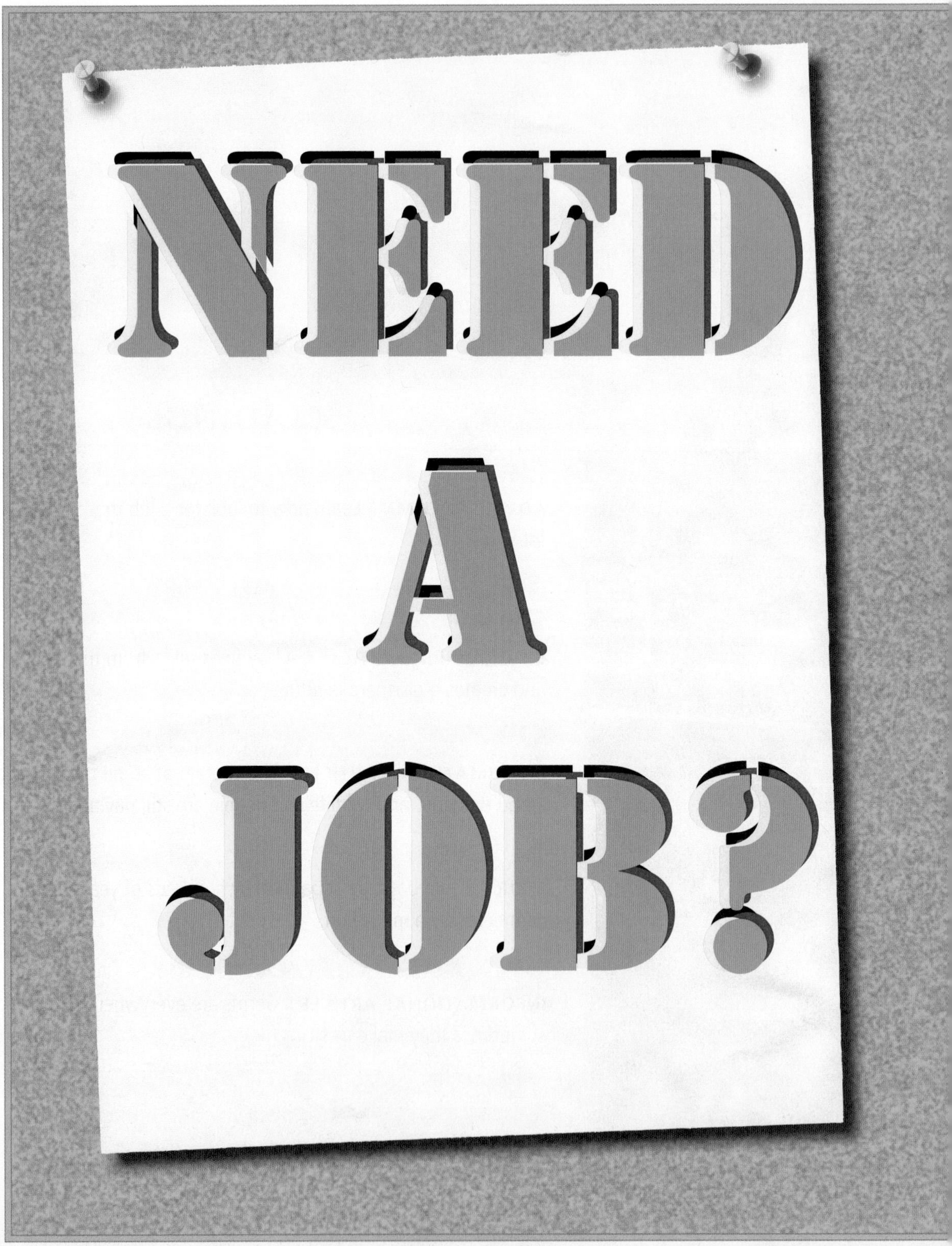
NEED
A
JOB?

- -

Check the listings! Your school may have job ads listed on a job board. In newspapers and online, there is a space just for jobs in the classified ads. Read them to see what's available. Then pick the job that fits you best.

For some jobs, you will need to work well in a team. For others, you will be working by yourself. Some jobs will be permanent, while some may not last long. Some jobs may take place inside. Others will be outside in fresh air. Which job would be best for you?

Computer Wiz

I need your computer skills! I need help checking my e-mail and searching the Web. I will pay $25 a week. You also get limited access to my pool.

Interviews will take place at my home, 23 Spain Road, at 4:00 P.M. all next week. Hope you can make it!

REREAD

Problem/Solution

What is this person's problem?

5

Bike Ride

My son has a bike, but doesn't know how to ride it. I am afraid he will hurt himself. I need someone to help him stay safe and have fun.

I will pay $10 an hour. Call me at 555-0807.

Best Pets

We need help at **Best Pets**. You will be responsible for:

- feeding

- grooming

- walking

We pay well!

See us at 57 Pine Road at 2:00 P.M. on Sat.!

Tune Town has the best jobs!

We will be **hiring** next week. Do not let this one slip by! Pop, jazz, swing, hip-hop … We've got it all! We need people like you to sell, **ship**, file, and shop for CDs.

Call us at **555-6234**.

JEANS, JEANS, JEANS

Get paid to look at jeans in a magazine! Rate each pair on a scale of 1 to 10. This job pays $25 a day and lasts six weeks. We'll ship you the jeans you like best as a bonus!

See us at Jeans, Jeans, Jeans
Sky Mall, West Wing

Job Checklist

When you apply for a job, you're probably not the only one. So how do you show that you are the best person for the job? Use this checklist when you go on a job interview.

- Do not be late.
- Make eye contact when speaking.
- Answer questions as well as you can.
- Ask a lot of questions.
- Think about your skills. Explain why you can do the job well.
- Smile!

■ ■ ■ STOP AND THINK

1. What are two ways to categorize jobs?

2. What job is good for you?

JUAN QUEZADA
and the
POTS *of* MATA ORTIZ

FOCUS: How can you take something you love to do and make it into a career?

A boy named Juan Quezada often walked the hills near the village of Mata Ortiz, Mexico, looking for firewood for his family. All around were scraps of pottery. These were the remains from a people who had disappeared from the area at least 500 years before.

One day when he was about 13, Quezada found a pot in a cave. It was not broken! It was beautiful. Quezada was fascinated and inspired. He guessed the materials to make the pot must have come from nearby. Maybe he could find them and make his own pottery. He began to experiment. He made pots using different soils. He tried different ways of forming and shaping the pots. He discovered new ways to make natural paints and paintbrushes. One time he used a brush made from children's hair!

At first Quezada copied the old designs. But soon he made his own. He was teaching himself to be a potter and an artist. He began to sell a few pots. He gave a couple to some salesmen. The salesmen took them to New Mexico. They traded the pots for clothes in a place called "Bob's Swap Shop."

One day, Spencer MacCallum walked into that shop. MacCallum was an anthropologist and art collector. He saw the pots. Right away, he knew they were special. "It's as if they stood up on their hind legs and they shouted at me, 'Look at us, we're made by someone who knows who he is,'" he said.

MacCallum went to find the man who made the pots. Quezada was now 36 years old. He had been working to improve the pots for more than half his life. MacCallum and Quezada made an agreement. Quezada quit his regular job. Now he could concentrate on making pots. MacCallum took the pots to museums and stores. Before long, Quezada's work was in great demand. His pots are collected all around the world.

Quezada wanted more. He wanted to help his village. "I remembered a proverb my mother used to say: 'You don't give a fish to the needy; you teach them how to fish.'" Quezada taught his brother and sisters how to make pots. Then he taught other people in the village. Each became an artist in his or her own right.

Today, the village of Mata Ortiz is full of artists. Collectors and tourists travel there. If they are lucky, they meet the man who started it all, the living legend, Juan Quezada.

Juan Quezada makes pots in the Mexican tradition.

■■■ STOP AND THINK

1. What inspired Quezada to become a potter?

2. What does Quezada's mother's proverb mean?

Oil Spill

FOCUS: What are the consequences of a single bad choice?

On March 23, 1989, the captain of a large oil tanker called the *Exxon Valdez* made a bad choice. He left his crew alone.

Earlier that night, the ship had left Alaska loaded with oil and set out for California.

Not long after, the captain and his crew noticed big chunks of ice floating in the boat's pathway. Huge ice chunks can sink a ship if the ship hits them. The captain steered his ship off its path so that it wouldn't hit the ice.

Then he made an awful choice. He told his crew to steer the ship back to its original path when they had passed the ice, and he left!

But his crew didn't turn the boat back as they were supposed to. A bit after 12 A.M., the ship hit a reef.

Quite a few ships hit reefs, but this wasn't just any ship. It had 53,000,000 gallons of crude oil inside its hull. Most fuel is made from oil. That much oil could drive a car to the sun and back five times!

The reef cut a deep hole in the ship's side. Oil gushed from this hole. The oil slick went on for miles and miles, spoiling the deep blue sea and wrecking the fragile coast.

A clean-up crew at work

Wildlife at risk

Before the oil spill, this area was filled with wildlife. Sadly, the oil killed much of this sea life. It killed plants, such as kelp. It killed sea birds, such as ducks and gulls. Birds flew by and then landed in a sea of oil. It stuck to them like glue, and few made it back up. Fish floated belly up, poisoned. Whales got sick and died. Oil coated the pelts of otters and seals, killing them as well.

REREAD

Cause ➕ Effect

How did the oil spill change the area?

Quite a few men and women joined in to help clean up the mess. They helped stop the oil gushing from the ship's side. But by this point, 11,000,000 gallons had spilled. People threw in nets and scooped oil off the top of the sea. They burned oil off with fire and cleaned the water with soap. They cleaned shores and beaches as well. These men and women cleaned up as much as they could.

Today, we can visit this site and enjoy its wildlife once more. But it still hasn't fully recovered from that bad choice made on March 23, 1989.

STOP AND THINK

1. What accident caused the oil spill?
2. Who do you think should take responsibility for the oil spill?

Shipwreck

FOCUS: How can a shipwreck 250 years ago affect someone living today?

It is 1750, somewhere off the coast of Assateague Island.
A Spanish ship, La Galga, *is fighting through a storm.*

The wave crashed right over the deck. Felipe clung to the rail with both hands. His body trembled from cold and fear. The waves had soaked his heavy clothes. The wind and waves filled him with terror. How much longer could they hang on in this storm? How much longer would the ship hold together? They were so close to shore! At any moment they could run aground.

Felipe touched the gold medallion hanging around his neck. He held it tight and closed his eyes. He was thinking of his family in Spain.

The captain was shouting. Every hand was on deck. They were struggling with the sails. It was almost impossible to bring them down and tie them fast. The wind was too strong. The waves were too high. The boat was tossing too wildly.

Suddenly, the boat lurched to one side. There was a sound like a groan or a roar, then a crack.

"We've hit bottom," shouted the captain. "The ship is lost! Lost! Abandon ship! Swim for shore! Swim!"

Felipe dove. He tried to swim clear of the wreck. It was cold! He felt heavy in his wet clothes. He struggled against the wind and the waves. Where was the shore? Would he make it? He felt himself sinking. Everything went dark.

Felipe groaned and turned over. His head and body ached. He rubbed his eyes. The rising sun shone right into his face, hot and bright. He brushed the sticky sand from his lips and whispered to himself, "I'm alive." Then his hand reached for the medallion. Where was it? He sat up and searched with both hands. "My medallion is gone. Lost in the sea. But I am alive. I am alive."

LOOK IT UP

More on shipwrecks: Titanic 1912, Andrea Doria, Gulf of Mexico shipwrecks, shipwreck treasure, wreck diving

It is 250 years later. A boy is running down the beach along Assateague's shore.

The wind blew into Paul's face. He kicked the sand and watched it blow. The cool October day was perfect for a walk along the shore. As always, his eyes scanned the sand for treasure. You never knew what the waves might bring ashore. He had found beautiful shells and stones. And there was interesting beach trash, too, like shoes, light bulbs, and wooden signs.

A glint in the sand made him stop. Paul leaned over and scratched the sand. He saw a chain, crusted with sand. He pulled. At the end, something round and heavy . . . .

STOP AND THINK

1. Why is Felipe's medallion important to him?

2. How important is saving an object of value if your life is at risk?

Comprehension

✓ **TARGET SKILL** **Main Idea and Details** Every passage or selection contains a topic that can usually be stated in just a few words. A topic is what a passage or selection is about. Passages and selections also contain a main idea. A main idea is the most important idea about the topic. Usually the main idea can be stated in a sentence. Sometimes it is stated in a sentence that comes near the beginning or the end of a passage or a selection. Other times, readers must figure out the main idea from details provided in the selection. Details are small bits of information found in a passage or a selection. Details that support or tell more about the main idea are called supporting details.

The following paragraph is taken from the selection "Sick and Tired of Germs." The topic of this paragraph is how germs are passed on. The paragraph contains both a main idea and details that support that main idea.

> The main idea of the paragraph is in the first sentence.

Germs can be passed on in many ways. When a sick person sneezes, coughs, or exhales, germs fly into the air. Germs can also be left on a surface, such as a desktop or a doorknob. Germs lie waiting on phones, in beds, in sinks—everywhere.

> The other sentences provide details supporting the main idea.

Topic:
Transfer of germs

Main Idea:
Germs can be passed on in many ways.

Coughing or exhaling

Being left on surfaces

In unexpected places

✔ TARGET STRATEGY **Summarize** A summary sums up a story.

When you summarize, you tell in your own words what a selection is about.

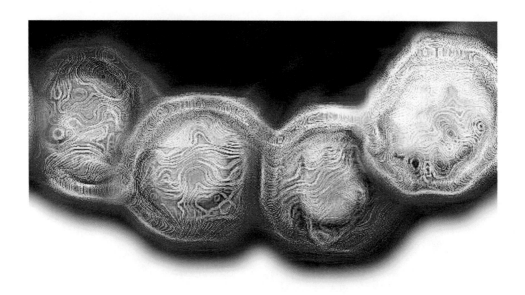

Sick and Tired of GERMS

FOCUS: How do germs affect people?

What is smaller than a flea
but can knock you off your feet?

What can make you sick
but can help you feel better, as well?

Germs!

Most germs are so small that we need a microscope to see them. But they make up for their size with their numbers. A single grain of soil is full of germs—it may hold up to 100,000,000 of them! Some germs live inside us without bringing us harm. But bad germs can sneak inside our bodies and make us sick. Two types of germs that can make us sick are viruses and bacteria.

Viruses

On its own, a virus is quite helpless. But when it sets up camp inside a living thing, it can take over. Each tiny virus can copy itself. In no time, a virus forms an army that kills or harms cells in a body. This is what makes a person sick. If you've ever spent a day stuck in bed with a cold or flu, you can blame these tiny invaders. These germs can cause diseases such as chicken pox and mumps as well.

Bacteria

This germ is a bit bigger than a virus, but it is still quite small. The biggest kind is as big as the period that ends this sentence. That is quite big for a germ! Like a virus, bacteria can go inside a living thing and cause harm. Bacteria in raw meat can make a person quite ill. Other kinds can cause a bad sore throat.

But some bacteria can help us. In fact, we have bacteria inside us that help break up food when we eat. Also, scientists in labs can use these germs to make drugs that help kill disease. When we get sick, these drugs may help us feel better!

REREAD

Main Idea

What is the main idea of this paragraph?

ASPIRIN

100 TABLETS

How Germs Make Us Sick

Germs can be passed on in many ways. When a sick person sneezes, coughs, or exhales, germs fly into the air. Germs can also be left on a surface, such as a desktop or a doorknob. Germs lie waiting where you least expect them: on phones, in beds, in sinks—everywhere.

But germs must go inside a body to make it sick. Germs can go in through a person's eyes, nose, or mouth. We can eat them, drink them, or breathe them in. Germs can sneak inside a cut on the skin. Or they can enter a body when a bug bites.

When germs enter a living thing, they steal from it. Germs take things a body needs, like nutrients and energy. A body will work hard to try and stop them. This is why a sick person can feel so tired. Germs can form toxins inside a body as well. A toxin acts as a poison. It brings harm to a body.

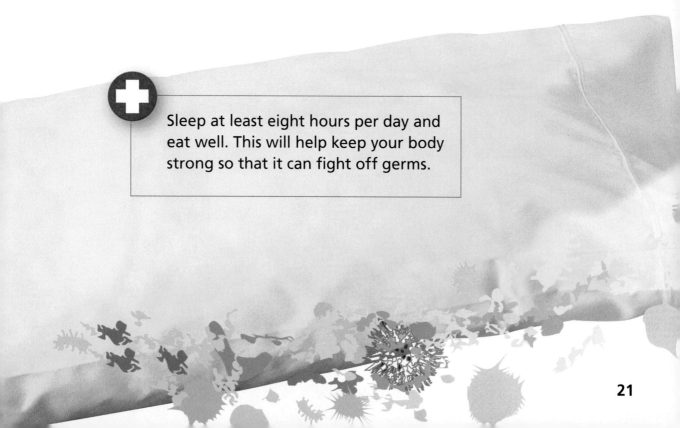

Sleep at least eight hours per day and eat well. This will help keep your body strong so that it can fight off germs.

Wash Those Hands!

Germs lurk everywhere. You cannot avoid them. But washing your hands with soap and water can help keep germs from getting inside you and making you sick.

Wash your hands BEFORE
- preparing a meal
- eating
- brushing or flossing your teeth

Wash your hands AFTER
- getting dirt on them
- sneezing
- visiting a restroom
- picking up trash
- playing with a pet

Germs in History

We fought germs a long time ago, and we still fight them to this day.

 **LOOK IT UP**

More on germs in history: bubonic plague, history of yellow fever, Dr. Walter Reed, history of smallpox, Edward Jenner, typhoid fever

The Black Death

In the 1300s, one kind of bacteria killed more than a third of the people in Europe. It gave them scorching fevers and limb pain. They got big red spots on their skin. These red spots then turned black. That is why this disease got the name "The Black Death."

Ebola Virus

This deadly germ can cause burning fevers, joint pain, and bleeding. It was first discovered in 1976. It is dangerous, but it is quite rare. We are still working on finding a cure for this virus.

STOP AND THINK

1. How do germs make people sick?
2. What do you do to fight germs?

Jenner and the Smallpox Vaccine

A PLAY

FOCUS: How can one disease be used to prevent a more serious disease?

SCENE I: *A doctor's office in England, in 1796. Edward Jenner (**EJ**), is examining a dairymaid, Sarah Nelmes (**SN**). He is looking carefully at each of her hands.*

EJ: Yes, I see those spots. But don't worry. It doesn't look like smallpox to me.

SN: *(smiling with relief)* Oh! Thank you doctor. I was a bit frightened. Even though, you know, people say we dairymaids never get smallpox.

EJ: Yes, I've heard that too. Now, tell me. Have any of the cows you milk had cowpox lately?

SN: Yes, sir. Blossom had a few spots a week or so ago. Do you think I might have cowpox?

EJ: Yes, I'm sure that's what you have, Sarah. Cowpox is not a bad illness. You'll feel better in a few days. Would you mind if I took some of the fluid from these spots? You see, I think it could help me with some research I'm doing. It's my idea that once you've had cowpox, you can't ever get smallpox. Maybe we can use this mild illness to help keep people from getting a very dangerous one. Do you see?

SN: I'm not sure, sir. But I'm glad if I can help …

SCENE 2: *Dr. Jenner is talking to his friend Roland Smith (***RS***).*

RS: Are you telling me that you plan to test your idea on a healthy person? You're going to infect someone with smallpox on purpose?

EJ: Yes. I have already infected him with cowpox. I think the cowpox will protect him.

RS: Won't it affect his health? Are you sure it's safe?

EJ: I can't be 100 percent sure. But I truly believe that he will be safe. None of the people who have had cowpox ever seem to get smallpox. This is the way to prove it once and for all.

RS: But what if you're wrong? Can't you test your idea on yourself?

EJ: You know I would if I could. I have already been inoculated against smallpox. I did it the dangerous way, with smallpox itself. Every time someone is inoculated that way there's a danger they will catch the disease and die. I want to use cowpox instead. It could save so many lives. We might even win the war against smallpox.

RS: Come off it! We'll never beat smallpox! It has killed millions. And it will continue to kill millions. That's just the way it is.

EJ: No. If we take some risks, we can beat it. I think we are going to change history.

POSTSCRIPT: In 1980, smallpox was officially declared dead. It is the only disease in history to have been totally eradicated.

STOP AND THINK

1. Why do you think dairymaids didn't get smallpox?

2. Can you take a vaccine to prevent catching a cold? How can you help to prevent catching a cold?

25

UNIT
2 OLD WAYS

WHAT CAN WE LEARN FROM OLD TRADITIONS?

READINGS

HOW PAST TRADITIONS HELP SHAPE WHO WE ARE

What things can our grandparents teach us?

Our grandparents can teach us...

☐ about our family.

☐ about our traditions and cultures.

☐ what life was like when they were young.

☐ a craft they learned from their grandparents.

What would you have to do without if you lived 200 years ago?

If I lived 200 years ago I'd have to do without...

☐ electricity.

☐ cars, buses, and trains.

☐ telephones and cell phones.

☐ pizza and other fast foods.

If you lived on a farm 200 years ago, what things would you have to do yourself?

If I lived 200 years ago, I'd have to...

☐ grow my own food.

☐ make my own clothes.

☐ make soap.

☐ make butter.

How do we learn about our traditions?

We learn about our traditions...

☐ from our families.

☐ by attending ceremonies.

☐ by reading about them.

☐ by helping to prepare for traditional ceremonies.

When a town has a big party or fiesta, what can you expect to find?

When a town has a big party or fiesta, I can expect to find...

☐ good food to eat.

☐ music and dancing.

☐ games, rides, and other activities.

☐ contests.

LEARN THE WORDS

Literature Words

appreciate

craft

draw

echo

heritage

plow

pluck

reservation

sow

toil

---

appreciate

Appreciate means to be thankful or grateful for something.

❝ I appreciate the help you gave me on my project. ❞

craft

A **craft** is an art or job that requires special skill.

❝ You can make sweaters if you are good at the craft of knitting. ❞

plow

A **plow** is a tool used by farmers to turn over the soil.

❝ The plow cut deep ridges in the soil. ❞

pluck

Pluck means to pull off or out from where a thing grows.

❝ I'll pluck the apples from the tree when they are ripe. ❞

draw

Draw means to bring, take, or pull out from a source.

66 To get water we had to draw it from the well. 99

echo

An **echo** is a sound that is heard again after it bounces off a surface.

66 In the mountains I can hear the echo of my own voice. 99

heritage

Heritage refers to traditions or traits that are passed down through generations.

66 Traditional music and dancing are important parts of our heritage. 99

reservation

A **reservation** is a piece of land that is set aside for use by an American Indian group or nation.

66 Grandfather lived on the Navajo reservation. 99

sow

Sow means to plant or scatter seeds for growing.

66 If we sow corn in the spring, it will be ripe by summer. 99

toil

Toil means to work hard.

66 The farmers toil in the field from sunup to sundown. 99

Poetry About Old Ways

Lineage

by Margaret Walker

My grandmothers were strong.
They followed plows and bent to toil.
They moved through fields sowing seed.
They touched earth and grain grew.
They were full of sturdiness and singing.
My grandmothers were strong.

My grandmothers are full of memories
Smelling of soap and onions and wet clay
With veins rolling roughly over quick hands
They have many clean words to say.
My grandmothers were strong.
Why am I not as they?

UNTITLED

BY SHAWNETAIYE WYNETT DUBOISE (NAVAJO)

Voices as silent as the winds
That blow through the piñon trees
And make swirls throughout
The hogan's earth top
Clinking sounds **echo**
Through the lonely hills

A child stands quietly
And watches her father
Make shapes into the silver
His eyes so wise and knowledgeable
The **craft** sent down
Through the many generations

And silently the girl stands
Eager to learn from him
Eyes so keen watching every move
Though the voices are silent
Only the wind blows throughout

I sat here quietly
To learn from my grandfather
As he once learned
When he was still my age

And in the future
My children and grandchildren
Will stand where I stand
And learn from me
Like I learned from my grandfather.

DOWN ON THE
OLD TIME
FARM

by Mia Lewis

Mark stared out of the car window. "I don't see why I have to go out to a farm before I write a report on farming," he said. "I can look everything up on the Web."

"Isn't your assignment to do at least one farm task and then write about it?" asked Mom.

The car pulled up at Old Time Farm. A woman came to greet Mark and Mom. "I'm Mrs. Dane," she said. She wore a long dress and an apron. "Here, we work the way people did long ago."

Mom went to sit and read. Mrs. Dane brought Mark to a wooden butter churn with a long wood pole. "Move this pole up and down," she said.

Mark sat at the churn. Moving the pole wasn't easy work. "How long do I have to do this before the cream becomes butter?" he asked.

"About an hour," said Mrs. Dane.

Mark almost dropped the pole. "An *hour*? My

LOOK IT UP

For more on old-time farming: churning butter, sheep shearing, Colonial farming

arms will fall off by then." Mrs. Dane laughed and took the pole back.

"Now I can write about churning butter for my report," said Mark.

"What will you write?" asked Mrs. Dane. "All you did was hold the pole."

Nearby, a man sat on a wooden stool, milking a cow. Only about an inch of milk was in the pail. "This doesn't look like a fast job, either," said Mark.

"You're right," said the man.

All morning, Mrs. Dane explained farm tasks to Mark. Mark learned about how people used to **pluck** goose feathers to fill pillows. He found out that sheep have their wool shorn, or cut, once a year. He tried several farm tasks himself. Each time, he gave up before he finished.

At lunchtime, Mark went into the kitchen. There was a sink but no water tap. "We **draw** our water from the well out in the back," said Mrs. Dane.

About then, Mom said, "We can only stay for another hour."

An hour—where had Mark heard that before? Then he remembered. That was how long it took to make butter. That job was starting to seem like the easiest one. "May I try the churn again?" he asked Mrs. Dane.

So Mark worked at the churn until the cream became butter. Then he wrote down the steps for using a churn. He had something to report on at last!

On the way home, Mom said, "I guess you learned a lot today."

Mark laughed. "One thing I learned was that I'm glad I live in this century!"

STOP AND THINK

1. What are some things the family saw at Old Time Farm?

2. What was harder about preparing food the old way?

Comprehension

✔ **TARGET SKILL** **Story Structure** Most stories contain *characters*, a *setting*, and a *plot*. The plot begins with the **rising action**, which tells about the problem and the main character's attempts to solve it. The events of the rising action lead to a **climax**, which is usually the point at which the main character solves the problem. Whatever happens after the climax is called the **falling action**, which leads to the **resolution**, or ending.

The following excerpts are from the story "Down on the Old Time Farm."

Mark stared out of the car window. "I don't see why I have to go out to a farm before I write a report on farming," he said. . . .

"Isn't your assignment to do at least one farm task and then write about it?" asked Mom. . . .

> This is the **rising action** of the story. In this part, readers learn about the main character, Mark, and the setting, Old Time Farm. Readers also learn that Mark's problem is that he must perform a farm task before he can write about it for a school report and that he gives up on each task before he can finish it.

All morning, Mrs. Dane explained farm tasks to Mark. . . . He tried several farm tasks himself. Each time, he gave up before he finished. . . .

About then, Mom said, "We can only stay for another hour."

An hour — where had Mark heard that before? Then he remembered. That was how long it took to make butter. That job was starting to seem like the easiest one. "May I try the churn again?" he asked Mrs. Dane.

> The **climax** occurs when Mark decides to try churning the butter again and succeeds at a farm task at last.

So Mark worked at the churn until the cream became butter. Then he wrote down the steps for using a churn. He had something to report on at last!

> The **falling action** tells what happens after the climax and leads to the resolution.

The plot line shows the events that make up the rising action, climax, and falling action of "Down on the Old Time Farm." Each point along the plot line carries the story along.

Climax

Mark tries churning again
and succeeds

Rising Action

Mark learns about and tries
other tasks but can't
finish any of them.

Mark writes down
the steps for
using a churn.

Falling Action

Mark starts
to churn butter but quits
before finishing.

Mark and Mom
ride home.

Mark and his mother
drive to Old Time
Farm.

Problem

Mark must perform a farm
task that he can write about
for a school project

Resolution

Mark has something to
write about for his report.

✔ TARGET STRATEGY **Summarize** A summary of a story is a restatement in your own words of the most important elements of the story. The summary identifies the main character, the setting, and important events. As you read, think about the important events that happen. Ask yourself the following questions:

- Who is the main character?
- What is the problem the main character must solve?
- Where does the action take place?
- What important events make up the rising action of the story?
- How does the main character solve the problem?

Your Turn

Use Your Words:

altar	response
burden	shrewd
constantly	shrivel
gasp	sly
greedy	thatch
legend	weave
persistent	workmanship
pierce	

- Read the words on the list.
- Read the dialogue. Find the words.

MORE ACTIVITIES

1. Take a Survey
Graphic Organizer

Ask twelve classmates whether they are persistent about completing their homework. Tally their responses. Share your findings with your class.

Are you persistent about completing your homework?	
Yes	No

2. You Are the Author
Writing

Look at the piece that is hanging. Write a paragraph describing it. Share your paragraph with your partner.

3. Make a List
Vocabulary

Think of the kinds of art you would see in an art gallery or museum. With a partner make a list. Share your list with the class.

4. Write About Animals

Writing

Animals are sometimes given human traits. Think of an animal that is said to be brave, sly, or greedy. List each animal and give your reasons for thinking the way you do.

5. Tell the Stories

Listening and Speaking

The guides talk about the legend behind the piece hanging in the picture. Tell the legend to your partner. Add your own details.

6. Dialogue

Listening and Speaking

Make believe you are one of the guides in the picture. Have your partner ask you three simple questions about the piece that is hanging. Answer the questions. (You can make up the answers if you want to!)

NIGHT CHANT
from Racing the Sun

by PAUL PITTS

FOCUS: How can an old man get a young boy to understand the importance of traditions?

Brandon Rogers is just a regular kid who lives in a house in the suburbs. Brandon's parents, though, were born on a Navajo **reservation** *. When Brandon's father went to college and became a professor, he even changed his name—from Kee Redhouse to Keith Rogers. Brandon's Shinali, or grandfather, has continued to live in the traditional way on the reservation.*

Now, however, Shinali is old and ill. He has come to stay with the Rogers family for a while. In fact, he is sharing Brandon's bedroom. Shinali was not able to pass Navajo traditions down to his son. He feels that he still has a chance to get his grandson Brandon to **appreciate** *his* **heritage** *. One tradition, taking a run before sunrise, hasn't thrilled Brandon at all. When Shinali took him outside to "race the sun," Brandon even cheated and walked part of the way! He told his parents how much he disliked running so early in the morning. Now, long after nightfall, Brandon is about to learn about another tradition.*

LOOK IT UP

For more on the Navajos: Navajo language, Navajo code talkers, Navajo art, Navajo Nation, Navajo legends, Navajo culture

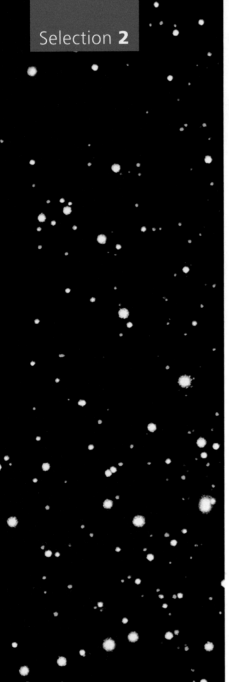

Mesa Monument Valley

Late that night, I woke up to familiar, quiet chanting.

"Grandpa?" I said.

No **response**.

"*Shinali!*"

The noise stopped.

"We've got to reach some agreement about all this praying you do."

"I'm not praying," Grandpa said. "I'm singing."

The bed trembled as he rolled over and sat up. "I'm singing of home ... of the little goats and how they lie down under a sagebrush and might get left behind. A herder must be careful and watch after them."

I sighed. "I need to get some sleep."

"When I sing, it makes me ready for sleep."

"How about singing it just once more and then calling it quits?"

"Quits?"

"You know, stop singing and go to sleep."

"If you listen, you'll be ready for sleep, too."

"I don't know about that, Grandpa."

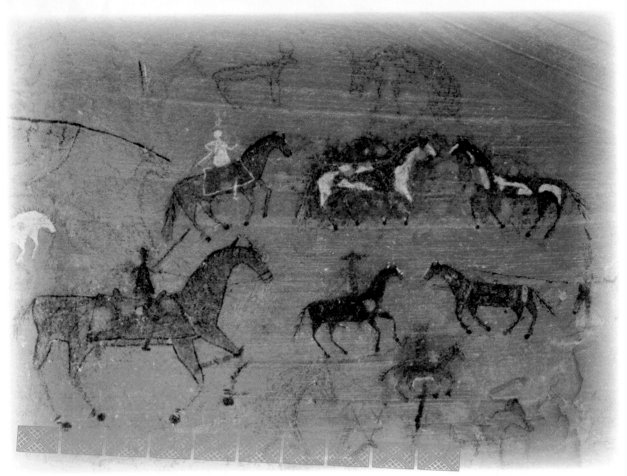

Navajo pictograph

"Listen for these words and you will know what the song says: *kl'izi yazhi*—that's a little goat—and *ts'ah*—that's a sagebrush—and *na'nithkaadi*—that's the sheepherder. Say the words with me."

I repeated the vocabulary with him a couple of times until I could say the words myself.

"Are you trying to make me learn Navajo?" I asked.

"It's a difficult language. People must learn it from birth."

"What about all the traditional stuff, the **legends** and stories that Dad says you know—are you going to tell me all that?"

"There isn't time."

"I mean, if you decide to stay here."

He laughed quietly. "There still isn't time."

The room was silent while I tried to figure out what he meant. Maybe there were so many legends that it took a lifetime to learn them all.

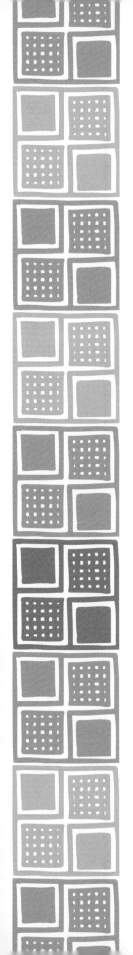

"I'm going to teach you only the important things," Grandpa interrupted my thought. "Language and legends you can learn on your own. Those things are in books. What I want you to learn is inside of me, in my heart."

"Oh" was all I could think to say.

"Are you ready for the song?" he asked.

"Go ahead."

"Should I sing?"

"Yes! Sing!" I was feeling less and less ready for sleep.

He started the song very softly, and I strained to hear the words he'd taught me. It's funny, but I was disappointed when he stopped.

After a minute of silence, Grandpa asked, "Should I sing it again?"

"Go ahead," I said. "But only a couple of times or we won't be able to get up and race the sun tomorrow."

"Your mother said you didn't want to race anymore."

"I'll try it once more … if I get enough sleep."

The room was silent for a minute.

"Grandpa?" I whispered.

"Mmmm?"

"I'm going to really race tomorrow … run the whole way."

"I thought you would," he said, and started singing the little-goat song softly.

STOP AND THINK

1. How do Brandon's feelings about *Shinali*'s traditional ways change?

2. What are some ways to learn about family traditions?

43

PREPARING FOR THE

FIESTA

from *The Corn Grows Ripe* by Dorothy Rhoads

Words You Need to Know

to bush to cut down plant growth
corrida bullfight
fiesta festival
huipil dress worn by native women
milpa cornfield
vaquero herder, cowboy

FOCUS: How can a community's traditions help young people show others that they are becoming adults?

Tigre lives in a Mayan village in Mexico. The time is about 100 years ago. Earlier, Tigre's father broke his leg. Though Tigre is young, he took over his father's work in the family's cornfield. Alone, he prepared the land for planting. He had to bush the field—cut down young trees and underbrush. Tigre has completed this task, and he looks forward to planting the corn in May. For now, there is a fiesta to prepare for. This year, Tigre wants to take his place with the older boys and lead a bull into the bull ring. He thinks he has earned that right. First, though, he must show that he can make the rope he will use to lead his bull.

For three days there would be prayers and ceremonies in the church, feasting and dancing. People would come from all the villages around. And on the very last day there would be a *corrida*, a bullfight, for which the bulls would be rented or borrowed, and not killed. The older boys, many of them for the first time, would be *vaqueros*, leading the bulls into the bull ring. Already many of the boys were working on their ropes. At the dance the evening before the bullfight the ropes would be judged.

Tigre began thinking about making a rope. "I too will make a rope," he said to Father.

"You are too young," Father started to say. Then he stopped. Had not Tigre already taken on a man's responsibilities? Who was he, Father, to say the boy should not enter the bull ring?

Great-Grandmother gave Tigre a **shrewd** look, and he felt as he always did that her sharp bright eyes were reading his thoughts, summing up all his faults. He had never been one to sit quietly and work with his fingers.

"I think we could arrange it," Great-Grandmother said to Father. "Only let it be a good rope, Tigre. Do not disgrace us with poor **workmanship**. And let it be finished if you begin."

*Tigre begins **weaving** his rope. The work is harder than he expected. He puts it aside for awhile. There are so many other things to do! Weeks pass.*

"How is your rope coming, Tigre?" Great-Grandmother asked **slyly**. "You have not forgotten, have you, that you asked to join the other boys in the bull ring?"

"It is coming," Tigre said. But he did not offer to show it. He had not worked on it for some time.

He determined to start again the next morning and keep at it until it was finished.

* * * *

April was dry. Every day was hotter than the day before. Gray dust settled on the houses and in the streets and clung to the **shriveled** leaves of the trees like swarms of tiny insects. The trees of the bush were only skeleton trees, gray bony trunks and limbs.

Everything **gasped** for water. Mother drew bucket after bucket of water from the well to give to her thirsty plants. They sucked in the water with a **greedy** gurgling, and in a little while the earth around them was cracked again and dry.

Father sat in his hammock or limped about the house and yard.

Tigre worked on his rope. Several times he had to unravel it and start again, but each time it was a little easier. A few months ago, he thought, he would have given it up as not worth the trouble. But his **persistence** in keeping on with the bushing had done something more for him besides getting down bush. As using his muscles **constantly** had strengthened his arms, so doing the hard thing had exercised and strengthened his will. It was easier now for him to stick to unpleasant things.

I am growing up, I think, Tigre said to himself. When two days went by without work on his rope he felt guilty.

Everyone was looking forward to May.

"Soon now the rains will come," people said to one another.

And Tigre thought, In May I will face the bulls in the *corrida*. In May I will sow my *milpa*.

Then it was May.

May third came, the day of Holy Cross. This was the day when the rains should begin. But from dawn to darkness the sun rode across a clear bright sky.

The men of the village had cut down trees for the bull ring the week before. They had built the ring, placing each tree a little apart from the next, so people could look through at the fight. The church floor had been scrubbed, the **altar** newly painted. The dance platform too was ready, in the street before the church; and held up by four poles, one at each corner of the platform, was a covering of **thatch** to protect the dancers from the almost certain rain.

Every man in the village had a haircut and wore a red handkerchief about his neck. Every woman had a new hair ribbon and a new embroidered *huipil* freshly washed and ironed.

The fourth of May came, and visitors began to pour into the village. The bush trails were choked with travelers **burdened** like ants, bundles of clean clothing and hammocks on their backs.

The bulls arrived.

The orchestra came.

The village was jammed with people.

Every house had twenty or thirty sleeping at night in the room where four or five usually slept. The hammocks were strung like cobwebs, over and under one another. Men slept four and five in each hammock. Women sat up or slept with the children on the floor. The schoolhouse too was full. And many people slept in the open, hanging their hammocks from trees.

Tigre's uncle Pedro and his family came, and Mother's mother and father and her sisters.

For three days the village was filled with music and laughter. Skyrockets exploded and spattered the sky with stars without pause. Every family had bought dozens. There was dancing and feasting and prayer.

The night of the last dance came. All the village was gathered around the platform—the men in their stiff white suits and silk shirts, the women wearing their gold fiesta jewelry, the girls as pretty as butterflies in their white dresses and little straw hats with gay ribbons and flowers.

The orchestra began the music for the dance of the *vaqueros*. The boys came on with their ropes. Tigre saw at once that his rope could not win. Some were so true, so beautiful, woven as smoothly as glass. But his was not the worst one either. There were others as rough and even more misshapen.

After the dance the boys went to the house of the fiesta leader. There must be no sleep for any of them during the night. This was the ceremony *vigil*, a test of their physical and mental endurance.

The next day they went together to the bull ring.

Ai! It was exciting.

The bulls bellowed and pawed the ground and ran at the boys and men with lowered horns. Pancho Noh had his shirt **pierced**, the horn just missing his shoulder. Felipe Dzul fell down and had to be dragged away quickly. Tigre jumped on top of one of the tree-posts of the bull ring just in time.

Outside around the bull ring the villagers watched and shouted. "Bravo, Pancho! Bravo, Juan!"

Even Father was there, leaning on Uncle Pedro's shoulder. Great-Grandmother stood straight and proud, never moving, even when once the bull's horns came through the ring almost in her face.

Concha's eyes shone. "Bravo, Tigre! Bravo, Tigre!" she yelled.

And Dog ran back and forth madly, making as loud a noise as any.

Father tired easily, and he and Mother and Chan Tata left early. But Great-Grandmother and Concha stayed until the very end.

Then it was over. Tigre went home. Mother's father and mother and the aunts and cousins had left. Mother had hot chocolate for Tigre, and he sat in his hammock and drank it. He was so tired he could hardly hold the bowl.

Great-Grandmother mentioned the rope. She was the only one who did.

"You were too impatient," she said. "I watched you. Always in a hurry to get it finished. But it was not the worst one," she added kindly.

Tigre's head dropped lower over his chocolate. His eyes closed. "Another time I will do better," he said sleepily.

"That I believe," Great-Grandmother said.

STOP AND THINK

1. Why did Tigre's family allow him to be a *vaquero* this year?

2. How do old traditions help some communities mark important events?

UNIT 3

SEEKING THE NEW WORLD

Christophorus Columbus
Genuensis. 1492.

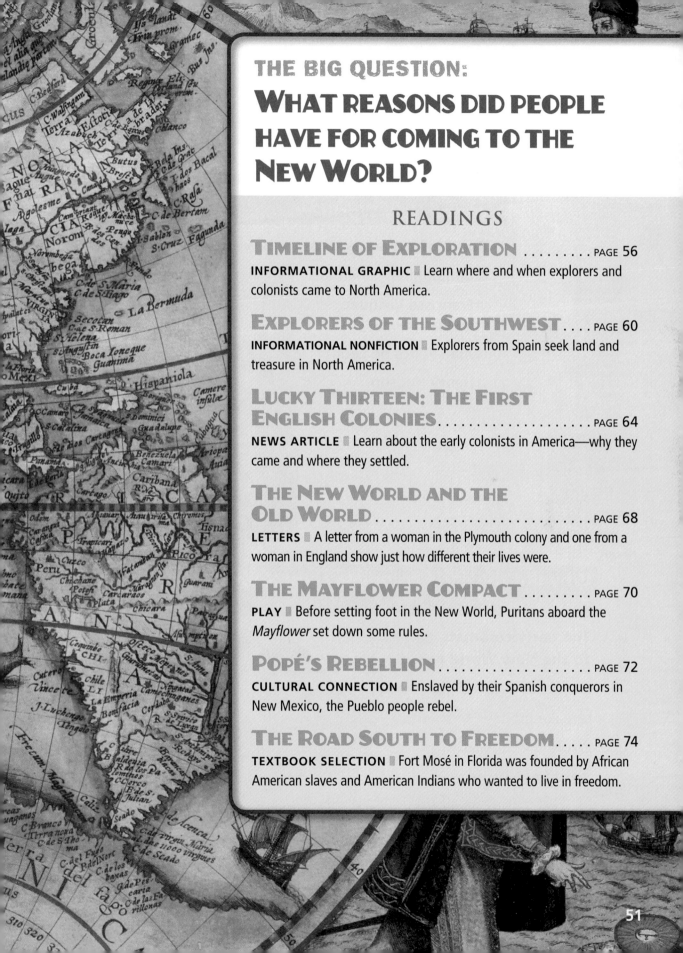

LOOK TO THE NEW WORLD

Who were some of the early explorers of the New World?

Some of the early explorers were...

☐ Christopher Columbus.

☐ Francisco Vásquez de Coronado.

☐ Juan Ponce de León.

☐ Henry Hudson.

Why did the early colonists come to the New World?

The early colonists came to the New World to...

☐ practice their religion freely.

☐ make money.

☐ rule themselves.

☐ start a new life.

What did colonists have to do to survive in the New World?

To survive in the New World, colonists had to...

☐ grow their own food.

☐ build their own houses.

☐ make their own clothes.

☐ make laws to govern themselves.

Why were American Indians and Africans enslaved in the New World?

American Indians and Africans were enslaved because...

☐ more people were needed to populate towns and villages.

☐ they were forced to do the hard work.

☐ their rights were not respected.

Which people rebelled against harsh rules that took away their freedom?

The people that rebelled against harsh rules were...

☐ the Puritans.

☐ the Pueblo people.

☐ African Americans.

☐ the Pilgrims.

History Words

- **agriculture**
- **ancestor**
- **found**
- **frequent**
- **occupy**
- **port**
- **presence**
- **rival**
- **trade**
- **volume**

agriculture

Agriculture is a word that describes the process of raising crops and animals.

" I studied agriculture in college because I wanted my own farm someday. "

ancestor

An **ancestor** is a person from whom one is descended. The person is more distant than a grandparent.

" My ancestor settled in Texas and became a rancher. "

port

A **port** is a harbor or place on a waterway where ships can load and unload, or stay safe from storms.

" Juan guided the sailboat into port, just ahead of the squall. "

presence

A **presence** is being or existing in a place, or having influence there, such troops or representatives.

" Once Charlotte joined the Girl Scouts, she had a presence in that organization. "

found

To **found** is to set up, provide money for, or establish an organization or institution.

❝ The committee met to found a neighborhood watch group. ❞

frequent

Frequent means occurring often or on a regular basis.

❝ Linda is a frequent visitor to the library and is usually there three times a week. ❞

occupy

To **occupy** is to dwell or reside in, or have possession of by settling in or conquering.

❝ Phil decided to occupy the tree fort he discovered. ❞

rival

A **rival** is a person or thing competing with another.

❝ Whitney's top rival for lead singer in the band was Alicia. ❞

trade

To **trade** is to exchange goods for money or other goods.

❝ Donte decided to trade some of his baseball cards for a concert ticket. ❞

volume

A **volume** is a book.

❝ The volume was too long to read in one afternoon. ❞

TIMELINE OF EXPLORATION

THE **ANCESTORS** OF HUMANS LEFT AFRICA almost two million years ago, and we've been exploring the world ever since. It seems that humans have always wanted to know what lies on the other side of the next mountain.

When modern humans settled in **agricultural** communities, they began to **trade** with their neighbors. Over time, these villages and towns developed better means of transportation—and longer trade routes. Explorers no longer just traveled over the next range of mountains. They started to cross continents and even oceans.

Coronado explores what is now the southwestern United States.

Sir Francis Drake reaches the west coast of North America by sea.

1450

1500

1550

1600

Christopher Columbus reaches the New World, landing on the island of Hispaniola.

Alvar Núñez Cabeza de Vaca begins an eight-year trek across what is now the southeastern United States.

The history of exploration of our world would fill many **volumes**. And there will always be more to write. Most of Earth is covered by oceans, and most of those oceans remain unexplored. For now, let's focus on just one part of the world. The timeline on these pages shows some important events in the exploration of North America.

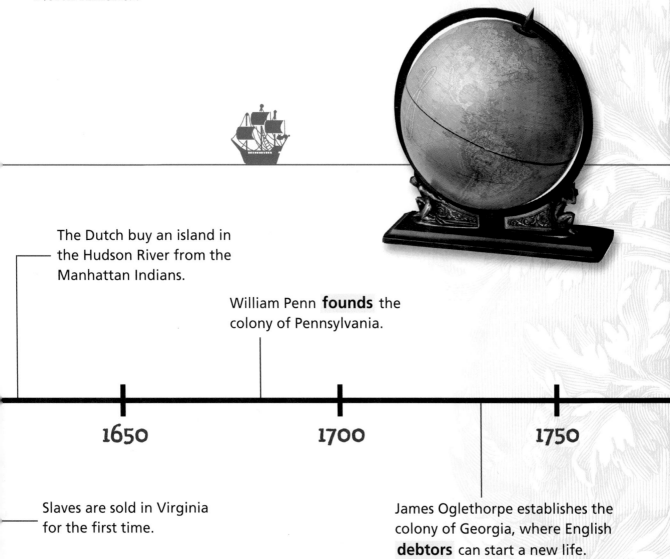

The Dutch buy an island in the Hudson River from the Manhattan Indians.

William Penn **founds** the colony of Pennsylvania.

1650

1700

1750

Slaves are sold in Virginia for the first time.

James Oglethorpe establishes the colony of Georgia, where English **debtors** can start a new life.

Comprehension

✔ **TARGET SKILL** **Cause and Effect** When you read about why an event happens, you are reading about cause and effect. The cause is *why* something happens. The effect is *what* happens as a result of the cause.

Here is one example of a cause-and-effect pattern with a signal word:

Cause

Effect

Puritans wanted to "purify" the Church of England. Therefore, they got rid of ceremonies that they felt were too close to those of the Catholic Church. Puritans had strict views about religion. They came to North America for their own religious freedom, but they didn't want to live with people who had different religious beliefs.

Roger Williams was a Puritan living in Massachusetts. He did not believe in forcing others to follow his beliefs. As a result, many of his fellow Puritans wanted to send him back to England. Instead, he bought land from some Indians and started the colony of Rhode Island.

Cause

Effect

Graphic organizers can help show cause and effect. Look at the boxes below.

The first box shows the *cause*, or why something happened. The second box shows its *effect*, or what happened.

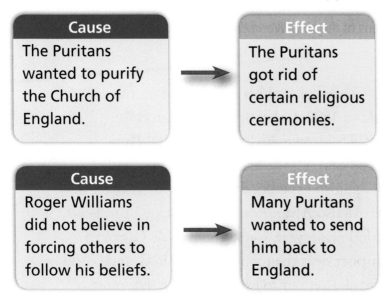

Cause
The Puritans wanted to purify the Church of England.

Effect
The Puritans got rid of certain religious ceremonies.

Cause
Roger Williams did not believe in forcing others to follow his beliefs.

Effect
Many Puritans wanted to send him back to England.

✔ **TARGET STRATEGY** **Ask Questions** Asking questions as you read can help you better understand cause and effect. Ask yourself these questions:

• What happened?

• Why did it happen? or, What caused it to happen?

These questions will help you find cause and effect.

Explorers of the Southwest:
❖ Conquest and Conflict ❖

FOCUS: What regions of the New World did Spain explore and claim?

Christopher Columbus and his men landed on the island of Hispaniola in 1492. Other Spanish explorers followed Columbus. They conquered vast territories. From Florida to Mexico and beyond, the Spanish empire expanded.

The earliest Spanish expeditions were sent to discover new lands. The mariner Alonso Alvarez de Piñeda mapped the Texas coast in 1519. The following year, Captain Diego de Camargo established a small **port** near the mouth of the Rio Grande. And in 1527, Pánfilo de Narváez set out to explore Florida. For most of Narváez's men, the expedition ended in disaster. However, a few survived. They became the first Europeans to explore Texas and other parts of the American southwest.

The region was already **occupied**. Many groups of American Indians lived there. Narváez's men lived with these people for eight years. They slowly made their way across the continent, **trading** and talking. They heard stories of great wealth. Farther west and north, they were told, cities were built of gold and silver. Amazing animals were said to live in these remote places. When they finally got back to Mexico and Spain, they recounted these stories.

The tales of riches had a big effect on the Spanish. Explorers now wanted to do more than discover new lands. They wanted to find great treasures.

MEXICO

Francisco Vásquez de Coronado was the governor of a province in Mexico. In 1540, he organized an expedition to find the Seven Cities of Cíbola. These cities were supposedly so rich that the women wore belts of pure gold. Coronado took more than 300 Spanish soldiers on his expedition. A thousand Tlaxcalan Indians worked as guides and servants. Herds of cattle supplied the expedition with food.

Coronado and his men journeyed north into what is now Texas. They traveled west to the Colorado River, today's border between California and Arizona. They explored parts of what is now New Mexico. They even made their way to present-day Kansas. However, they never found cities of gold and silver.

By the late 1500s, Spain's conquests in the New World had begun to worry Queen Elizabeth I of England. England and Spain were **rivals**. Elizabeth wanted England to have a **presence** in the New World, but the English navy wasn't very strong. Elizabeth chose the **privateer** Francis Drake to command a voyage around the world. She instructed him to attack Spanish towns and ships along the western coast of the Americas. Conflicts between the two nations became **frequent**. For the time being, though, the Southwestern part of North America remained Spanish.

Five present-day U.S. states lie along Coronado's 1540 route.

....
privateer the commander of an armed private ship permitted by his government to make war on ships of an enemy country

■■■ STOP AND THINK

1. Why did later Spanish explorers believe they would find great riches?

2. How do you think American Indians felt about the Spanish expeditions in the southwest?

Your Turn

Use Your Words:

able	monarch
ceremony	native
cherish	oppose
civilized	purify
culture	reason
debt	relieve
democracy	revolt
document	right
hearth	vow
maintain	worship

- Read the words on the list.
- Read the dialogue. Find the words.

People settled here for many <u>reasons</u>. Who can tell me one reason?

People <u>opposed</u> the king and <u>revolted</u>.

One reason was that people didn't have some important <u>rights</u> under the <u>monarch</u>, such as the right to <u>worship</u> the way they wanted and hold specific <u>ceremonies</u>.

<u>Democracy</u> was another reason.

MORE ACTIVITIES

1. Make a Chart
Graphic Organizer

Look at the chart. Write down how people got things they needed back then. Write how you get them now.

How did/do people…	Back then	Now
get water?		
get milk?		
get from place to place?		
get food?		
get money?		

2. What Are Your Rights?
Listening and Speaking

With a partner, talk about the rights you have. Take turns describing your rights. Write them down. Share your list with your class.

3. Life Back Then
Writing

Suppose you were among the first settlers to come to the New World. What would your life be like? Write a letter to a friend back home telling about your life in the New World.

The people <u>cherish</u> this old house. They have made a <u>vow</u> to <u>maintain</u> it.

Including the historic <u>hearth</u> used for heating. And if you look around you'll see plants <u>native</u> to this area.

We can learn things about their history and <u>culture</u> through old <u>documents</u>.

Yes, and people in the future will be in <u>debt</u> for this knowledge.

Wouldn't this ability make them feel more <u>civilized</u>?

Water was pumped from the ground. People were <u>relieved</u> that they were <u>able</u> to <u>purify</u> it by boiling.

4. Play "I Am Going to the New World"

Listening and Speaking

Play this game with a partner. Think of the things you would need in the New World. The first player starts by saying, "I'm going to the New World and taking a _____." The second player repeats what the first player said and adds a second item. The first player repeats what the second player said and adds a third item. Play continues like this until a player forgets an item on the list.

5. Take a Poll
Writing

Ask ten classmates to imagine that they could move to a new, totally unknown land. Would they do it or not? Write their responses in the tally chart. Share your findings with your class.

Would you move to a totally unknown land?	Yes	No

6. Tell About Your Culture
Listening and Speaking

Draw a picture of a special item or event from your culture. Show your picture to a partner. Describe it.

LUCKY THIRTEEN: The First English Colonies

FOCUS:

How did the thirteen English colonies in North America get started?

What is now the United States started out as thirteen English colonies. A colony is a settlement in a new territory that is controlled by the parent country. Some of the colonies were businesses. Others were founded by people who wanted religious freedom.

Massachusetts

REREAD

Cause ➡ Effect

Why did the Pilgrims come to America?

The Pilgrims settled Plymouth Colony in 1620. Many of the Pilgrims were Separatists. They wanted to "separate" from the Church of England. Since the king of England would not let them practice their religion, they came to America. In 1630, another religious group, the Puritans, founded the Massachusetts Bay Colony near Plymouth Colony.

New Hampshire

In 1623, the king of England sent John Mason to establish a settlement in New Hampshire. The settlement was part of Massachusetts until 1679, when it became a colony.

New York

In 1626, the Dutch bought the island of Manhattan from a local Indian tribe for goods worth about $24. The Dutch called the island New Amsterdam. It was part of New Netherland, a Dutch territory. In 1664, a British army led by the Duke of York captured New Netherland, and it became New York.

Map of the original thirteen colonies

Rhode Island

The Puritans wanted to "**purify**" the Church of England. Therefore, they got rid of **ceremonies** that they felt were too close to those of the Catholic Church. Puritans had strict views about religion. They came to North America for their own religious freedom, but they didn't want to live with people who had different religious beliefs.

Roger Williams was a Puritan living in Massachusetts. He did not believe in forcing others to follow his beliefs. As a result, many of his fellow Puritans wanted to send him back to England. Instead, he bought land from some Indians and started the colony of Rhode Island.

Connecticut

Thomas Hooker was a Puritan minister. He left Massachusetts to start a colony in Connecticut. He thought that people had a right to choose their own representatives in government. Many Puritans joined his colony.

William Penn

Pennsylvania

As a young man, William Penn rebelled against the Church of England. He joined the Quakers, a church that **opposed** war and slavery. In 1681, the king of England had a **debt** to Penn's father. To pay the debt, the king gave William Penn land in the New World. William called the new colony Pennsylvania, or "Penn's woods." He had good relations with the American Indians and created a **democratic** form of government.

New Jersey

When the Duke of York captured New Netherland, some of the territory was given to Sir George Carteret. He was from the English island of Jersey, so he named the colony New Jersey. The new colony had laws that gave people the right to practice different religions. The laws also gave men the right to vote for representatives in government.

Delaware

Delaware was colonized by many countries. It began as a Dutch colony. Then it was a Swedish colony. Later, it became a Dutch colony again. Then it became part of the English colony Pennsylvania, and finally separated from Pennsylvania in 1704.

Maryland

Sir George Calvert was a Catholic. The Catholic Church and the Church of England were **rivals**, but the English **monarch** was friendly with Calvert. The king gave Calvert a colony, Maryland. Calvert worked to make sure Catholics and other Christians could live peacefully in Maryland.

 LOOK IT UP

For more on the thirteen colonies: Colonial times, daily life in the colonies, Colonial Williamsburg, Colonial slavery

Virginia

Jamestown, Virginia, was the first permanent English colony in America. The early Virginia colonists almost starved to death. When they started growing and selling tobacco, their fortune changed. Tobacco made a lot of money for the colonists and for the king of England. In 1619, Virginians brought the first African slaves to America to work in the tobacco fields.

North Carolina

In 1653, colonists from Virginia moved to North Carolina. In 1677, people from North Carolina refused to pay taxes to England. This was one of the first times that a colony and England argued about taxes.

South Carolina

North and South Carolina were once a single colony, Carolina. The king of England gave Carolina to eight English nobles, who were supposed to make money for the king. Later, the colony was split into North Carolina and South Carolina. South Carolina soon became the wealthiest of England's colonies. Both Carolinas depended on the work of slaves.

Georgia

In the early eighteenth century, people in England who couldn't pay their debts were often sent to prison. James Oglethorpe, a wealthy soldier, had an idea. He wanted to send these debtors to America, where they could start a new life. The king of England liked the idea and gave Oglethorpe a new colony, Georgia. According to Oglethorpe's rules, the settlers were not supposed to drink alcohol or own slaves. But they soon broke both rules.

Tobacco plant

STOP AND THINK

1. How was the establishment of Pennsylvania similar to the establishment of Georgia?

2. If you were an English colonist, which colony would you choose to live in? Why?

THE NEW WORLD AND THE OLD WORLD

FOCUS: How was life in colonial Massachusetts different than life in England?

Almost 400 years ago, 102 men, women, and children set sail for the shores of an unfamiliar land. On December 26, 1620, their ship, the *Mayflower*, landed in Plymouth, Massachusetts.

Two friends, separated by the Atlantic, kept in touch by writing letters.

June 1624

Dearest Jane,

I cannot write a very long letter. There is much work to do in these warm months of summer. Today, I must help to plant our Indian corn. It is not grown in the same manner as English wheat and rye. Our Indian friends have shown us what we must do. First, we dig a hole. Into the hole, we drop a fish. We then mound soil upon the fish and plant the corn seeds in the mound. This makes the corn grow better.

There are no shops in our town. So we must provide everything we eat, most of the clothes we wear, and even the furnishings in our houses. We get a few goods on the ships from England. However, except for a few cherished pieces from our old homes, everything we have was made here.

There is plenty of land here. The trees grow well and thick, so we have plenty of wood to make roaring fires in the hearth.

The morrow is Sunday, and the whole town will attend services in the meetinghouse. It is a great pleasure to be able to worship according to our beliefs.

Did you know that men from our very colony make the laws that govern us? This is a big change from our lives in England. The men chosen to make our laws are farmers and craftsmen, like us.

The part of England I miss most of all is you, my dear friend.

With loving thoughts to you and your family,

Emily

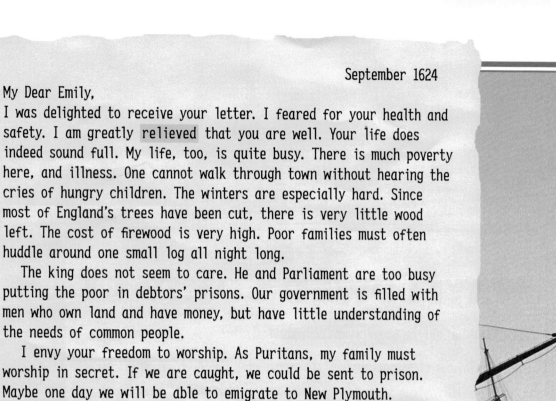

September 1624

My Dear Emily,

I was delighted to receive your letter. I feared for your health and safety. I am greatly relieved that you are well. Your life does indeed sound full. My life, too, is quite busy. There is much poverty here, and illness. One cannot walk through town without hearing the cries of hungry children. The winters are especially hard. Since most of England's trees have been cut, there is very little wood left. The cost of firewood is very high. Poor families must often huddle around one small log all night long.

The king does not seem to care. He and Parliament are too busy putting the poor in debtors' prisons. Our government is filled with men who own land and have money, but have little understanding of the needs of common people.

I envy your freedom to worship. As Puritans, my family must worship in secret. If we are caught, we could be sent to prison. Maybe one day we will be able to emigrate to New Plymouth.

Missing you greatly,

Jane

STOP AND THINK

1. How did Emily and her family get food and clothing?

2. Would you have preferred to stay in England or sail to Plymouth? Why?

THE MAYFLOWER COMPACT

FOCUS: What did the Mayflower Compact describe?

The Mayflower Compact was a **document** signed by 41 men on board the *Mayflower*. One group of colonists, known as Pilgrims, or Saints, came to the New World seeking religious freedom. The other group, known as Strangers, came for other reasons, such as to make money. Before going ashore at Plymouth, the two groups needed to reach an understanding.

Miles Standish: It is not right. We are not in England anymore. Why should we not live as we want?

John Carver: We are still **civilized** men, Miles Standish. Would you live with no laws at all, like wild animals?

Men: Ha, ha!
That could be a lot of fun! No laws! Hooowwwl! I'm a wild animal!

Standish: Hush your nonsense! We are men of **reason** , not animals.

Carver: Well, Miles, if we are men of reason, then we should be able to work together to write the laws we shall live by. The Saints and the Strangers, side by side.

Friend of Standish: But we are just carpenters and barrel makers. What do we know of laws?

Standish: What he says is true, John. We have never had a say in the laws that govern us.

Carver: I know. I have often thought it unfair that only men of wealth can make laws. We may not all be here for the same reasons, and we may have different beliefs. But here we are in this new land where we must live together peacefully. Can the Saints and the Strangers not reach an agreement?

Woman: We need more than an agreement. We need a written compact, a document to help create a new kind of government in a new land.

Friend of Standish: We should…*combine ourselves into a civil body…*

Friend of Carver: And…*frame such just and equal laws…*

Carver: Wait, slow down…*for the general good of the colony…*Okay, got it.

The people who signed the Mayflower Compact were men with equal **rights** . They agreed to work together to make laws that were for the good of the colony. With the Mayflower Compact, the colonists began to govern themselves.

STOP AND THINK

1. Why did the colonists think they needed a compact?

2. What change would you have suggested for the compact?

POPÉ'S REBELLION

FOCUS: How did the Pueblos defend their rights?

While the English were colonizing the eastern part of North America, the Spanish were colonizing the western part. By the middle of the 1600s, Spain had colonies in present-day Texas, California, Arizona, and New Mexico.

Mission San Jose

Spanish Missions

The king and queen of Spain wanted to spread Catholicism across the New World. Missions were built in the Spanish territories. The priests at the missions converted American Indians to the Catholic religion. The priests gave the Indians gifts such as knives, clothing, and food. In return, the Indians had to work and be baptized.

The Pueblo Indians lived in New Mexico. They were frustrated and angry with the Spaniards. The Pueblos had to do all the work. They grew the crops. They **maintained** the missions. They even had to pay taxes to the Spaniards. Worst of all, they were not allowed to practice their own religion. Popé, a religious leader and healer, decided this had to end. It was time to fight for freedom.

The Spaniards made the Pueblo Indians work for them.

Rise Up!

Popé had been imprisoned for leading secret religious ceremonies for his people. Now he **vowed** to help the Pueblos regain control of their lives. In 1680, he organized a **revolt**. He got the Pueblo tribes to agree on a time to fight. He even got the Apaches, enemies of the Pueblo Indians, to join the fight. Then he fooled the Spaniards by sending their spies false information. Three days before the Spaniards expected it, the Pueblos revolted.

REREAD

Cause ➡ Effect

How did Popé fool the Spanish?

When the revolt was over, many Spaniards had been killed. Popé told the rest to go back to Mexico. Then the Pueblos burned down the missions. The Indians began practicing their ancient religion again. They lived freely for 12 years. At that time, the Spaniards returned to New Mexico. But the Spaniards realized that they could not repeat their mistakes. They were more tolerant of the Pueblos' customs. Even today, the Pueblo people have been able to maintain much of their **native culture**.

STOP AND THINK

1. Why did the Pueblos revolt?

2. Why do you think the Spaniards wanted to convert American Indians to Catholicism?

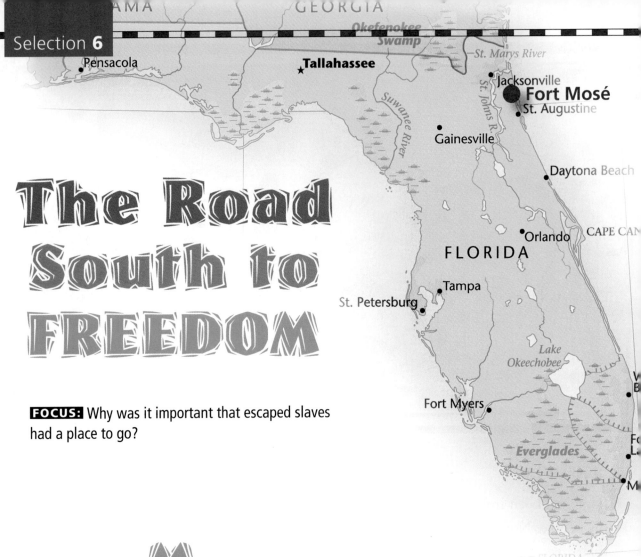

The Road South to FREEDOM

FOCUS: Why was it important that escaped slaves had a place to go?

ost newcomers to the North American colonies traveled there to find freedom. There was one exception. Beginning in 1619, many Africans were brought to North America against their will. There, freedom was taken away from them. They were forced to work as slaves. By the early 1700s, many enslaved Africans worked on plantations in the English colonies of Carolina and Georgia. (Later, Carolina became two separate colonies, North Carolina and South Carolina.) The enslaved Africans tended crops such as rice, sugar, and cotton. Their labor made plantation owners rich. Yet the hardworking Africans received no part of that wealth.

Music and dance helped enslaved Africans remember their past.

There was one chance for the slaves. If they could escape southward, they would reach a place where a better life awaited them. This place was Florida—the only Spanish colony on North America's east coast.

REREAD

Cause → Effect

Why did enslaved people escape southward?

In 1693, King Charles II of Spain said that Florida would shelter runaway slaves from English colonies. They would not be returned to their masters. This gave hope to enslaved African workers. Some tried to make their way from the English colonies to Florida.

The Africans weren't the only ones to benefit from their new life under the flag of Spain. The Spanish colony was always in danger from English raiders. Spanish settlers needed help defending their land. Escaped Africans were eager to pitch in. They formed a militia, or military band, to fight the raiders.

REREAD

Cause → Effect

Why did the escaped Africans form a militia?

75

In 1738, the Spanish governor of Florida, Manuel de Montiano, granted some land to Florida's black people. He gave them permission to form a settlement. About a hundred men, women, and children began households on the land and put up a fort. The settlement became known as Fort Mosé (moe-SAY). Fort Mosé was the first known free black community in North America. It was also the northern line of defense for the nearby Spanish city of Saint Augustine.

Reaching Fort Mosé wasn't easy. Few made it. Escaping slaves might be recaptured by the English and returned to a life of slavery. Yet some brave runaways took the risk. Along the way, they were sometimes helped by local Indians who were allies of Spain. Once the Africans reached Florida, if they agreed to become Catholics and promised to fight for Florida, they could live there as free people.

Life at Fort Mosé was hard but rewarding. The settlers built the fort's walls of tightly packed earth. They put up huts with roofs of palm fronds woven together. The people of Fort Mosé had varied skills. There were farmers, carpenters, blacksmiths, builders, and other workers. The settlers grew crops and caught fish and shellfish. They traded with the people of Saint Augustine. The fort's settlers had come from West Africa, the Caribbean, and the southern English colonies. Their food, music, and clothing reflected the many cultures. Fort Mosé's leader was Francisco Menéndez. Menéndez was an African-born escaped slave from the Carolina colony. He was a fierce fighter in defense of Spanish Florida.

This community did not last long. In 1763, Spain lost Florida to England. The Spanish had to give up the colony as part of an agreement following the French and Indian War. England was eager to gain Florida. English colonists wanted to create more plantations like those in Georgia and the Carolinas. The crops would be planted, tended, and harvested by African slave labor. This new Florida had no place for a free black community.

So the settlement of Fort Mosé came to an end. Yet Spain did not abandon the people who had defended Florida so well. The black people of Florida, and any Indians who wanted to come, sailed to Spanish Cuba to live.

REREAD

Cause ➡ Effect

Why did Spain take care of the people from Fort Mosé?

During the next seventy years, Florida was ruled by England, then Spain again, then the United States. Throughout this period, some of Florida's Indians remained in the swamps and wilderness areas. Other Indian groups joined them. The new groups came from what are now Georgia, Mississippi, and Alabama. More African American runaways also slipped into Florida. The mixture of different Indian groups, including Creeks and Muskogees, joined together for protection. They formed a new Indian nation, the Seminoles. The Seminoles welcomed and hid many of the escaped slaves. In time, these black people became allies of the Seminoles. Some actually joined Seminole bands. So Florida remained a place where African Americans had a chance to live in freedom.

STOP AND THINK

1. Why were the people of Fort Mosé willing to risk their lives to protect Florida?

2. How was Fort Mosé like a modern city?

UNIT 4

ALL SYSTEMS GO!

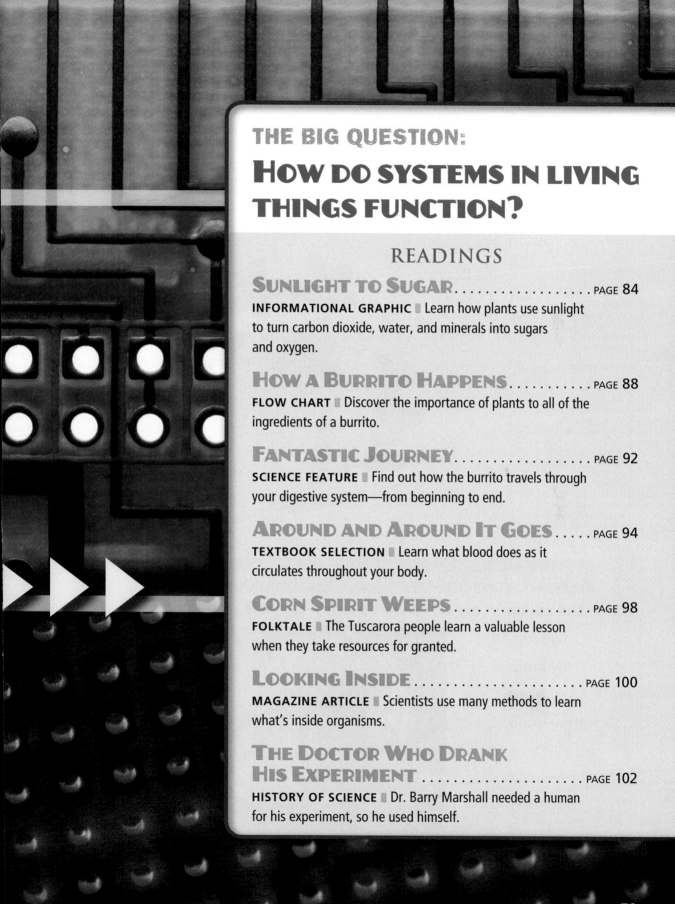

What plant parts can you see?

A plant part I can see is...

☐ a stem.

☐ a flower.

☐ a leaf.

☐ a fruit.

Which organ in your body pumps blood?

The organ in my body that pumps blood is...

☐ my stomach.

☐ my lungs.

☐ my heart.

☐ my brain.

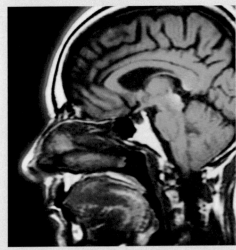

What parts of your body help digest food?

The parts of my body that help digest food are...

☐ my mouth.

☐ my heart.

☐ my stomach.

☐ my intestines.

How do scientists learn about internal organs?

Scientists learn about internal organs by...

☐ examining dead bodies.

☐ taking x-rays.

☐ doing CAT scans.

☐ looking at DNA.

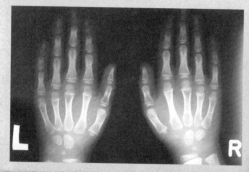

What causes ulcers?

Ulcers are caused by...

☐ too much stress.

☐ bacteria.

☐ spicy food.

☐ genetics.

bacteria

churn

dejected

depend

descend

esophagus

function

generate

minerals

mucus

bacteria

Bacteria are tiny one-celled organisms. They sometimes cause disease.

66 The doctor told Bobby that his illness was caused by bacteria. 99

churn

Churn means to stir or swirl vigorously.

66 A stomach churns the food inside it, moving it around and breaking it down. 99

esophagus

The **esophagus** is a tube in the throat that pushes food down into the stomach.

66 Always chew your food very well so it doesn't get stuck in your esophagus. 99

function

A **function** is a specific job.

66 The function of the heart is to pump blood. 99

dejected

Dejected means to be sad or depressed.

66 The boy was dejected when he learned that he had received a C on the test. 99

depend

Depend means to need or to rely on.

66 Plants depend on sun, rain, and soil in order to live and grow. 99

descend

Descend means to go down from a higher place to a lower place.

66 From the mountaintop they will descend by way of a path. 99

generate

Generate means to make or create.

66 Water flowing over turbines can generate enough electricity to run a factory. 99

minerals

Minerals are non-living things that provide nutrients to living things.

66 It is very important to eat foods filled with minerals like calcium and iron. 99

mucus

Mucus is a slimy mixture in the body. It protects body surfaces and keeps them moist.

66 A coating of mucus protects cells in the stomach's lining from digestive acid. 99

Sunlight to Sugar

Photosynthesis

SUNLIGHT

CARBON DIOXIDE

CHLOROPHYLL

WATER AND MINERALS

OXYGEN

SUGARS

Food Factories

Plants use the energy of sunlight to turn water, **minerals**, and carbon dioxide into sugars and oxygen. The sugars are food for the plants. They use them to make things that we and other animals eat: roots, leaves, fruits, and seeds.

How do plants transform sunlight into sugars? The process is called photosynthesis, and it **depends** on chlorophyll, a pigment in leaves that absorbs light.

Plant Circulation

LEAF

The leaf's work is done by structures called chloroplasts. That's where the chlorophyll is, so that's where photosynthesis happens.

STEM

Tiny tubes called xylem carry water and minerals throughout the plant. Other tubes, called phloem, carry the plant's sugars, or sap.

ROOTS

Roots have hairs that help draw water from the soil. Plants need a lot of water, so they have a lot of roots. A rye plant can have more than 13 million roots.

Parts of a Plant

Plants are complex organisms. Each part of a plant has a job to do. The roots keep the plant secure and pull water and minerals from the soil. The stem supports the plant. The leaves are the factories, capturing light and **generating** sugars. And flowers, seeds, and fruits are the plant's way of reproducing.

85

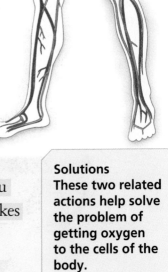

Comprehension

✔ TARGET SKILL **PROBLEM/SOLUTION** Writers of articles often tell about problems and how they are solved. A writer may tell about one problem or several related problems. Sometimes a problem has more than one solution. Sometimes several related problems may have one solution.

The following paragraphs from the selection "Top Eight Things Your Blood Does for You" contain problems and solutions.

Problem

Cells throughout your body need oxygen. You breathe in oxygen through your lungs. Blood takes it the rest of the way, dropping off oxygen and picking up the waste gas, carbon dioxide.

Solutions
These two related actions help solve the problem of getting oxygen to the cells of the body.

Problem

When your body is invaded by a foreign substance such as bacteria, your blood helps fight it off. White blood cells rush to the scene. Some "eat" the invaders. Others make proteins that attack the invaders.

Solutions
These three related actions all help solve the problem of fighting off a foreign substance.

You can use a graphic organizer to show problems and solutions.

Solution
The blood takes the oxygen the rest of the way to the cells of the body.

Problem
Cells throughout your body need oxygen.

Solution
White blood cells rush to the foreign substance.

Solution
You breathe in oxygen through your lungs.

Problem
Your body must fight off foreign substances such as bacteria.

Solution
Other white blood cells produce proteins that attack the foreign substance.

Solution
Some white blood cells destroy, or "eat" the foreign substance.

Each box on the left shows a problem. The boxes on the right show solutions. The arrows pointing from the boxes on the left to the boxes on the right show that each problem has more than one solution.

✔ TARGET STRATEGY **Summarize** A summary contains only main ideas and details that tell about the main ideas.

You can use the problem/solution graphic organizer to help you summarize an informational article. To do so, ask these questions:

- What are the main ideas of the article? (Remember, the main ideas are the problems and solutions.)
- Which details are relevant to the problems and solutions?

HOW a BURRiTO HaPPens

FOCUS: Can all the ingredients in a burrito be traced back to plants?

The sun powers photosynthesis, which is how plants make the sugars they need to live. In turn, we eat fruits and vegetables that come from plants. But how do we get other foods? Could the meat in the Deluxe Guacamole Burrito you ate for lunch also **depend** on photosynthesis? How about the cheese? Let's look at the burrito's ingredients.

88

The Photosynthetic Burrito

The chart shows that each ingredient in a burrito comes from plants, either directly or indirectly. It's easy to see the plant connection for guacamole and tortillas. Guacamole is made from avocados, which are the fruit of the avocado tree. Tortillas are made from flour, which comes from wheat. But cheese is made from milk, and we get milk from cows, not plants. What do cows eat? Plants such as alfalfa. The chicken filling in your burrito also has an indirect connection to plants. What do chickens eat? Grains such as corn.

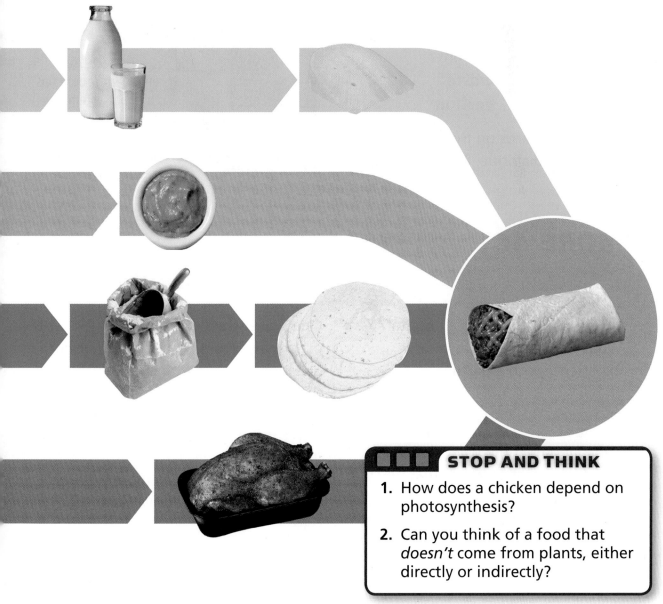

STOP AND THINK

1. How does a chicken depend on photosynthesis?

2. Can you think of a food that *doesn't* come from plants, either directly or indirectly?

89

LEARN THE WORDS

Your Turn

Use Your Words:

branching	limitation
circulate	network
clot	radiation
convention	reduce
foreign	solution
hypothesis	sufficient
image	symptom
internal	system
isolate	waste
key	version

- Read the words on the list.
- Read the dialogue. Find the words.

X-RAY DEPT

The hospital has been branching out. Now there's a large network of doctors.

With an x-ray image there is very little radiation, right?

Correct. This emergency room has a good system, but there is a limitation. It won't show a blood clot or injury to internal organs.

MORE ACTIVITIES

1. Dialogue
Listening and Speaking

Have you ever been to a hospital? What was it like? Share your experience with a partner.

2. You Are the Author
Writing

Think about a time when you were sick. Make a list of words that describe your symptoms. Use the words to write a poem that tells how you felt.

3. Play "Guess My Job"
Listening and Speaking

One player thinks of a hospital job. The other player asks up to five yes-or-no questions to try and figure out what the job is.

4. Make a List
Vocabulary

What are ways you can reduce waste? Make a list. Share your list with the class.

5. What's Your Version?

Listening and Speaking

One person in the picture is going to have an x-ray. Tell a partner what happened and how it could have happened. Then have your partner give a different version of how it happened.

6. Make a Graph

Graphic Organizer

Ask ten classmates if they have ever had an x-ray. Tally their responses. Make a bar graph showing your results.

Have you ever had an x-ray?		
10		
9		
8		
7		
6		
5		
4		
3		
2		
1		
	yes	no

Fantastic Journey
Through the Digestive System and Beyond

FOCUS: How is food absorbed by the human body?

5... 4... 3... 2... 1... The Deluxe Guacamole Burrito has taken off! But instead of going up, it's going down—into the digestive **system**! We'll follow the burrito on its mission.

Mission Status Report

Time: 0 hours 0 minutes 6 seconds
Location: mouth
Food status: pulverized
Mission status: Teeth are chewing up the burrito; tongue is helping. Saliva is beginning to break down sugars.

Mission Status Report

Time: 0 hours 0 minutes 24 seconds
Location: esophagus
Food status: mushy blob
Mission status: Muscular **esophagus** is squeezing and pushing the burrito down to the stomach.

Mission Status Report

Time: 1 hour 33 minutes 17 seconds
Location: stomach
Food status: soupy sludge
Mission status: Stomach acid is killing most of the **bacteria** in the burrito. **Churning** muscles are breaking down the burrito. And digestive juices are preparing the burrito for digestion.

Digestion Question

Can I swallow food while standing on my head? Yes, the muscular action of the esophagus will make sure the food goes in the right direction. But don't be surprised if you feel a little sick!

Digestion Question

Why doesn't all that stomach acid hurt my stomach? The walls of your stomach are coated with **mucus** to protect it from the acid.

92

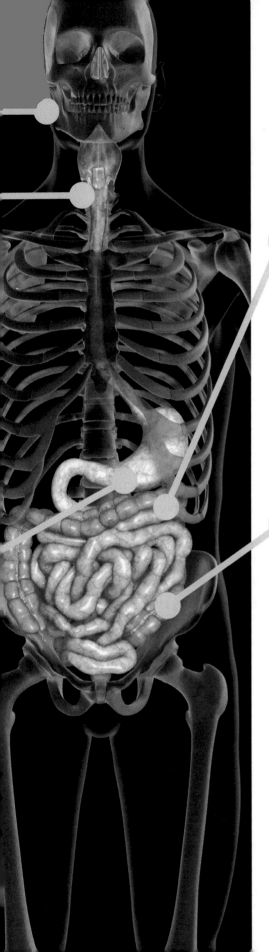

Digestion Question

What happens to the food after it enters my bloodstream?
The sugars and fats provide energy for cells throughout your body. This energy keeps your heart beating, your lungs breathing, your legs walking, and your brain thinking. Proteins have a different **function**. They help make new cells and tissues.

Mission Status Report

Time: 4 hours 1 minute 53 seconds
Location: small intestine
Food status: thin liquid

REREAD

Problem + Solution
What is the problem here? How is it solved.

Mission status: In the upper part of the small intestine, food sugars are flowing into tiny blood vessels called capillaries. Proteins and fats will need more time to be absorbed by the blood. But there's plenty of time—the small intestine is about 23 feet long.

Mission Status Report

Time: 8 hours 30 minutes 6 seconds
Location: large intestine
Food status: **waste**
Mission status: Mission accomplished! Almost all of the burrito's nutrients have entered the blood. Waste has gone to the large intestine, where water is being absorbed by the body. Bacteria are helping digest any leftover nutrients. The large intestine is only about 6 feet long, but the waste will need up to 20 hours to travel through it.

STOP AND THINK

1. Which part of digestion takes the longest?

2. What kinds of food do you think are digested most easily?

93

AROUND AND AROUND IT GOES

A Short Course on the Circulatory System

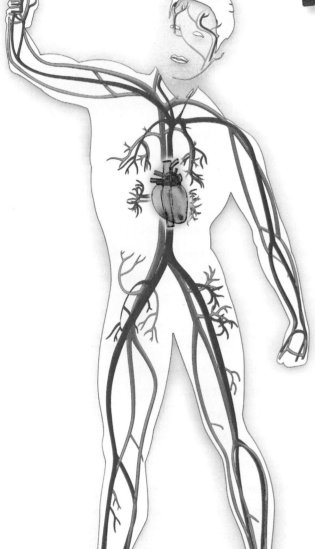

FOCUS: What does the circulatory system do?

Now that we've followed a burrito through the body, there's still one big question. How do nutrients from the burrito reach all the parts of your body? Blood does the job. It travels through the **circulatory system**, a **network** of blood vessels that stretches throughout your body. The system has two main loops. In the first loop, blood moves from your heart to your lungs, where it picks up oxygen and drops off carbon dioxide. Then the blood returns to your heart and starts the second loop. In this loop, it goes to your digestive organs, such as the small intestine. After picking up nutrients from the burrito, it travels to other parts of your body. Then it drops off nutrients for the cells—and picks up **waste** products. Finally, the blood travels back to your heart.

The Muscle

The heart is the center of the action. It's a strong muscle that pumps blood throughout the circulatory system. You can feel how your heart works by pressing a finger to the side of your neck. That's blood flowing through an artery. The pulse is the rhythm of your heart. Whether you're studying, playing basketball, sleeping, or eating a burrito, your heart is at work, pumping blood through your body.

How many times does my heart beat in a minute?

If you're resting, it will probably beat 68 to 80 times in a minute. You can check by counting your pulse as you time a minute. About how many times will your heart beat in a year?

The Transfer

Blood flowing away from the heart travels in arteries. The arteries **branch** off, getting smaller and smaller. Finally, they become tiny vessels that connect with other tiny vessels leading back to the heart. These tiny, interconnecting blood vessels are called capillaries. They are where the **key** exchange happens. As blood moves through the capillaries, it gives up oxygen and nutrients to your body's cells. At the same time, the cells give up carbon dioxide and waste products to the blood.

Blood flowing toward the heart travels in veins. Like arteries, veins form a branching network. So, as the blood gets nearer the heart, it moves through bigger and bigger veins.

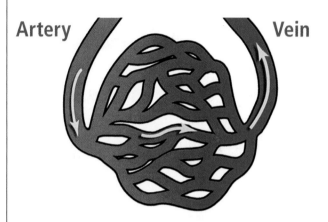

Artery   **Vein**

Capillary Network

The Clean-Up

Finally, your blood has to be cleaned. All those waste products it picked up in the capillaries have to go somewhere. Your kidneys filter the blood. Your liver removes most of the other waste.

> REREAD
> **Problem** + **Solution**
> What problem do the liver and kidneys solve?

Why are the arteries colored red and the veins blue?

Blood carrying oxygen is bright red. Blood that has given up its load of oxygen is darker red. So blood flowing in arteries is brighter than blood flowing in veins. As a **convention**, diagrams show arteries as red and veins as blue.

Top Eight Things Your Blood Does for You

1 **It feeds you.**

The food you digest wouldn't be much help if it just sat in your stomach and intestines. How do the nutrients get to the cells of your body? Blood carries them.

2 **It helps you breathe.**

Cells throughout your body need oxygen. You breathe in oxygen through your lungs. Blood takes it the rest of the way, dropping off oxygen and picking up the waste gas, carbon dioxide.

3 **It clots.**

When you have a cut or an injury, blood vessels are broken. The circulatory system starts to leak. Blood flows out. Your body needs a way to stop the bleeding—fast! Special blood cells cause the blood to thicken and harden into a **clot**, which plugs the cut and stops the bleeding.

4 **It takes out the trash.**

Just as your body's cells always need fresh nutrients, they also need something to take away the waste products. That's another job for your blood.

5 It fights invaders.

When your body is invaded by a **foreign** substance such as bacteria, your blood helps fight it off. White blood cells rush to the scene. Some "eat" the invaders. Others make proteins that attack the invaders.

6 It remembers.

Special proteins made by your white blood cells "remember" foreign invaders. So the next time your body is attacked by the same invader, your white blood cells can respond more quickly. That's what happens when you get a vaccination. You are given a weak **version** of a disease germ. Your white blood cells make a "record" of the germ and are ready to fight it when the actual germ invades your body.

7 It tells your body what to do.

Your blood carries special chemicals called hormones. They tell organs when to work, when to grow, what to produce, and many other things. Some hormones affect your moods, thoughts, and emotions.

8 It sounds the alarm.

Life was dangerous for our ancestors, who lived by hunting and gathering. At a second's notice, they had to be ready to fight an enemy—or flee. Blood carries the hormone that gives your body the strength to fight or run. It's called adrenaline, and today it's more likely to make you feel a little nervous before you take a test or swing at a baseball.

LOOK IT UP

For more on the circulatory system: capillary, artery, heart muscle, human heart, aorta, heart and lungs

STOP AND THINK

1. What are the key parts of the circulatory system?

2. How many times did your heart beat in the last minute?

Red blood cells

CORN SPIRIT WEEPS

A TUSCARORA LEGEND

FOCUS: Could the Tuscarora survive without corn?

Long ago, a village had excellent corn harvests. However, the people got used to having plenty of corn and started to take it for granted. They didn't weed their fields very well. Their children played in the fields and damaged the plants. At harvests, the people didn't bother to pick all the corn. They gave some of the corn to their dogs. And when they stored corn for the winter, they were careless. They didn't bother to make good storage baskets or dig holes deep enough to protect the baskets.

"There are plenty of animals to hunt," the people said. "We don't need all that corn."

One man continued to weed his fields, harvest all of his corn, and store it carefully. His name was Dayohagwenda. Each harvest, he gave thanks to Corn Spirit for his good fortune.

One fall, the village's hunters came back from the forests with empty hands. They couldn't find any deer or moose. They couldn't even find any rabbits. So the people went fishing in the streams and lakes. No luck. As winter **descended** on the land, the people began digging up their baskets of corn. But the baskets were already falling apart. Some of the corn had spoiled; the rest had been eaten by mice.

"We shall surely starve," the people said.

Dayohagwenda went for a walk in the forest. He found a lodge that was falling apart. The lodge was in a clearing, but the clearing was thick with weeds. An old man sat crying in front of the lodge. His clothing was torn and dirty.

"Grandfather, why are you crying?" asked Dayohagwenda.

"I am sad because your people have forgotten me," replied the old man. "Since they no longer respect me, I will have to go away."

Dayohagwenda realized that the old man was Corn Spirit. He went back to the village, where people were sitting on the ground, **dejected**. "Our corn is gone," they said. "Our hunters and fishers have failed. We will starve!"

"Maybe not," said Dayohagwenda. He told them about his encounter with Corn Spirit. "If we treat our corn with respect, I am sure Corn Spirit will help us survive the winter." Then Dayohagwenda dug up his stored corn to share with the village. He had made good, strong baskets and buried them deeply. The corn was still in good condition. He noticed something curious—his baskets held much more corn than he remembered harvesting. In fact, there was enough corn for the whole village, all through the winter.

Never again did the people take their corn for granted. They planted, hoed, and weeded their fields carefully. They made strong storage baskets and dug deep holes for the baskets. And they remembered to thank Corn Spirit during each harvest.

The Tuscarora

When Europeans settled North America, the Tuscarora lived in a region that is now part of North Carolina. Although they were excellent hunters, their society **depended** on the cultivation of maize, or corn.

STOP AND THINK

1. Why did the people of the village start to take corn for granted?

2. What is something that you take for granted?

Looking Inside

FOCUS: How do scientists study what's inside the human body?

In biology class, you may have dissected a frog to learn about its **internal** organs.

Dissection has also been an important way to study the human body. But people used to believe that dead bodies shouldn't be cut up.

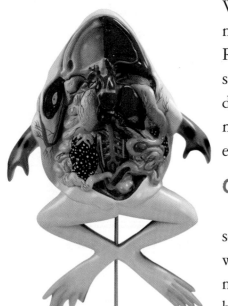

Where did early medical students get the bodies they needed? In the eighteenth century, England's Parliament passed a law to solve the problem. The law stated that the bodies of executed murderers could be dissected by medical schools. There weren't many medical schools then, and there were plenty of executions. So the supply of bodies was **sufficient**.

Grave Robbing

By the early nineteenth century, medical science was taking off. More and more medical schools were opening in England, and all the new students needed bodies to study. But fewer murderers were being executed. There was a shortage of bodies.

Grave robbers solved the problem. They snuck into cemeteries at night and dug up fresh corpses. They were careful to replace the dirt and sod so that no one would notice. Then they sold the bodies to doctors and medical schools. The business was so good that two men, William Burke and William Hare, started killing people to sell the bodies. After a great public outcry, Parliament passed a new law. This law made it legal for doctors and students to study "unclaimed corpses." Most unclaimed corpses came from prisons and workhouses. As the supply of dead bodies increased, the business of grave robbing died out.

REREAD

Problem + Solution

How did grave robbers solve the problem of the shortage of bodies? What steps did they take?

Inside the Living

Doctors often need to see what's going on inside a living patient. X-rays, discovered in 1895, gave doctors their first good look inside living people. X-rays are a kind of **radiation** that travels at the speed of light. They go through soft matter, such as flesh and muscles, but are absorbed by hard matter, such as bones. So doctors can use x-rays to take pictures of patients' bones and organs. Film is placed behind the patient's body, and then a machine fires x-rays at the patient. The result is an **image** that shows bones as white and soft tissues as dark.

X-rays were a great advance, but they have their **limitations**. They don't show soft tissues very well. And they don't show parts of the body that are behind other parts. Computers helped solve the problem. A new kind of x-ray machine was developed in the twentieth century—CAT, for "computerized axial tomography." To get a CAT scan, a patient is put inside the machine. Then a beam of x-rays is swept across the patient. Many images are taken, each from a different angle. Finally, a computer records the images and combines them to make a three-dimensional view.

With x-rays, doctors can tell whether or not a bone is broken.

STOP AND THINK

1. What are some of the limitations of dissection?

2. How has technology helped doctors?

The Doctor Who Drank His EXPERIMENT

Dr. Barry Marshall, University of Western Australia

FOCUS: How did this scientist test his hypothesis about the human body?

Would he do it? Would he drink the **solution** that contained the **bacteria**? The test tube in Dr. Barry Marshall's hand contained *Helicobacter pylori* bacteria. He thought these bacteria were the cause of stomach ulcers, painful breaks in the stomach's protective coating. But he couldn't test his idea on someone else. The only way to test his **hypothesis** was to swallow the bacteria himself.

Ulcers: A New Clue

The story began in 1982, when Marshall's colleague, Dr. Robin Warren, noticed large amounts of bacteria in the stomachs of ulcer patients. Warren wondered whether the bacteria were the cause of ulcers.

Medical views about ulcers hadn't changed much in a hundred years. Doctors believed that ulcers were caused by stress and bad diet. The logic seemed clear. The more a person worried, or ate greasy or spicy food, the more acidic the person's stomach became. Over time, the acid would eat away at the stomach lining, causing an ulcer.

The cause of ulcers?

102

A stomach ulcer

According to the best available science, there wasn't a real cure for ulcers. Doctors could prescribe medicines to **reduce** the acid in a patient's stomach. This would help the patient feel better, but it wouldn't get rid of the ulcer.

Prove It

Warren's questions about the cause of ulcers caught Marshall's attention. If bacteria caused ulcers, then ulcers might be cured with antibiotics, drugs that kill bacteria.

Marshall and Warren began to investigate. They found an unknown **bacterium** in the stomachs of many ulcer patients. They were able to **isolate** and grow the bacteria: *Helicobacter pylori,* or *H. pylori* for short. But when they told scientists that they thought the new bacteria caused ulcers, nobody believed them.

"Well," Marshall recalls other scientists telling him, "that's all very nice, but let's face it... These bacteria are so common that they must just be harmless."

"So I had to prove that the bacteria could infect a normal, healthy animal," Marshall says.

Helicobacter pylori

....

bacterium The singular form of *bacteria.*

A Dangerous Test

Marshall thought about who that "normal, healthy animal" might be. He decided that he was the only person who understood the risks of the experiment. So one morning he mixed up some of the bacteria. "Down the hatch," he said. A horrified lab worker watched him drink the mixture. Marshall calculated that he'd swallowed a billion *H. pylori.*

Not much happened for several days. On the fifth day, though, Marshall started feeling sick. He ran to the bathroom to vomit. "Wow, this is weird," he told himself.

He kept on working. Each day he felt a little bit sicker. But the sicker he felt, the better he felt about the experiment. Finally, on the fourteenth day, Marshall's wife said, "Barry, there's something wrong with you. You look terrible."

Marshall confessed that he had swallowed the bacteria. "What?" his wife cried. She ordered him to take antibiotics immediately.

The experiment ended. Marshall took antibiotics, the *H. pylori* were eliminated from his stomach, and his **symptoms** disappeared. Other scientists began to take Marshall and Warren's research seriously. It took more years of research, but eventually the medical world accepted the idea that *H. pylori* weren't harmless. The new bacteria caused infections that, if not treated, created stomach ulcers.

In 2005, Marshall and Warren were awarded the Nobel Prize in Medicine. Today, patients with stomach ulcers can be cured quickly and easily, thanks to Dr. Barry Marshall's remarkable experiment.

STOP AND THINK

1. Why were other scientists skeptical of Marshall and Warren's hypothesis?

2. Why were Marshall and Warren awarded the Nobel Prize in Medicine?

UNIT 5 INTO THE UNKNOWN

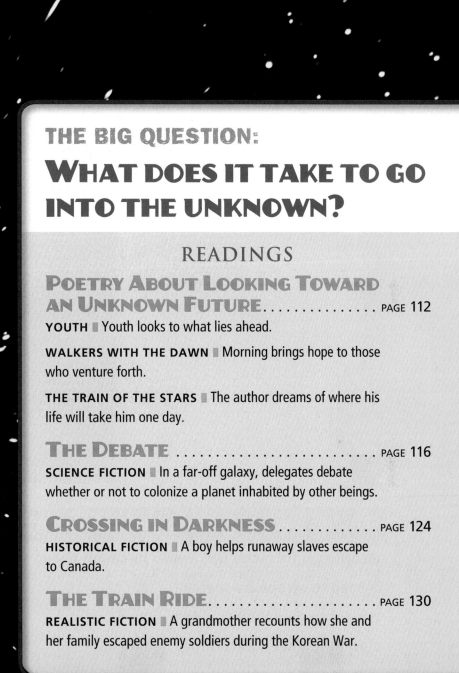

WHAT DOES IT TAKE TO GO INTO THE UNKNOWN?

READINGS

LOOK TO THE UNKNOWN

What can the unknown be?

The unknown can be...

- ☐ a new place to live.
- ☐ a new friend.
- ☐ the future.
- ☐ a new beginning.

Why do people go into the unknown?

People go into the unknown because they...

- ☐ need to escape an enemy.
- ☐ want to gain their freedom.
- ☐ want to have a better life.
- ☐ can't survive where they are now.

What can you find in a science fiction story?

In a science fiction story you can find...

- ☐ events that happen in the future.
- ☐ travel between planets and galaxies.
- ☐ advanced technology that doesn't exist today.
- ☐ unusual beings from other planets.

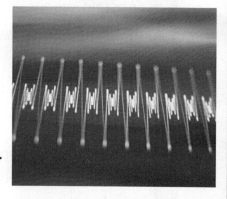

How did slaves escaping to freedom find their way?

Slaves escaping to freedom found their way...

- ☐ by following the North Star.
- ☐ with help from former slaves who had escaped.
- ☐ by following streams and rivers.
- ☐ with help from people who lived along the way.

How can people escape a dangerous place?

People can escape a dangerous place by...

- ☐ walking.
- ☐ riding a train.
- ☐ taking a plane.
- ☐ crossing a river.

LEARN THE WORDS

Literature Words

- **abstain**
- **alternative**
- **conclude**
- **current**
- **install**
- **primitive**
- **probe**
- **propose**
- **slight**
- **survey**

abstain

Abstain means to hold back from casting a vote.

66 Council members can vote for or against the bill, or they can abstain. 99

alternative

An **alternative** is one of two things or actions that can be chosen.

66 The alternative to taking the highway is to travel through the mountains. 99

primitive

Primitive means simple, unrefined, or at an early stage of development.

66 The people on the new planet lived in primitive houses. 99

probe

A **probe** searches or examines something thoroughly.

66 The space probe sent back data from Jupiter. 99

conclude

Conclude means to bring to an end or to reach an end.

" The ceremony will conclude with a song. "

current

Current means new or most recent.

" The current weather report says that it will rain. "

install

Install means to place in position or connect for use.

" We'll install the new television in the living room. "

propose

Propose means to suggest or present a matter for others to consider.

" I propose we spend the day in the park. "

slight

Slight means small in amount or degree.

" There was a slight amount rainfall overnight. "

survey

Survey means to look over.

" I survey the room each day to see where my friends are sitting. "

Youth

by Langston Hughes

We have tomorrow
Bright before us
Like a flame.

Yesterday
A night-gone thing,
A sun-down name.

And dawn-today
Broad arch above the road we came.

We march!

Walkers with the Dawn

by Langston Hughes

Being walkers with the dawn and morning,
Walkers with the sun and morning,
We are not afraid of night,
Nor days of gloom,
Nor darkness—
Being walkers with the sun and morning.

The Train of the Stars

by Abdul-Raheem Saleh al-Raheem
Translated by Adil Saleh Abid

The night is a train that passes,
Up on my house I watch it
Its eyes smile to me.

The night is a train that passes,
Carrying moons and stars
Clouds, flowers,
Seas and rivers that run.
The night is a train that passes.
The night is a train that passes,
I wish, oh, how I wish!
I could take it one day:
It would take me away,
To see where it's going,
Oh, where's that train going?

Comprehension

✓ **TARGET SKILL** **Inference** Stories do not always state directly the information you need for a complete understanding. As you read, you can use clues in the story and knowledge from your own experiences to make inferences. Story clues can include the words and actions of the characters.

Here is an excerpt from "Crossing in Darkness." Louis, a young white boy, is about to row a family of runaway African American slaves (Sarah, Tyler, and Lucy) across a river to freedom.

> Clues in this passage help you infer that the African Ameirican boy, Tyler, is reluctant to trust the white boy, Louis. What you know about the lives of enslaved people also helps you make this inference.

Louis gave the warm clothes, the quilt, and the chocolate bread to Sarah and her children. The boy looked like he wasn't going to put the jacket on, then he did.

"Don't mind my boy, he's stubborn," Sarah said. "I tell him there are good white people. Plenty of them helped us along our way."

> The question that Louis asks Tyler helps you infer that Louis does not exactly trust Tyler either.

Together the two boys pushed the skiff into the water, breaking a thin skin of ice. . . .

"You sure you can row a boat?" Louis asked Tyler.

"I'm sure. I rowed the boat for Master Harmon when he went cat fishin'. I rowed him all over Mud Lake." . . .

When the patrol boat was out of hearing the boys began to row again. . . .

Tyler was as worried as Louis. To break the silence he asked, "What kind of fish you catch in this river?"

> You can infer that Louis and Tyler are not having a casual conversation about fishing. Rather, they are beginning to trust one another and may be trying to calm each other down.

"Whitefish, herring, perch, sturgeon . . ."

"That's a big fish. You got to be strong to catch it . . ."

This graphic organizer can help you keep track of story clues and inferences you make as you read.

Clues	Inference
Tyler looked like he wasn't going to put on the jacket that Louis had given him. Then Tyler put on the jacket. → "Don't mind my boy, he's stubborn," Sarah said. "I tell him there are good white people." →	Tyler does not quite trust Louis or understand his motives.
"You sure you can row a boat?" Louis asked Tyler. →	Louis does not quite trust Tyler either.
Tyler was as worried as Louis. To break the silence he asked, "What kind of fish you catch in this river?" → The boys discuss the fish. →	Tyler and Louis are trying to calm each other down. They are beginning to trust one another.

✓ TARGET STRATEGY   **Predict** You can use clues from a story and knowledge from your own experience to predict what will happen next in a story. As you read, ask yourself the following questions:

- What do story clues tell me about the important characters?
- What do I know from experience that can help me predict what will happen next in the story?
- What do I predict will happen next?

Think about which clues were most helpful in making your prediction.

THE DEBATE

BY

STEVEN L. STERN

In this science fiction story, a planet's people get ready to take
a new and disturbing path.

FOCUS: How can people tell what results a big decision might have?

     The huge assembly hall buzzed with voices. The Chairman
had to bang his gavel a number of times to get everyone's attention.

     "To order! To order!" he said, raising his voice only **slightly**.
The splendid new sound system, **installed** in the year 2621,
transmitted his voice clearly around the entire hall.

     "We are here this morning to complete the debate and take a
final vote." The Chairman **surveyed** the room, waiting until he had
everyone's full attention. Every seat was filled. The Chairman's main
concern, however, were the 100 people sitting closest to the podium.
These were the 100 elected representatives of the Global Union.
There were equal numbers from the Northern, Southern, Eastern,
and Western regions.

116

"Delegate Kalin," the Chairman said, once the hall was silent. "I believe you had some remarks you wanted to make before the vote."

A gray-haired representative from the Northern Region rose from his chair.

"Thank you, Chairman. Yes." He cleared his throat. "I continue to be troubled by this **proposal**. I do not see how we have the right to take such a drastic step. It goes far beyond the Code of Acceptable Action that this assembly adopted in 2466. Simply having the *power* to do something does not give one the *right* to do it."

Several small red lights began to blink on the Chairman's control panel. There were 100 lights in all. They were connected wirelessly to built-in controllers on the 100 representatives' chairs. A representative who wanted to speak touched a button on his or her controller.

"Delegate Abben," the Chairman said.

A representative from the Eastern Region rose.

"The Code of Acceptable Action has nothing to do with our **current** problem. These are desperate times. We have no choice. We are out of time."

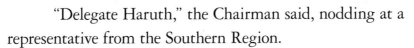

"There is *always* a choice," Delegate Kalin said.

The Chairman banged his gavel. "Delegate Kalin, you will not speak until recognized, please, " he said.

"My apologies," Kalin said, sitting back in his chair.

"Delegate Haruth," the Chairman said, nodding at a representative from the Southern Region.

"I respect my colleague from the Northern Region," Haruth began in his low, gravelly voice. "But I, too, must disagree with him. The facts make it clear that we have run out of choices. Despite our advanced technology, our air and water remain polluted. Our planet's population has multiplied far beyond what our land and other natural resources can support. Colonizing planet K-3 in the Dithram Galaxy offers us our only chance for survival."

The Chairman gave Kalin a chance to respond.

"But survival at what cost, Haruth?" Kalin said. "K-3 is not some uninhabited rock in space. As our **probes** have revealed, there are living creatures there. **Primitive** life forms, yes, but living creatures nonetheless. Colonizing K-3—what you really mean is *invading* K-3—will destroy existing life on the planet."

"You would rather that our own people be destroyed?" Abben asked.

"Of course not," Kalin replied quietly. "But we should think about other solutions."

"We already have," Haruth said. "You know that as well as

I do. K-3 is the nearest planet with a suitable atmosphere and environment. There are others, yes. But they are too distant to be of use."

Kalin did not respond. He had heard all this before. Yet although he still disagreed with the arguments in favor of invasion, he could propose no **alternative** .

The Chairman called upon a dozen other representatives. Only two sided with Kalin, although several expressed understanding of his position. Finally, the Chairman banged his gavel.

"I believe that we have heard enough. As Chairman, I therefore propose that we are ready to take a vote on this matter. All in favor of ending the debate now and taking a vote, please touch the green button on your controller. All against ending the debate, please touch the blue button. If you wish to **abstain** from voting, touch the white button."

When the last vote had been cast, an electronic display screen mounted above the podium displayed the results.

"The vote to end the debate is 87 in favor, 13 against, no abstentions. The debate is now **concluded** . We are ready to vote on the issue at hand."

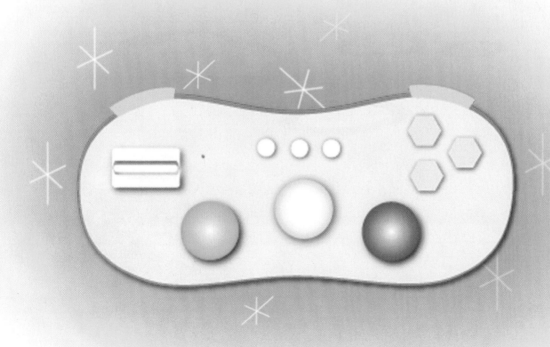

The hall quieted. The Chairman continued, "The proposal before this assembly of the Global Union calls for the **immediate** colonization of planet K-3 in the Dithram Galaxy." The Chairman paused. He wanted the complete attention of everyone in the hall. "Such colonization will be carried out with the full might of our Unified Interspace Forces. This is not a course of action to be entered into without full recognition of its consequences." He paused once more. He wanted everyone to weigh his words carefully. "For the proposal to pass, it must receive a minimum of 75 votes—three-quarters of the representatives. I ask you now to **cast** your vote as follows. If you are in favor of the proposal, touch the green button on your controller. If you oppose the proposal, touch the blue button. To abstain, touch the white button."

A number of **spectators** began whispering. The Chairman slammed down his gavel. "There will be silence in this hall until the vote is completed. This is an extremely serious matter. It requires complete concentration."

A hush fell over the hall. One by one, the representatives registered their votes. Some touched their electronic buttons without **hesitation**. Others held back, frowning, still **conflicted**.

When the last vote had finally been cast, the display screen above the podium showed the results. The hall erupted with reactions from representatives and spectators alike. The Chairman had to pound his gavel repeatedly to restore order.

"The vote to colonize planet K-3 in the Dithram Galaxy is complete. There are 79 votes in favor, 16 against, and 5 abstentions. The proposal passes. The Global Union approves the colonization plan."

Kalin's young daughter greeted him when he arrived home. "What's the matter?" she asked. "You look sad."

Kalin sighed heavily. "The assembly took its vote today."

"About what you were explaining to me last night? About colonizing that planet with the living creatures?"

"They *call* it colonizing. It's nothing less than an invasion."

"So everyone voted against it?"

Kalin sat down and rubbed his eyes. "No," he said, lowering his voice. "It was approved."

His daughter was quiet for a long time. She had many questions, but her father looked so tired and unhappy that she did not want to trouble him.

She sat down beside him, wondering what he was thinking.

"What's the planet's name?" she asked after a while.

He looked at her, puzzled. "What do you mean?"

"Well, *we* call it K-3. But those living creatures there must have their own name for it, right?"

Kalin smiled at her. "Yes. Of course."

"So?" she persisted. "What do *they* call it?"

"*Earth*, my daughter. They call their planet *Earth*."

> ### ■■■ STOP AND THINK
> 1. What important fact don't you learn until the end of the story?
> 2. In what way will the global vote change both of these planets?

Your Turn

Use Your Words:

aroma	hesitate
brittle	immediate
cast	rustle
chance	scarce
conflicted	scowl
flicker	shoal
flimsy	shudder
fugitive	spectator
glimpse	swept
grim	wake

- Read the words on the list.
- Read the dialogue. Find the words.

I hear a <u>rustle</u> in the reeds. Look, a <u>flicker</u> of silver in the water!

Quick! Row! A <u>fugitive</u> fish! It's getting away.

MORE ACTIVITIES

1. Draw a Picture

Listening and Speaking

Suppose you entered the fishing contest and won! Draw a picture of yourself holding the winning catch. Show your picture to your partner. Talk about it.

2. Play "Who Is It?"

Listening and Speaking

Choose to be one of the people in the picture. Have your partner ask up to five yes-or-no questions to figure out which person you've chosen. Then change places.

3. Take a Survey

Graphic Organizer

What kinds of things make your classmates shudder: a scary movie, a test, a worm? Ask ten classmates which of the following things make them shudder. Let them choose as many as they want. Tally their answers and make a bar graph to show your results.

What makes you shudder?

Worms	
Stormy night	
Scary movie	
Test at school	
Spider	
Chores	
Other	

122

4. You Are the Author

Writing

With a partner, think of words that describe fish and where they live. Write down the words. Use the words to write a poem about a fish. Share your poem with your partner.

5. Pick the Contests

Writing

Think about all the contests you would like to enter and win. Choose your two favorite contests. Write a paragraph describing the contests and why you think you would win. Share your writing with your class.

6. Make a List

Vocabulary

Flimsy and *brittle* are two words that are used to describe things. With a partner, brainstorm things that are flimsy and things that are brittle. Make a list. Share the list with your class.

Flimsy	Brittle

Crossing in Darkness

from

Friend on Freedom River

by Gloria Whelan

Illustrated by Gijsbert van Frankenhuyzen

FOCUS: How can someone find the courage to try a new and frightening task?

 The time is 1850. Louis lives on a farm at the edge of the Detroit River. Canada lies just across the river. **Fugitive** *slaves often pass through the area on their way to Canada, where there is no slavery.*

 One evening, Louis is working alone outside. Winter is coming, and the river is starting to ice over. Louis hears a **rustling** *noise nearby. A woman, Sarah, steps out from the bushes, along with her son Tyler and her daughter Lucy. Tyler* **scowls** *distrustfully at Louis. But Sarah explains that the three are escaping to Canada.*

 Louis's father has always helped any runaway slaves who asked. However, Papa is away. Louis knows the river's **shoals** *and currents. But it takes three hours to row to Canada. Slave catchers are traveling close behind the family, so the trip cannot wait until morning. Is Louis strong enough for this task? Is he brave enough? Should he take this* **chance***? Louis's father has told him, "Just do what you think I would have done." So Louis makes the decision to take the family across.*

 Louis spends a moment in the farmhouse kitchen. It is full of the **aromas** *of supper cooking. He takes some chocolate bread for the trip. He gets out warm clothes and a quilt. He says goodbye to his mother. Then he goes back outside.*

Louis gave the warm clothes, the quilt, and the chocolate bread to Sarah and her children. The boy looked like he wasn't going to put the jacket on, then he did.

"Don't mind my boy, he's stubborn," Sarah said. "I tell him there are good white people. Plenty of them helped us along our way."

Together the two boys pushed the skiff into the water, breaking a thin skin of ice. They held the boat steady while Sarah and Lucy climbed in.

"You sure you can row a boat?" Louis asked Tyler.

"I'm sure. I rowed the boat for Master Harmon when he went cat fishin'. I rowed him all over Mud Lake."

Louis and Tyler slipped the oars into the locks. Like a hand reaching up out of the water the strong current grabbed hold of the skiff. The river that was such a friend to Louis in the daytime was a dangerous stranger at night.

"To fight the current we got to paddle upstream as we paddle across," Louis said. The icy wind stung their faces. The light from the farmhouse faded.

"How did you get here?" Louis asked Sarah.

"We crossed the Ohio River and come station to station on the Underground Railway."

"We followed the North Star," Lucy said.

"They sent big dogs sniffing and growling after us," Tyler said.

Sarah said, "There were kind folk took us in, hungry, and sent us off full."

LOOK IT UP

For more on the Underground Railroad: Harriet Tubman, slavery in the United States, Compromise of 1850, Underground Railroad songs, abolitionists, Civil War

The boat **shuddered** as it plowed through the thin ice. In the daytime Louis had the gulls and the other fishermen to keep him company, but in the winter night it seemed to Louis the four of them were the only people left on earth. Louis's teeth were chattering and his fingers were numb. Sarah held Lucy close to protect her from the wind.

The light from the farmhouse had long since disappeared but now another light wavered on the river. It was the lantern of a patrol boat. Louis felt as if he had swallowed a piece of the ice. If they were discovered, Louis would be sent to jail. Sarah and her children would be sent back to slavery.

"Stop rowing," Louis whispered to Tyler. "We got to be quiet."

As soon as they stopped rowing, their boat began drifting away from Canada. The voices of the men carried across the water as the patrol **swept** by. The **wake** from the patrol boat splashed against the skiff, but the boat's lantern didn't catch them.

When the patrol boat was out of hearing the boys began to row again. Their arms ached from trying to make up the distance they had lost.

Tyler was as worried as Louis. To break the silence he asked, "What kind of fish you catch in this river?"

"Whitefish, herring, perch, sturgeon. My papa caught a sturgeon that weighed 80 pounds."

"That's a big fish. You got to be strong to catch it. You got to be smart to catch a catfish. The best thing is just to put on a heavy sinker and let some crawlers bump along the bottom of the lake."

The wind was against them and the ice was thickening. For every foot they gained, the boat seemed to slip back a foot into the black water. He had never been so cold.

Louis wished he could ask his papa if he had done the right thing to risk their lives.

Sarah began to sing and the children joined her.

O Lord, O my Lord, keep me from sinkin' down
I tell you what I mean to do
Keep me from sinkin' down
Sometimes I'm up, sometimes I'm down
Keep me from sinkin' down
Sometimes I'm almost on the ground
Keep me from sinkin' down
I look up yonder and what do I see?
I see the angels beckonin' me
Keep me from sinkin' down

After a minute Louis sang, too. The wind tossed the words back at them and they sent them back into the wind.

They all saw the light at the same time. "That another patrol boat?" Tyler whispered.

But the light stayed still.

"That's Canada!" Louis shouted.

He and Tyler pulled on the oars. They jumped out and dragged the skiff onto the shore.

The group reaches a farmhouse. There, people welcome Sarah and the children inside. Louis returns to the river to begin the long trip home. As he heads for the other shore, he knows that he has done what his father would have done.

STOP AND THINK

1. What gave Louis the strength to try to make the journey?

2. What can make a familiar task become unknown and frightening?

THE TRAIN RIDE

From PEACEBOUND TRAINS *by Haemi Balgassi*
Illustrated by Chris K. Soentpiet

FOCUS: Why might an ordinary family be
forced to leave their familiar way of life?

> Sumi, a young girl, listens to her grandmother tell about a
> frightening train ride into the unknown. This trip occurred during the
> Korean War in the early 1950s. Grandmother, or Harmuny, was young
> then. She was traveling south to the Korean city of Pusan to escape enemy
> soldiers. With her were her husband, son, and baby daughter.
> The daughter would grow up to be Sumi's mother, or umma.
> The son would become Sumi's uncle.

Korean words you need to know

Harmuny (HAR muh nee) grandmother
Harabujy (HAH rah buh jee) grandfather
Oppa (OP pah) papa
Umma (UM mah) mama
Yuh-bo (YUH bo) a term of endearment

Harmuny breathes a hollow-sounding sigh. "Harabujy had arranged for us to cross the river by boat. We had to go before light, so no one would see. We walked briskly, through a chalky grayness cast over the woods by night's fading hours. Harabujy carried the two heaviest bundles. I held the small bundle in one hand, your uncle's hand in the other. A sling made out of my thickest apron wrapped your sleeping umma to my chest.

"We couldn't afford the risk or the energy to talk on the way. Only our shoes murmured soft shuffling words to the ground. Around us the night was still, except for the creaking of **brittle** tree branches stooped low with icicles.

"A fisherman was waiting for us in the shadows of the riverbank. His boat was behind him, and I remember thinking, *It looks so **flimsy**. Surely we will all be toppled by the river's current.* But to escape to the south, we had to cross the river. As Harabujy and the fisherman rowed, I fixed my eyes on the shifting sky and prayed that we would reach the other bank safely. Luck was with us that night, for we set foot on land soon after.

"Throughout the next days we continued our journey on foot. We saw many others doing the same. Some were riding ox carts. Others struggled to pedal rusted bicycles on harsh winter soil. Occasionally we saw a car or truck, but not often.

"We heard about a train going south to Pusan. Harabujy was determined that we be on it. He feared there would be no more trains after this one. It could be our last chance for a safe passage.

"At last, on a frigid morning thick with fog, we **glimpsed** the looming shadow of the train ahead. As we drew closer, we could see people huddled alongside. So many people, thousands. Like us, they were dusty from travel by rural roads. Hungry babies wailed for their mothers' milk. Shivering children tugged on their mothers' and grandmothers' skirts. Everywhere I looked, a sea of **grim**, pained faces stared back.

"Suddenly, Harabujy turned to me, his face pale as the moon. 'Yuh-bo, you and the children must ride this train,' he said. His words clutched at my heart. 'What about you?' I demanded to know. And your uncle cried, 'Come with us, Oppa!'

"But Harabujy gripped my hand, so tightly that my knuckles ached, and said, 'I must go and do my part in this war, as a soldier. It is my duty, Yuh-bo.' If there had been more time, I would have argued with him further. But there was no time left."

Harmuny tells her granddaughter that Harabujy put the family on the train. Since the train was already packed full, the family climbed onto the equally crowded roof. It was hard to say goodbye.

"Then, before I knew what was happening, the train was moving. Harabujy was on the ground, waving to us and looking so brave. He smiled as wide as he could. The wind tried to bully me with its frosty breath, yet my eyes never moved from my husband. I wanted to wave back, but I couldn't for I had to hold on to the children and the bundles…to keep us all from plummeting off the slippery roof.

"Your umma was too little to know, but her brother began to cry as the train gained speed passing the crowd on the ground. 'Oppa, Oppa,' he moaned. 'Come with us, Oppa.' I consoled him the best I could, but it was no use. I knew he wanted his father. I knew because I did, too. Our tears froze on our cheeks as the train rumbled southward, rushing us away from war, away from home, away from the man I loved."

I reach with the cool cloth to wipe Harmuny's tears from her cheeks, just as she'd done for me earlier. "Tell me about the train ride, Harmuny. Did you make it to Pusan?"

Harmuny nods slowly. "Yes…but the journey was long. It was sad to see so many deserted farm fields and rice paddies. War had intruded on everyone's life, it seemed. The people we did see were all southbound, like us. Old people with tired bones and crooked canes did their best to keep up with their children and grandchildren. Those dogs not left behind panted alongside their exhausted masters.

LOOK IT UP

For more on the Korean War: Korean War timeline, Korean War battles, Forgotten War, Harry S Truman

"Young girls clutched bright folded blankets, and their brothers carried lumpy bundles in their skinny arms. Some people pushed carts, others pulled wagons. Most carried satchels and water canteens. Several times I saw young men sprint to grab on to the train, hoping for a ride, a chance for a brief rest.

"Those on the roof found it impossible to rest. Your umma was still a baby, so she wailed loudly throughout much of the trip. And her big brother fidgeted about, as young boys do. People complained. Room was **scarce**, and those without children resented the discomfort they caused. But I held my head high.

"When we saw sea gulls circle the skies, we knew we were approaching Pusan. After we left the train, the children and I found shelter in a school building. We met old neighbors and friends there, from Seoul."

Harmuny chuckles, remembering. "The local boys taught your uncle how to fish and dig for clams. Once he was pinched by a crab. But he didn't cry. He wanted to be brave, like his father."

Suddenly a light goes out of Harmuny's eyes, like a candle **flickering** dark. Her voice faint, she says, "And every time the soldiers came through, I searched their faces for Harabujy's." A whisper of a sigh flutters through her, and her small body seems to sag. "But I never found him. No, I never did."

STOP AND THINK

1. How was Harabujy's journey into the unknown different from the journey taken by the rest of the family?

2. Why are people sometimes able to do brave things at a time of great danger?

UNIT

6 IT'S A REVOLUTION

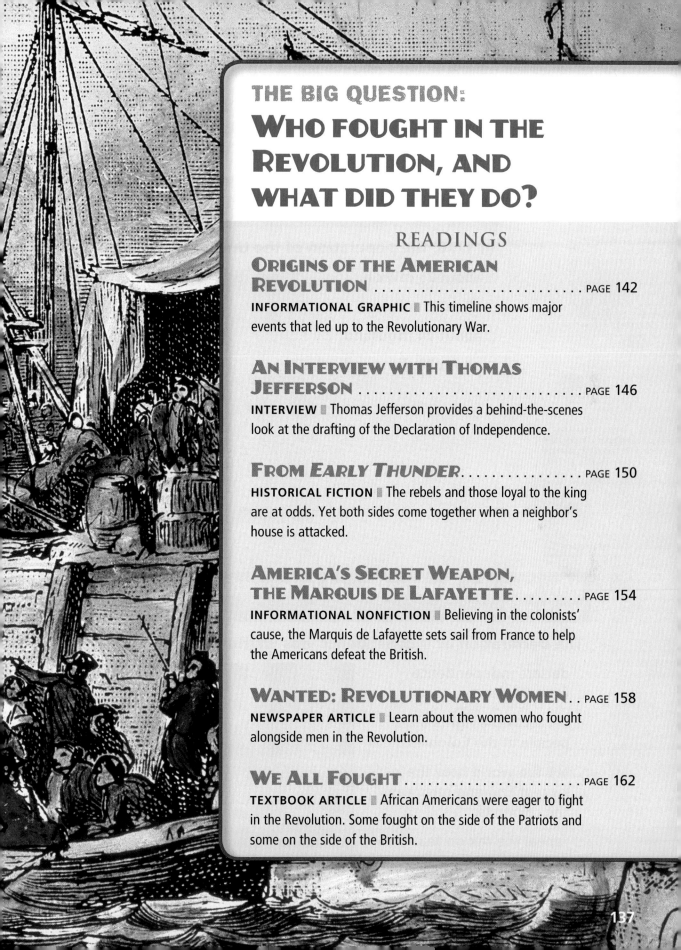

LOOK AT THE AMERICAN REVOLUTION

In 1776, what was the population of the United States?

In 1776, the population of the United States was...

- ☐ about 25 million.
- ☐ about 2 million.
- ☐ about 74 thousand.
- ☐ about 20 thousand.

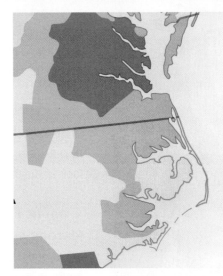

Why was the Declaration of Independence written?

The Declaration of Independence was written to...

- ☐ declare independence from England.
- ☐ set forth the rights of people in the Colonies.
- ☐ tell the world how the king of England mistreated the colonists.
- ☐ repeal the tax on tea.

How did Loyalist and Patriot ideas differ?

Loyalist and Patriot ideas differed in that...

□ Loyalists wanted to remain under English rule.

□ Patriots wanted to break with England.

□ Loyalists felt that problems with England could be settled.

□ Patriots wanted to set up an independent country.

Who fought in the American Revolution?

The people who fought in the American Revolution were...

□ farmers.

□ enslaved African Americans.

□ French noblemen.

□ laborers.

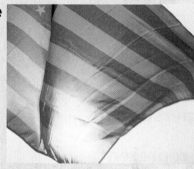

In what ways did women participate in the Revolution?

Women participated by...

□ bringing water to men on the front lines.

□ fighting alongside their husbands.

□ disguising themselves as men in order to fight.

□ intercepting messages from the enemy.

History Words

ally

An **ally** is a person, group, or nation that works with another for a common cause or purpose.

66 During the Revolution, France was an ally of the United States. 99

alter

Alter means to change or make different.

66 If I alter the dress, it will fit better. 99

motto

A **motto** is a sentence, phrase, or word that conveys the spirit or purpose of an organization or nation.

66 'In God We Trust' is the motto of the United States. 99

persuasive

Persuasive means able to convince by reasoning or urging.

66 People began volunteering when they heard his persuasive speech. 99

declaration

A **declaration** is a document that sets forth an announcement or proclamation.

66 The declaration stated that the people wanted to form their own government. 99

drastic

Drastic means forceful and extreme.

66 The people took drastic measures in their fight against the king. 99

merchant

A **merchant** is a person who buys and sells goods for profit.

66 The merchant bought tea and sold it in his shop. 99

represent

To **represent** means to act on behalf of a state, a person, or a group of people.

66 The delegate will represent the United States at the world summit. 99

significant

Significant refers to something important or of consequence.

66 The Declaration of Independence is a very significant document. 99

urgent

Urgent means requiring immediate action or attention.

66 General Washington received an urgent message from Congress. 99

Origins of the
AMERICAN REVOLUTION

Paris Treaty Ends French and Indian War

Britain and its American colonies defeat France and its American Indian **allies**. But the victory comes at a cost: war debt.

Townshend Acts

These acts place new taxes on the American colonies. Colonists avoid the taxes and attack British tax agents.

1765

1763

1767

Stamp Act

British Parliament sets a tax on colonial newspapers, almanacs, legal papers, and cards. The tax will help pay for Britain's war debt. In response, American colonists riot, burn stamps, and attack stamp agents. Since the colonists don't have **representatives** in Parliament, their **motto** becomes, "No taxation without representation."

142

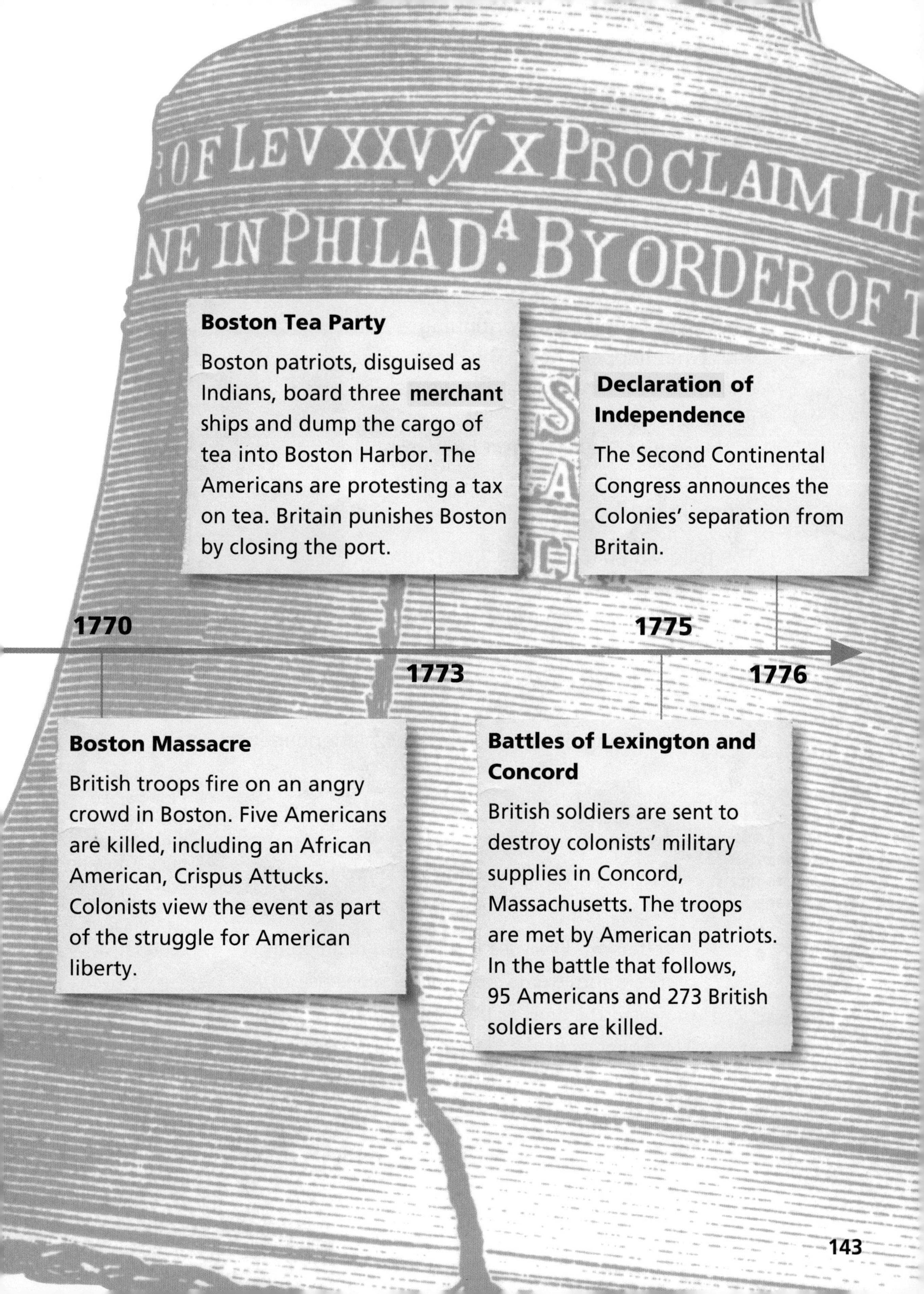

Boston Tea Party

Boston patriots, disguised as Indians, board three **merchant** ships and dump the cargo of tea into Boston Harbor. The Americans are protesting a tax on tea. Britain punishes Boston by closing the port.

Declaration of Independence

The Second Continental Congress announces the Colonies' separation from Britain.

1770

1773

1775

1776

Boston Massacre

British troops fire on an angry crowd in Boston. Five Americans are killed, including an African American, Crispus Attucks. Colonists view the event as part of the struggle for American liberty.

Battles of Lexington and Concord

British soldiers are sent to destroy colonists' military supplies in Concord, Massachusetts. The troops are met by American patriots. In the battle that follows, 95 Americans and 273 British soldiers are killed.

Comprehension

☑ **TARGET SKILL** Sequence of Events

Every passage or selection tells about **events** that happen. These events happen in an **order**, beginning with what happens first and continuing with what happens next. The order ends when there are no more events in the selection. This order is known as the **sequence of events**. **Clue words and phrases** help tell you how to put events in order.

The following paragraph taken from the selection "An Interview with Thomas Jefferson" contains clue words and phrases that help tell the sequence of events. The interviewer is asking Thomas Jefferson for information about the writing of the Declaration of Independence.

> **Clue word** *when* gives a time when something happened.

> **Clue phrase** *and then* tells what happened next. Knowing what happened next also tells which event comes first.

Interviewer: What happened when your draft was presented to the committee, and then to the whole congress?

Jefferson: Everyone was entitled to an opinion. Our committee of five made alterations before we presented the draft to the Continental Congress. The Congress made 39 more changes before the document was finally accepted on the morning of July 4.

> **Clue word** *finally* tells what the happened at the end.

> **Clue word** *before* tells when something was done.

First: Committee of five made alterations to the draft.

Second: The draft was presented to the Continental Congress.

Third: The Congress made 39 changes.

Fourth: The draft was accepted on the morning of July 4.

The first box tells the first event that happens in the sequence of events. The second box continues the sequence and names the next event. The third box tells the event that happens after that. The fourth box tells the last thing that happens.

✔ TARGET STRATEGY **Summarize** In a summary, you give the main points or events of a selection. You can use what you know about sequence to write a well-organized summary. As you read, ask yourself:

• What exactly happened?

• In what order did the events happen?

• Why is the sequence of events important?

An Interview with
THOMAS JEFFERSON

FOCUS: Who wrote the Declaration of Independence?

Interviewer: Mr. Jefferson, what was the background to the writing of the **Declaration** of Independence?

Jefferson: It was a time of great danger and uncertainty about the future of the Colonies. We were already at war with the British. Now we were about to take a **drastic** step.

Interviewer: Please tell us, sir, how the Declaration of Independence came about.

Jefferson: The **delegates** of the Continental Congress believed that we should have a formal document declaring the Colonies' independence. We had to write a statement of our rights. We needed to tell the world how the English king was abusing us. The Congress formed a committee of five men, of whom I was one, to draft the declaration.

Interviewer: How did you get the writing job?

Jefferson: I wanted John Adams to do it, because he was so forceful and **persuasive**. But he thought I was the right man for the job, because of other writing I had done. People say I have a way with words. So I agreed to do the rough draft.

Interviewer: In my **capacity** as a writer myself, I know that important details are often taken out of one's writing before it is published. Was anything cut out of the draft you wrote?

Jefferson: Yes. I said that slavery was wrong, but many slave owners didn't want that in the document. They would have refused to sign it, and we had to have **unity**. So that part was cut. The slavery issue was probably the most hotly contended topic of all. I also said that King George was a tyrant, and that the British people were wrong to side with him. The Congress wanted the British people to support our efforts. So they didn't want to criticize them. That part was also taken out.

Interviewer: How was it possible to create a document of such **significance** in so short a time? You wrote the draft in a little more than two weeks!

Jefferson: I had done a great deal of thinking and writing on the topic already. Nevertheless, it was a heavy task. There was **urgency** and pressure.

Interviewer: What happened when your draft was presented to the committee, and then to the whole Congress?

Jefferson: Everyone was **entitled** to an opinion. Our committee of five made 47 **alterations** before we presented the draft to the Continental Congress. The Congress made 39 more changes before the document was finally accepted on the morning of July 4. I was not happy with all the changes, but I understood that this document had to **represent** the views of the entire Congress.

Interviewer: When you signed the Declaration, why didn't you sign in letters as large as John Hancock's? Many people think he wrote the Declaration.

Jefferson: Let them think so. John was president of the Congress and a bold man.

■■■ STOP AND THINK

1. Which of Jefferson's ideas did not remain in the Declaration of Independence?

2. What steps do you take when writing a report?

A draft of the Declaration of Independence

LOOK IT UP

For related information:
Thomas Jefferson, Declaration of Independence, Founding Fathers, Colonial Virginia history, Louisiana Purchase

147

LEARN THE WORDS

Your Turn

Use Your Words:

advance	flannel
capacity	grieve
crucial	invalid
delegate	lack
disguise	patriot
eloquent	pension
endure	rebel
entitle	treaty
eventual	unity
fateful	upstanding

- Read the words on the list.
- Read the dialogue. Find the words.

I remember that <u>fateful</u> day. The cannon went off and I became an <u>invalid</u>.

You are an <u>upstanding</u> soldier. When this is over, you will be <u>entitled</u> to a <u>pension</u>.

MORE ACTIVITIES

1. Make a List
Vocabulary

With a partner, think of all the words you would associate with winter. Make a list of the words. Write each word in the correct category. Share your list with your class.

Weather	Clothing	Activities

2. Draw a Picture
Listening and Speaking

Think of an outstanding person you know. Draw a picture. Share the picture with your partner. Explain why the person is outstanding.

3. Write a Letter
Writing

Suppose you were camped with the Patriot soldiers. Write a letter home to your family telling of your experience. Share your letter with your partner.

4. Play "Guess It"

Listening and Speaking

One player picks an object in the picture above. The other player asks up to five yes-or-no questions to try to figure out what it is.

5. Be an Actor

Listening and Speaking

With a partner, take turns reading the dialogue in the picture aloud. Use your best acting voice.

6. What Is a Patriot?

Listening and Speaking

Think about what it means to be a patriot. Write down two qualities a patriot might have. Share the qualities with your class. Explain why you chose them.

From *Early Thunder*

by Jean Fritz

FOCUS: Are political beliefs stronger than friendship?

In stories about the American Revolution, it often seems that everyone in the Colonies supported independence. In fact, between one-fifth and one-third of colonists remained loyal to England. These Loyalists, or Tories, believed that problems with the English government could be settled peacefully. The Patriots, or Whigs, wanted to break away from England and form a new country. The disagreements between the two sides caused painful splits in communities and even families.

This story tells of Daniel West. His Loyalist father is the town doctor in Salem, Massachusetts. The year is 1774. Both Whigs and Tories are angry at the tax on English tea. In protest, people are refusing to buy or drink tea. However, Judge Ropes, a neighbor, is very sick with smallpox. He has asked for tea, which makes him feel better. Daniel and his friend Beckett find some tea hidden in his father's things. If Whigs find the boys carrying the tea, they might be attacked. So they have made plans to sneak over to the Judge's house in the darkness of evening.

But as soon as Daniel and Beckett stepped out the back door, these plans were forgotten. The town was no longer quiet. The boys ran around the corner of the house to the main street, the part that was called Paved Street because it was the only street in town that was paved. To the right, in the next block where Beckett and Judge Ropes lived, lanterns were moving around. They didn't seem to be going anyplace—just moving back and forth, up and down. To the left there was nothing to see, only to hear. From the direction of the Common came the sound of singing. Daniel couldn't quite catch the words but he knew what they'd be. From the Liberty Song:

"Our right arms are ready,

Steady, men, steady!"

It was the Whigs celebrating the repeal of the stamp tax, acting as if it were *their* holiday, as if only *they* had a right to mark it.

Daniel and Beckett took to the middle of the road and ran to the right toward the lanterns. Ten or fifteen people were in front of Judge Ropes' house. They had coats on over nightclothes. Men had their bare feet thrust into boots; few had even taken time to put on hats. As Daniel and Beckett ran up, no one spoke. Mr. Foote, Beckett's father, simply pointed to Judge Ropes' house. It was dark except for a light in the kitchen on the right side. It took Daniel a minute to see what was wrong. Then he drew in his breath. Every window in the front of Judge Ropes' house was broken. Mr. Foote stepped closer and held up his lantern. Glass was strewn all over the lawn. Along with the glass were rocks and bricks: the rest, Daniel figured, were in the house.

Mr. Foote tried to describe what had happened but all that came out was how quick it had been. A gang evidently had crept up quietly, let loose all at once with the bricks and rocks they had come armed with, and by the time the neighbors were outside, they'd pounded off. It had all taken place, Daniel guessed, while he and Beckett were in the pie room.

"Didn't anyone go after them?" Daniel cried.

Mr. Foote nodded. "Yes, Nathaniel, the Judge's son. And some others. But they won't find them. By now they're all part of the big crowd celebrating on the Common."

Daniel looked around at the people standing on the street—neighbors, Whigs and Tories together, helpless, angry. Some of the women were crying; the men were pacing, talking in short, shocked sentences.

Beckett stepped near the house. "Miranda!" he called. His voice didn't come out very loud but even so Daniel winced. It was as if the night itself had somehow been hurt and any sound, no matter what kind, was more than it could stand. "Miranda! Come on out here. Daniel West has something for the Judge."

Slowly the kitchen door opened. At first there was just a square of light on the steps; then Miranda stepped out into the light, holding a lantern over her head and squinting nearsightedly at the street. Like everyone else, her clothes were in disarray and she wasn't wearing her mobcap. Her shoulders sagging, she obviously didn't know or care that under the lantern, folks could see that she was all but bald.

BURNING OF STAMP ACT,
Boston.
Stamp-Act passed by Parliament.
March 22, burned Aug. 1765; re-
pealed, March 19, 1766.

"They've gone, Miranda," Beckett said gently. "It's all right. We're all friends here." Daniel set the jar down in the middle of the street, then everyone backed up while Miranda walked slowly out from the house. It was the only way a person could send something into a smallpox house without spreading the disease. The line of onlookers, backed up as far as they could, stood quietly and respectfully as Miranda approached the jar.

As she bent down, Mrs. Foote spoke. "Tell the Judge, Miranda, that the damage was done by a few ruffians. Tell him the town loves him."

Miranda straightened up. "I did tell him that, Mrs. Foote."

"What did he say?"

"He didn't say anything. His heart is broken."

Miranda made her way back to the house. No one moved until the kitchen door closed.

Then Captain Pickering spoke. He was one of the town's leading Whigs and a good friend of the Judge.

"What was in that jar?" he asked.

Daniel was standing on the edge of the group. He whirled around.

"Tea!" he shouted. "It was a blasted jar of English tea!"

STOP AND THINK

1. Why did the gang attack Judge Ropes's house?

2. Have you ever stood up for a friend? How did you do it?

153

America's Secret Weapon,
The Marquis de Lafayette

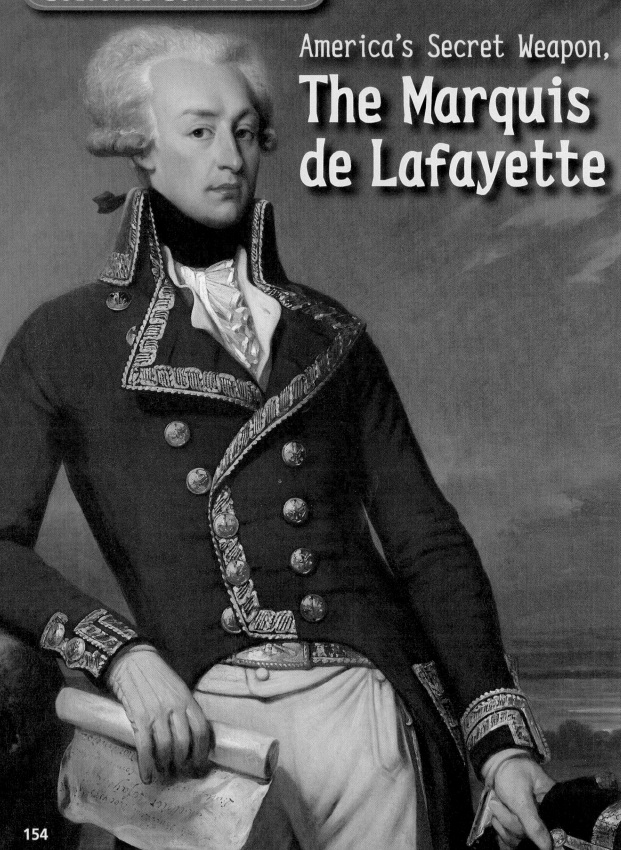

The American Revolution seemed doomed to failure. The thirteen British colonies had few trained military officers. The new army was filled with farmers and laborers, not soldiers. And worst of all, the Colonies **lacked** a navy, while the British navy commanded the oceans.

A 19-year-old French nobleman helped solve these problems. His full name was a mouthful: Marie Jean Paul Joseph Roche Yves Gilbert du Motier. "Marquis de Lafayette" was his title. He believed deeply in the rights of man and the idea of liberty. He also wanted to form a bond with the young country.

Lafayette was born in 1757. His family was rich and powerful. When he was young, his father was killed in battle. When he was 13, his mother and grandfather died and he inherited a fortune. By 17, he had already commanded men in battle. In 1776, Lafayette attended a **fateful** dinner. There he met the Duke of Gloucester, who told him of the **Declaration** of Independence and General George Washington's recent victories against the British army. Lafayette was electrified by the news. He wanted to help the colonial army.

France's king had no use for the American **rebels**. He would say jokingly, "I am a royalist by my trade, you know." But the queen, Marie Antoinette, was a supporter of the American cause.

The King and Queen of France, Louis XVI and Marie Antoinette

REREAD

Sequence of Events

What happened after Lafayette came to America but before the Battle of Brandywine?

Using his own money, Lafayette outfitted a ship. He obtained letters that would introduce him to the American Congress. He kept his movements secret, but **eventually** the English found out about his plan. They sent ships to try to stop him from reaching America.

When Lafayette made it to America, he offered his services for free. He soon became a major general and served as an aide to General Washington. The two became close friends. Lafayette was injured at the Battle of Brandywine. After he recovered, he helped Washington through a difficult time.

By 1778, Washington's position as commander in chief was questioned. Several people criticized Washington's performance. They sent letters to army generals and members of the Continental Congress. Lafayette spoke up, arguing that the French viewed Washington as **crucial** to the American cause. Lafayette was **eloquent**. His impassioned support of Washington helped win the day.

Lafayette suffered alongside Washington during the terrible winter at Valley Forge. He also fought bravely at Barren Hill and the Battle of Monmouth. Lafayette **endured** the freezing cold, the rain, the mud and mosquitoes, as well as the battles, that were part of the Revolutionary War.

Flag and uniform of the Revolutionary War

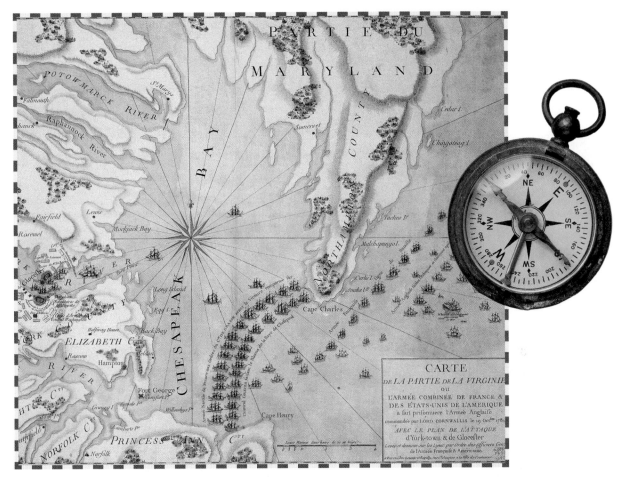

 French map of Battle of Yorktown, 1781

In 1778, Lafayette sailed back to Paris. On the way, he had to fight off sailors who wanted to turn him over to the British. When he arrived in France, he was received as a hero. Six thousand men and many ships were made ready for his return to America. France would provide what America so sorely needed—naval power.

Lafayette and his fellow Frenchmen proved key **allies** in the final stages of the revolution. Lafayette spent $200,000 of his own money to buy supplies for American troops. He also pinned down the British at the Battle of Yorktown. As the rebel army **advanced**, French ships kept the British from escaping by sea. When American and French forces were able to capture Yorktown, the war was over.

REREAD

Sequence of Events

What happened before Lafayette arrived in France but after he sailed for Paris?

STOP AND THINK

1. Why did Lafayette want to help the American colonies?

2. Do you think the Colonies would have won the Revolutionary War without help from the French?

WANTED:
REVOLUTIONARY WOMEN

FOCUS: Who are some of the women who played important roles in the Revolutionary War?

Philadelphia, December, 1800—This newspaper is creating an honor roll of women who helped bring about the successful end of the Revolutionary War. Everyone knows the names of men such as George Washington, Alexander Hamilton, and Paul Revere. The names of women who served the cause should also be known. Here are the women who are already on our list of honors. Remember their names. Tell them to your children and your grandchildren. Their names should be known to all future generations.

Margaret Cochran Corbin

In times of peace, Margaret Cochran Corbin worked alongside her husband. So when he became a soldier, she accompanied him. With other army wives, Margaret performed jobs around the camp, such as washing, cooking, and nursing the sick. John's task was to clean and load a cannon for another soldier to fire.

In November 1776, the colonial army met British forces in battle. John Corbin was killed by enemy fire. There was no time to **grieve**. Margaret took over his job of loading the cannon. Sometime during the battle, the gunner was also killed. There was no time to find another gunner. Margaret took on the job. She kept the cannon blasting against British troops.

Washington's army was trying to retreat. The job of the American gunners was to hold off the British troops while the rest of the American army got away. One by one, British attackers killed the American gunners and silenced their cannons. The last gunner standing was Margaret Cochran Corbin. Finally, she too was shot. She was badly wounded, but she survived.

Margaret later joined the "**Invalid** Regiment." This was a group of injured soldiers who continued to help the war effort. Later in life, she became very poor.

Ladies of Philadelphia working for Washington's army

In 1779, the United States government awarded her a half-**pension**. This was money paid to soldiers during the rest of their lives. Hers was the first government pension awarded to an American woman.

Mary Hays McCauly

Mary Hays McCauly lived with her husband, William Hays, in an army camp. Like John Corbin, William Hays was part of an artillery crew. Mary Hays entered the history books on June 28, 1778, when the Battle of Monmouth was fought. As the gunners loaded and fired their cannons, Mary Hays brought pitchers of water to the gunners. The water quenched their thirst and cooled the cannons. Mary Hays also tended to the wounded. She helped one injured soldier get to safety while cannon fire raged all around her.

Then William Hays fell wounded. Mary Hays took over his job of firing the cannon. She continued firing until the battle ended. The American line held. The British army ended up retreating.

According to contemporary accounts, Mary Hays earned praise from George Washington himself. He made her a sergeant in the Continental Army.

Mary Hays McCauly at the Battle of Monmouth

Molly Pitcher

When you say the name "Molly Pitcher," you may be talking about many women. It was a nickname used in stories about several different battles. It refers to women who went onto the battlefield carrying pitchers of water and ended up firing cannons. Mary Hays McCauly was most likely the "real" Molly Pitcher. However, there were other brave ladies who also did what McCauly did. Perhaps readers of this newspaper can give us more details about other "Molly Pitchers."

Deborah Sampson

Margaret Corbin and Mary Hays McCauly fought as women. Some female heroes **disguised** themselves as men. Deborah Sampson of Massachusetts signed up to fight under the name "Robert Shurtleff." She took part in several battles. She was wounded more than once. Instead of going to the camp doctor, she took care of her own wounds. She did this because a doctor would have figured out that she was not a man! Her secret caught up with her when she became ill with a fever. Then the doctor realized that she was a woman. After treating her, he passed her secret on to a higher commander. "Robert" got an honorable discharge from the Army without her secret being publicly revealed.

Grace and Rachel Martin

In South Carolina, the Martin family believed in the cause of the new nation. All the Martin sons signed up to fight. The wives of two sons were also heroes of the war effort. One night, they learned that some British soldiers were carrying important messages through their community. Grace and Rachel Martin disguised themselves in their husbands' **flannel** clothing. Pretending to be men, they ambushed the British soldiers. The captured soldiers handed over the messages. Grace and Rachel Martin got the documents to General Greene, the American commander. The British soldiers were let go. They never knew that they had been captured by two women.

Abigail Adams

Our own First Lady, Abigail Adams, was herself a hero of the Revolution. She stood up for the rights of Americans and for the rights of women. Her husband had a distinguished career. Before he was President, John Adams was a member of the Continental Congress; a diplomat representing the United States in Paris, France; the first United States

Abigail Adams

Minister to Great Britain; and Vice President. Throughout that long career, Mr. Adams considered Abigail Adams to be one of his most intelligent advisers.

Where Are the Other Ladies of Liberty?

We are sure that many other women performed brave deeds for the cause of liberty. Do you know any of them?

■ ■ ■ STOP AND THINK

1. Why were some women nicknamed "Molly Pitcher"?

2. Do you think female soldiers should be allowed to fight on battlefields today? Why or why not?

The Battle of Lexington, April 19, 1775

WE ALL FOUGHT

African Americans in the Revolution

FOCUS: How do you fight for freedom when you don't have freedom yourself?

The cry for freedom and liberty coming from the American **patriots** in 1776 must have sounded appealing to nearly 500,000 enslaved people. But most African Americans living in the British colonies were not allowed to fight for their freedom. Slave owners feared giving weapons to the people they enslaved. And making these enslaved people into an army that could turn against the slave owners worried many of the revolutionary leaders. At first, George Washington refused to allow African Americans to join the Continental Army. As a Virginia landowner and slave owner, he preferred to win the revolt without using freemen or the enslaved.

Ninety-two percent of the African American population were enslaved. Most lived in the South. Fewer than 25,000 African Americans lived as freemen or freewomen. Most free African Americans lived in the northern colonies. When war broke out, they had to decide where their loyalties lay.

Lord Dunmore was the British Governor of Virginia. At the start of the war, he offered wages and freedom to any African American who joined the British. Tens of thousands of men and women signed up, though only a few hundred actually took up arms.

When African Americans began joining the British side, General Washington decided to change his position. He too began enlisting African Americans into his army. He had suffered many defeats and needed more soldiers. Soon, one out of every four soldiers in his army was African American. In some cases, the enslaved served in place of their masters. Congress offered slave owners $1,000 for any slave that served in the army. The enslaved were promised $50 and their freedom at the end of the war.

REREAD

Sequence of Events

What sequence of events convinced Washington to allow African Americans to join the army?

Many of the African Americans who served with the British died in a smallpox outbreak. Others stayed with the British forces when they fled America. They were given land in Nova Scotia. But it was of poor quality. A colony in Sierra Leone, in Africa, was established for them. Yet this also proved to be a difficult place to resettle.

Peter Salem, black soldier and patriot, fought at the Battle of Concord on April 19, 1775.

Washington
Crossing the
Delaware
by Emanuel
Leutze

Black Heroes of the War

Five thousand African Americans fought for the rebels. Some became famous.

★ **James Armistead Lafayette** was a skilled spy. He volunteered for the role. He provided information on the traitor Benedict Arnold. Later, he worked as a double agent. He fooled the British general Cornwallis into thinking he was spying on the rebels. But instead, he passed information to the Marquis de Lafayette that helped to win the war.

★ **Crispus Attucks** is perhaps the most famous African American rebel. Most likely a runaway slave, Attucks was killed in the Boston Massacre, at the very beginning of the war.

★ The **1st Rhode Island Regiment** became famous as the only all–African American military unit in the army, though it served under the command of white officers. The regiment fought valiantly. At the end of the war, its soldiers were not granted pay or **pension** for their services.

★ **Salem Poor** was cited for his bravery during the Battle of Bunker Hill. Poor had purchased his freedom in 1769 for 27 pounds, about the value of a year's labor.

★ **Seymour Burr** first fought for the British in Connecticut. He was captured and returned to his master. After convincing his master that he would fight for the rebels, Burr gained his freedom.

★ **Agrippa Hull** was born a freeman in 1759. He served as an aide to General Kosciuszko, who came from Poland to help the rebels. After the war, Agrippa's strong character and wit made him famous.

Crispus Attucks was killed in the Boston Massacre.

★ **Prince Whipple** may have accompanied General Washington in the famous crossing of the Delaware River. Whipple received his freedom at the war's end.

★ **William Flora** fought bravely with a small force of Americans holding off a larger British force at Norfolk, Virginia. Flora later became an **upstanding** businessman.

On the other side of the conflict were equally famous African Americans. Colonel Tye fought a guerrilla war for the British across New Jersey. He commanded over 800 men and was never captured. Boston King, another escaped slave, joined the British as a way to stay free. He later wrote of his experiences, and became a teacher and scholar.

STOP AND THINK

1. Why did Washington change his mind about letting African Americans join the army?

2. How do you think enslaved people felt about the Revolutionary War?

UNIT 7

ECO DISASTERS

HOW ARE HUMANS, PLANTS, ANIMALS, AND RESOURCES ON EARTH CONNECTED?

READINGS

LOOK AT ENVIRONMENTAL ISSUES

What does a food chain show?

A food chain shows...

☐ the Sun as the source of energy.

☐ that plants use sunlight to grow and reproduce.

☐ that animals and insects eat plants.

☐ that some animals and insects are eaten by other animals.

How do invasive species threaten the environment?

Invasive species threaten the environment by...

☐ competing with native species for food.

☐ damaging the physical environment.

☐ killing native species.

☐ upsetting the food web.

What happens to animals when natural areas are destroyed?

When natural areas are destroyed, animals...

- ☐ are forced to move to a smaller, shrinking habitat.
- ☐ compete with other animals for limited food.
- ☐ try to stay and survive.
- ☐ begin to die off.

How are humans damaging the oceans' ecosystems?

Humans damage the oceans' ecosystems by...

- ☐ overfishing.
- ☐ dumping waste into the oceans.
- ☐ filling in wetlands and mangrove swamps.
- ☐ allowing fertilizers and pesticides to flow into the oceans.

What can humans do to help endangered species?

To help endangered species, humans can...

- ☐ make everyone aware of endangered animals living nearby.
- ☐ recreate a species' habitat.
- ☐ fight to preserve natural areas.
- ☐ discover what is threatening the species.

Science Words

decline

decompose

displace

exploit

fungi

organism

photosynthesis

physical

resource

species

---

decline

A **decline** means a decrease or a downward trend.

" The harsh winter caused a decline in the deer population. "

decompose

Decompose means to rot or decay.

" Over time, a dead plant will decompose with the help of fungi and bacteria. "

organism

An **organism** is a form of life, such as a plant or an animal.

" An amoeba is a one-celled organism found in pond water. "

photosynthesis

Photosynthesis is the process by which green plants use sunlight to produce carbohydrates.

" Photosynthesis relies on sunlight and carbon dioxide. "

displace

Displace means to put out of the proper or usual place, or to take the place of.

66 Cutting down the forest will displace a lot of animals. 99

exploit

Exploit means to use to one's advantage.

66 The government plans to exploit the river's current in order to produce electricity. 99

fungi

Fungi are organisms that include mushrooms, mildew, mold, and yeast.

66 The fungi on that dead tree are helping to decompose the rotted wood. 99

physical

Physical means of or relating to material things.

66 The pond, meadow, and forest made up the frog's physical surroundings. 99

resource

A **resource** is an available supply that can be used when needed.

66 The country's main resource was oil. 99

species

Species refers to a category of individuals that have some common characteristics.

66 The lake is home to a rare species of fish. 99

IT'S → ALL → CONNECTED

Think of a place such as a river, a plain, or a valley. Now think of all the **organisms** that live there, the relationships they have with one another, and their **physical** surroundings. That's an ecosystem. The living and nonliving parts are connected by two main processes. Energy flows through the ecosystem, and nutrients are cycled through it. The sun is the source of energy. Plants use **photosynthesis** to convert sunlight into sugars, which they use to grow and reproduce. Some animals eat plants. Other animals eat those animals. And still other animals eat those animals. Finally, bacteria and **fungi** consume dead plants and animals.

Scientists call this movement of nutrients and energy a food chain. A mouse might eat the seeds of a wildflower, a snake might eat the mouse, and a hawk might eat the snake. Then, when the hawk dies, it is **decomposed** by bacteria. Most food chains, however, are interrelated and overlapping. The mouse eats many kinds of plants and, in turn, may be eaten by many kinds of animals. Together, all the food chains in an ecosystem are called a food web.

mallard
duck

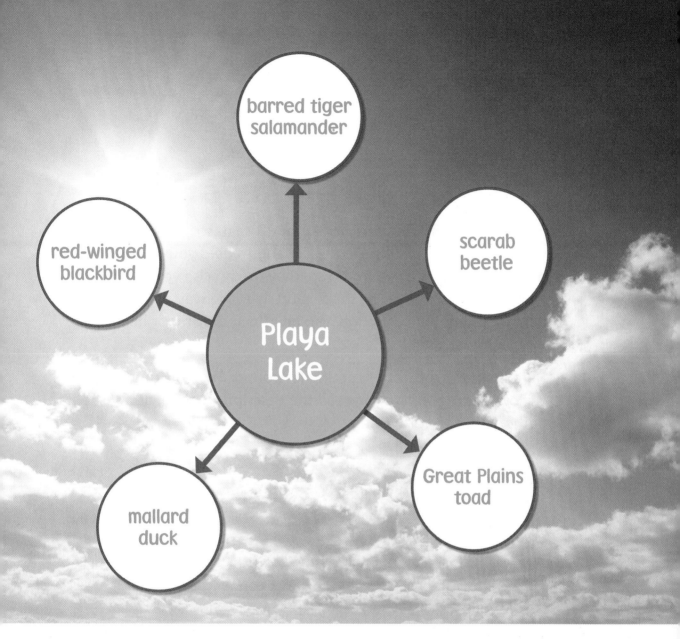

Playa Lake

The playa lakes of the high plains of Texas and neighboring states are a unique ecosystem. They provide wetland habitats for many species, including migrating water birds from northern North America. A playa lake is a shallow, circular basin. When it is filled by rainfall, a temporary lake forms. Playa lakes usually disappear for parts of the year. They can even dry out for years at a time, depending on rainfall patterns. Only plants and animals that have adapted to this pattern of flooding and drying out can survive there. For many migrating birds, playa lakes are just one of the habitats on which they depend for survival. Everything is connected.

Comprehension

✓ **TARGET SKILL** **Description** Authors use description to tell you what a place or thing looks like and to help you understand how something is done. To do so, they use precise verbs and words that describe color, shape, and size. The way an author describes something, though, can be affected by his or her motive for writing.

Here is an excerpt from "Turning It Around: The Return of the Willow Flycatcher." As you read the description, think about the author's motive for writing.

> It seems that David Ogilvie has proven the doomsayers wrong. He has created one of the healthier riverbank ecosystems in arid New Mexico.
>
> Ogilvie's success can be measured by inches and ounces. Those measurements record the dimensions of the southwestern willow flycatcher. This small bird is about 7 inches long, with just a 9-inch wingspan. It weighs just about half an ounce less than a letter that you'd mail with a first class stamp. The willow flycatcher isn't a glamorous bird. Its feathers are grayish brown, except for its pale yellow-gray underparts and some whitish bars on its wings. What makes it special is that, although its numbers are falling in most places, they are rising on David Ogilvie's ranch. Ogilvie has managed to protect this and other threatened species on a ranch where cattle are raised commercially.

These details help you see in your mind the small southwestern willow flycatcher.

Part of the author's motive in this article is to show that progress being made to restore ecosystems in the world is measured in small increments. Progress is not always dramatic, but any progress is significant. The description of the small bird helps support this idea.

You can use this graphic organizer to keep track of story clues that help you visualize in your mind what the author is describing.

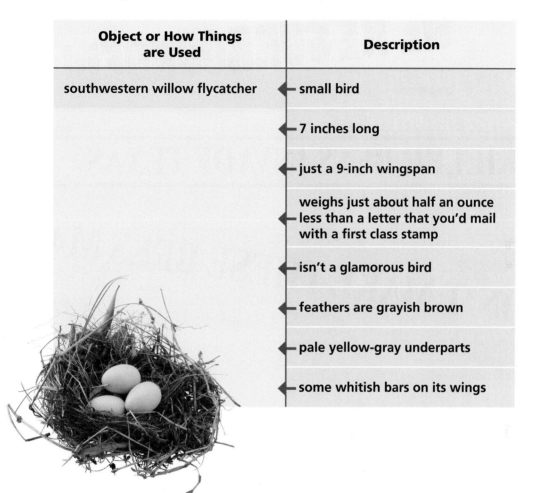

Object or How Things are Used	Description
southwestern willow flycatcher	← small bird
	← 7 inches long
	← just a 9-inch wingspan
	← weighs just about half an ounce less than a letter that you'd mail with a first class stamp
	← isn't a glamorous bird
	← feathers are grayish brown
	← pale yellow-gray underparts
	← some whitish bars on its wings

✔ **TARGET STRATEGY** **Analyze/Evaluate** To analyze and evaluate a descriptive text, you can ask the following questions:

• What is being described?
• What words help me see in my mind the thing being described?
• Why is the author writing this description?
• How does the author's motivation affect the description?

WE'RE SURROUNDED!

KILLER BEES INVADE TEXAS

DON'T MAKE THESE BEES MAD

FOCUS: How can one invading species affect an ecosystem?

These headlines may sound exaggerated, but they're serious. Animals and plants from one ecosystem can cause havoc when they are moved to a different ecosystem.

Plants and animals have always traveled to new lands. Seeds drift in the wind or float in water. Birds fly, wolves roam, and lizards swim. Most plants and animals don't survive very long in new environments. Some thrive, however. Their natural predators and competitors may not live in the new place. Or the new environment may have **resources** that the newcomer can **exploit** better than native **species** can. If the invading species does well enough, it can **displace** native species and change the ecosystem.

Humans also move plants and animals from one ecosystem to another. In the nineteenth century, for example, a group of New Yorkers brought 100 European starlings to Central Park. Today, starlings live throughout North America. Their population is estimated at over 200 million. Biologists think the starling's success has led to **declines** in many native bird species.

Killer Bees

So-called killer bees are actually honeybees from Africa. They were brought to Brazil so that scientists there could develop a better kind of honeybee. However, some of the bees escaped. They began to breed with native Brazilian honeybees. In 1990, the first swarm of these bees migrated from Brazil to Hidalgo, Texas.

These bees look a lot like a regular honeybee. Their sting is about the same, too. What makes them so dangerous? They attack in swarms, they chase their victims for great distances, and they are easily annoyed. Killer bees aren't really killers. Only a few people have died from the stings. One man even survived over 2,000 stings.

The greatest threat of these bees is to commercial beekeepers and to farmers. Beekeepers keep honeybee hives to make honey and other products. The aggressive "killer" honeybees can breed with or

killer bees

LOOK IT UP

For more invasive species: Hydrilla, kudzu in United States, Mediterranean white snails, giant salvinia, northern Pacific seastar

drive out the bees in commercial beehives. Unfortunately, killer bees tend to abandon a hive more easily and swarm off. They also do less well in cold weather. A beekeeper could end up with empty hives. The problem is greater than just honey production. Honeybees provide over 80 percent of the pollination needed for agricultural crops, such as melons. In this way, the presence of killer bees might endanger local agriculture.

Injurious Crabs

Chinese mitten crabs are named for their claws, which are covered with soft bristles. They aren't exactly warm and fuzzy. The first Chinese mitten crab ever found on the East Coast of the United States was collected from the Chesapeake Bay in Maryland in 2006. The federal government immediately issued an alert, like one of the FBI's "Most Wanted" posters. It told anyone who found a mitten crab *not* to throw it back into the water. That's because the crabs can multiply and spread quickly. They cause serious damage to riverbanks, levees, and ecosystems.

Chinese mitten crabs come from East Asia. They probably traveled by ship to the United States. They may have arrived in a ship's ballast water. The crabs are good to eat, so they may have been shipped to food markets. Or they may have been imported for the aquarium business. The crabs have already established themselves in California and Europe. They cause serious long-term damage to the environment. Huge numbers of the crabs burrow into riverbanks, causing erosion and mudslides. They displace native species, out-competing them for food. They also get into fishing and shrimping nets, damaging the nets and ruining the catches.

Chinese mitten crabs

Some Invasive Species in the United States

Species	Bad Habits	Estimated Costs
Leafy Spurge Purple Loosestrife Garlic Mustard Star Thistle	These plants mix with crops, make livestock sick, damage rangeland, crowd out native species, and kill trees.	$20 billion to control invasive weeds in the 1990s
Zebra Mussels Asian Clams	These mollusks eat native species, clog waterways and pipes, and damage ecosystems.	$5 billion per year to control zebra mussels and repair the damage $1 billion per year for the Asian clam
Balsam Woolly Adelgids Red Fire Ants Formosan Termites	These insects kill trees, hurt livestock, and damage wooden buildings.	95 percent of the Fraser firs in the Southern Appalachians destroyed by woolly adelgids $1 billion each year in livestock losses and control of the fire ant $1 billion per year in damages and control of the Formosan termite

STOP AND THINK

1. What makes the mitten crab a problem in its new environment?

2. What are two ways in which invading species force people to spend money on repairs?

Your Turn
Use Your Words:

aquatic	immense
balance	infinite
base	mechanize
compete	narrative
consequence	recover
decade	refine
deplete	respire
extinct	restore
extract	stock
fundamental	vast

- Read the words on the list.
- Read the dialogue. Find the words.

In the last <u>decade</u>, you've worked hard to <u>restore</u> <u>balance</u> in this ecosystem.

Yes. There were an <u>infinite</u> number of problems. So we started with some <u>fundamental</u> goals.

The water got so bad the fish couldn't <u>respire</u>.

Dennis tells an interesting <u>narrative</u> about the river's history.

Yes. When factories became <u>mechanized</u>, they began dumping into the river.

MORE ACTIVITIES

1. Venn Diagram
Graphic Organizer

In what ways can you help the environment at home? in school? in both places? Fill in the Venn diagram. Write the things you can do only at home. Write the things you can do only at school. Write the things you can do in both places. Then talk about the diagram with your class.

Helping the environment at home — Both — Helping the environment at school

2. Make a Drawing
Listening and Speaking

Suppose you could work, like the teenagers in the picture, to help restore a river. Draw a picture showing what job you would do. Show the picture to your partner. Talk about it.

3. Write a Letter
Writing

Is there a lake, pond, river, or stream in your area that needs help? Write a letter to an official, describing the body of water and what needs to be done to make it healthy. Share your letter with your class.

We pick up <u>vast</u> amounts of trash.

We <u>extract</u> water samples and test them.

We <u>refine</u> our methods as we learn. It will take an <u>immense</u> amount of work and time for this river to <u>recover</u>.

We <u>stock</u> the river with native fish and other <u>aquatic</u> animals.

At the <u>base</u> of the riverbank, we plant native plants.

Pollution <u>depletes</u> resources. Species must <u>compete</u> for food. In fact, many species are in danger of becoming <u>extinct</u>.

What are the <u>consequences</u> of pollution in this river?

4. It's Immense!

Vocabulary

Immense means "huge or very great." With a partner, think of other words that mean the same or almost the same as *immense*. Make a list of the words and share them with your class.

5. You Are the Reporter

Writing

Suppose you were a reporter covering the story of the river restoration. What questions would you ask? Write down five questions that would help you understand the project better. Share the questions with your partner. Talk about ways they can be improved.

6. Make a List

Vocabulary

People working to restore a river need tools and supplies. With a partner, make a list of the tools and supplies they might need. Share the list with your class.

Tools and Supplies
1.
2.
3.

181

WHAT HAPPENED HERE?

FOCUS: What "good idea" caused the Aral Sea disaster? What were some of the unexpected side effects?

Governments and companies often take advantage of natural resources or use them inappropriately. A government might decide to dam a river or allow gas exploration in a mountain range. A company might log a forest or build a mall on a wetland. The **consequences** of these decisions can affect many people for a long time.

The Story

REREAD

Description

What do these details show about the Aral Sea in 1960?

In 1960, the Aral Sea, really a saline lake, was the fourth largest inland body of water in the world. It was the size of Southern California. The sea was rich with many kinds of fish, and it supported an important fishing industry. The sea regulated the icy winds from Siberia in winter and eased the fierce summer heat. The sea was also a great "evaporator" that kept moisture in the air.

In the 1960s, the Soviet Union decided to use the land around the Aral Sea to grow cotton. There were millions of acres of flat land. All the land needed was water. The government ordered that water should be diverted from the AmuDarya River and the SyrDarya River to irrigate **immense** new cotton fields. The region became one of the world's largest cotton producers.

Abandoned boats rust near the Aral Sea.

The Aral Sea Disaster

What: When water was diverted from the rivers that feed it, the Aral Sea began to dry up.

When: The diversion projects began in the 1960s.

Where: Kazakhstan and Uzbekistan, in Central Asia

The Consequences

Once water was diverted from the rivers to the cotton fields, only a trickle was left to flow into the Aral Sea. The water in the sea kept evaporating. Salt does not evaporate with water, so as the sea shrank, it became more and more salty. The number of fish dropped. Four species became extinct. By the 1980s, there were not enough fish left to support a fishing industry. By 1995, seventy-five percent of the water in the Aral Sea was gone.

A huge salty desert has replaced the sea. Dust storms are frequent, and they carry the salt far. Without the sea, the local climate has become more severe. Winters are longer and colder, and the growing season is shorter and drier.

The impact on the people who live around the sea has been drastic. When the fishing industry collapsed, many families lost their livelihoods. Almost 5 million acres of once fertile land have become too salty to grow crops or vegetables. Grasslands where cows and sheep used to graze are now covered in toxic dust. Pesticides and fertilizers from the cotton fields have seeped into the groundwater, making people sick.

> **REREAD**
>
> **Description**
>
> What do these details show about the Aral Sea area?

Toxic Waste in Ecuador

What: As oil was **extracted** from Ecuador's rain forest, enormous amounts of toxic waste were spilled and dumped.

When: Drilling began in 1964, but most of the spills occurred between 1971 and 1992. Oil extraction is still going on in the area.

Where: In eastern Ecuador, a country in South America

Some of the rivers in Ecuador are polluted with oil and toxic waste.

The Story

Ecuador was in the middle of an oil boom in the early 1970s. The world was demanding more and more oil for industry and personal use. Large oil companies, including Ecuador's national oil company, were drilling and extracting oil in an area near the city of Oriente. The companies dumped large quantities of toxic wastewater into pits and swamps. In 1995, the companies signed an agreement to "remediate" the damage done. As part of the agreement, the company would clean up 160 of the more than 600 waste-filled pits. That part of the job was completed in 1998.

COLOMBIA

ECUADOR

Amazon

PERU

However, many large pits of toxic waste remain. Today, the surface of a river that feeds the Amazon River shimmers with an oily sheen. Children swim in the water; people eat fish caught in it. Some of the waste pits are in people's backyards. The fumes make them sick with **respiratory** infections and rashes.

The Future

Now a group of Ecuadorian citizens is suing the big oil companies again. They say that the oil waste has seeped into rivers and streams, poisoning animals and humans. They cite the cancer rate in the region, which is several times the nation's rate. The oil companies claim that the charges are unfounded. They refuse to negotiate a settlement. One way or another, two and a half million acres of rain forest have been damaged—or ruined. Many experts doubt whether the land can ever be cleaned up, since much of the toxic waste has already seeped into the ground.

What Can You Do?

We all need to make choices every day. Do we toss something away or recycle it? Do we walk to the corner store or ask for a ride in a car? How do these choices affect the world? If we recycle paper and clothing, not as much cotton has to be grown. If we walk to the corner store, not as much oil needs to be extracted and **refined**. Do you feel as though you should live "green"? What can you do to make a difference?

STOP AND THINK

1. What are some of the negative effects caused by wastewater from oil drilling?

2. What does toxic wastewater in Ecuador have to do with your life?

FERRET DOESN'T LIVE HERE ANYMORE

FOCUS: What ecosystem is as seriously threatened as the rain forest, and why?

Native to North America, the black-footed ferret is an endangered species. Less than two percent of its original grassland habitat still exists.

Following is the personal **narrative** of Oscar Anderson, an imaginary retired farmer from North Dakota, who might have seen some of the last black-footed ferrets in that state.

I was born in North Dakota in 1906. When I was growing up, there was still some prairie around here. I liked it. Used to lie on my back in the grass and watch the clouds sail by, listening to the meadowlarks.

I heard that the American prairie might be more endangered than the tropical rain forest that people make such a fuss about. We sure lost a lot of prairie, and we have to admit, we did it ourselves. There used to be grass as far as you could see, like an ocean of grass. Long ago, they say the prairie was black with buffalo. There were millions of those animals. Between the settlers and the government, they killed all but a few. Now people raise buffalo on ranches and sell them for meat, like beef. I've heard it's good, but I don't care to try it.

So what happened to the prairie? Folks like my grandparents are what happened. They settled here in the 1870s and 1880s and started their farms and ranches. Naturally, they came to make a living for themselves and their families, so they plowed the prairie under. And they drained the ponds and marshes where the ducks used to live. The problem is, all those wheat fields and cornfields were the end of the prairie.

Now, the ferret doesn't live here anymore. I heard there are a couple of groups out in Montana and Wyoming now. The ferrets nearly died out, you know. When that last group in South Dakota died, everyone thought they were **extinct**. Then in 1981 someone found 130 ferrets living in Wyoming. The conservationists got real excited, but most of those animals died of disease. Finally the scientists took the last eighteen and started breeding them in captivity.

What happened to the ferrets has a lot to do with what happened to prairie dogs. They're not related to dogs, but people call them dogs because they bark. When a prairie dog sees a hawk or a badger or a ferret, it jumps up and down and barks, "Yip, yip, yip!" to warn the others. Then they all dive into their holes. The prairie dogs are mostly gone now. Ranchers killed them. They thought prairie dogs were **competing** with their cattle for grass.

The ferrets used to eat prairie dogs, and they lived in old prairie-dog burrows. So when the prairie dogs disappeared, the ferrets did, too. It's all connected.

STOP AND THINK

1. The ferrets lost more than their land. What was the real cause of their disappearance?

2. Do you think it's important to keep animals like prairie dogs and ferrets alive? Explain your answer.

Oceans in Danger

Green sea turtle

Forum: What's Happening to Our Oceans?

FOCUS: How are oceans affected by human activities?

For most of human history, people have considered the oceans too large to damage. The number of fish living in oceans was practically limitless, so we didn't have to worry about them disappearing. Pollution that made its way into the oceans would be so diluted that it wouldn't matter. The ecosystems were **vast** and stable, so there wasn't any danger of upsetting the natural **balance**. But now we know that this isn't true. The oceans are not **infinite**. They are affected by human activities, and their ecosystems are surprisingly delicate.

OVERFISHING Since the 1970s, the number of factory fishing ships has risen dramatically. These giant, **mechanized** trawlers can sweep miles of ocean clean of fish. They have led to the collapse of many fisheries. When an important fish **stock** disappears, the food web is torn apart.

POLLUTION Runoff from crop fertilizers flows down rivers into the ocean. This leads to algae blooms that **deplete** the oxygen in the water, creating "dead zones" that extend for miles. When oil tankers run aground, the spills can damage coastal ecosystems for **decades**.

RISING TEMPERATURES Along with atmospheric temperatures, ocean temperatures are rising. The warmer temperatures cause damage to coral reefs. Warmer temperatures may also force some **aquatic** animals to move to colder waters. Scientists have also noticed a decline in the amount of tiny ocean organisms called plankton and krill, but they aren't sure what the cause is. Plankton and krill are **fundamental** to ocean food chains.

COASTAL DEVELOPMENT Much of the world's population now lives in coastal regions. Wetlands, estuaries, and mangrove forests, which act as nurseries for many ocean species, are filled in or paved over. Bays and beaches are polluted, further damaging coastal ecosystems.

Comments

1. Nikos (November 6) I live in Athens, Greece. I know that industrial waste and raw sewage are dumped into the ocean here. It's bad enough that our coastal waters are filthy and that fish are dying. It hurts to think that what we do here hurts the ocean in other places, too.

2. Darlene (November 8) I live in Greenville, near the Mississippi River. We aren't even close to the ocean. But I know that the water that flows from our land to the river is loaded with chemicals from fertilizers and pesticides. And the amount of animal waste a hog farm produces in a week is astonishing! All of it goes down the Mississippi and into the Gulf of Mexico. I've seen pictures of parts of the Gulf that are now officially dead. No sea creatures can live there because of the pollution.

3. Ben
(November 11)

I'm really proud of my state, Washington. We are part of a project to **restore** the Olympia oyster. It's the only oyster native to the Pacific Northwest. Landowners, tribes, community groups, and the shellfish industry have all worked together. More than 5 million oysters have been placed, or "seeded," in different areas across Puget Sound.

4. Maneh
(November 15)

In Bali, we have had a problem with sea turtles. Four of the five kinds of great sea turtles live around Indonesia. They have been hunted or accidentally killed in fishing nets, and now they are endangered. There is a big illegal trade in turtles and turtle meat here. And turtles are also used in some religious ceremonies. The World Wildlife Federation is working with Hindu priests to tell people that turtles don't have to be killed for the ceremonies. It is making a difference, I think.

5. Brenda
(November 21)

Doesn't everybody realize that the main danger for oceans right now is the decline of plankton and krill? Without plankton and krill, everything goes. They're the **base** of all the ocean's food chains. And scientists still don't know why the plankton and krill are declining, just that they are. I'm writing from Australia.

LOOK IT UP

For more on endangered sea life: southern sea otters, manatees, Guadalupe fur seals, monk seals, humpback whales, bowhead whales

Krill

6. Derek (November 29) I live near Mombasa in Kenya. We are losing coast and wetlands that are important to the health of our communities. In many places, the plants that held the soil in place have been cut down, so now the waves drag the soil into the ocean. Also, our beaches are very important to tourism. The United Nations and the Kenyan government are studying what to do about it.

7. Abigail (December 3) I'm from Massachusetts. Overfishing really cut the amount of cod all along the East Coast. Fishers have had to change the kind of fish they look for until the cod population **recovers**—if it ever does. I've heard that sometimes, when too many of a species die, the population can't recover. It's called a "tipping point." I really hope that hasn't happened.

STOP AND THINK

1. Why can fertilizers that help things grow create dead zones in the ocean?

2. Notice that the students who commented are aware of what's happening in the oceans near them. What do you know about what's happening to the oceans in North America?

191

Turning It Around

FOCUS: What did David Ogilvie do that helped preserve endangered species?

It seems that David Ogilvie has proven the doomsayers wrong. He has created one of the healthier riverbank ecosystems in arid New Mexico.

Ogilvie's success can be measured by inches and ounces. Those measurements record the dimensions of the southwestern willow flycatcher. This small bird is about 7 inches long, with just a 9-inch wingspan. It weighs just about half an ounce—less than a letter that you'd mail with a first class stamp. The willow flycatcher isn't a glamorous bird. Its feathers are grayish brown, except for its pale yellow-gray underparts and some whitish bars on its wings. What makes it special is that, although its numbers are falling in most places, they are rising on David Ogilvie's ranch. Even more significantly, Ogilvie has managed to protect this and other threatened species on a ranch where cattle are raised commercially.

What's the story? In 1994, Ogilvie decided to use some irrigation ditches from the old days, before the U Bar. When water flowed in the ditches, dying willow trees began to flourish. The same year, the U.S. government put the flycatcher on the endangered species list. Ogilvie was interested. He thought he had seen some willow flycatchers near the old ditches.

The rancher got a biologist to do a bird survey. The biologist found that there were indeed southwestern willow flycatchers on the ranch, and that it was the largest known population anywhere—64 pairs. Since then, Ogilvie has opened up more irrigation ditches. The willow trees have continued to thrive, and the bird population has grown. Now there are healthy forests and grasslands along the Gila River where it flows through the U Bar Ranch.

Some conservationists still think cattle should be removed from land where endangered birds and fish live. But Ogilvie's experience may lead to changing opinions. In his stretch of the Gila River, 99 percent of the fish are native species. That's not true elsewhere in the Southwest. And the U Bar supports what may be the healthiest habitat for songbirds in North America.

Willow flycatcher

New Mexico | Endangered Species List

Bat, Mexican long-nosed (Leptonycteris nivalis)

Bear, grizzly lower (Ursus arctos horribilis)

Chub, Chihuahua (Gila nigrescens)

Falcon, northern aplomado (Falco femoralis septentrionalis)

Flycatcher, southwestern willow (Empidonax traillii extimus)

leopard (Rana chiricahuensis)

Pecos (Gambusia nobilis)

hermosphaeroma thermophilus)

r (Panthera onca)

oach (Tiaroga cobitis)

de silvery (Hybognathus amarus)

Owl, Mexican spotted (Strix occidentalis lucida)

Rattlesnake, New Mexican ridge-nosed (Crotalus willardi obscurus)

STOP AND THINK

1. Some conservationists believe in an idea that Ogilvie's ranch disproves. What is the idea?

2. What does the story suggest to you about animals and ecological systems?

UNIT

8 BEYOND BOUNDARIES

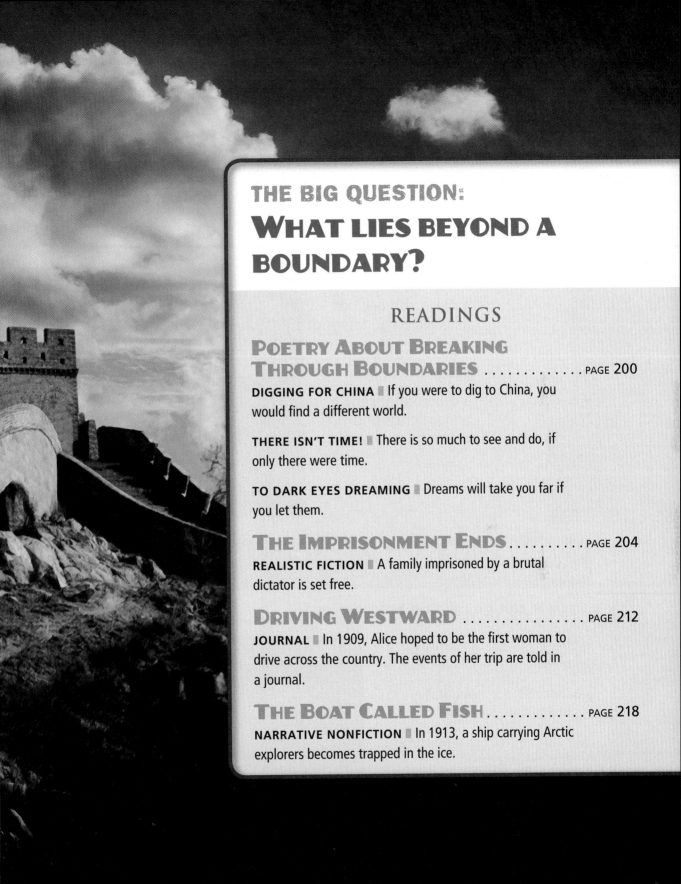

LOOKING BEYOND BOUNDARIES

Think about a boundary. What can a boundary be?

A boundary can be...

☐ a fence.

☐ a place you are not allowed to go beyond.

☐ a limit you put on yourself.

☐ a place where the known ends and the unknown begins.

What are some ways people can go beyond boundaries?

People can go beyond boundaries by...

☐ trying to do something new.

☐ exploring a new and unknown place.

☐ finding strength to change their lives.

☐ doing something no one has done before.

What happens when a dictator rules a country?

When a dictator rules a country...

- ☐ there are no free elections.
- ☐ there is no free speech.
- ☐ people can be arrested without cause.
- ☐ people must follow the dictator's rules.

In 1909, what problems did people have driving cross-country?

In 1909, people driving cross-country...

- ☐ had no road maps.
- ☐ had to travel on bad roads.
- ☐ had to repair their cars themselves.
- ☐ had few gas stations where they could buy gasoline.

What would people need to survive in a very cold place like the Arctic?

To survive in the Arctic, people would need...

- ☐ very warm clothing.
- ☐ a lot of food.
- ☐ some sort of shelter.
- ☐ fuel for stoves and lamps.

Literary Words

accustom

aggravate

array

burrow

dictator

editorial

fatigue

neglect

plod

thrust

accustom

Accustom means to familiarize by use, habit, or constant practice.

66 John tried to accustom himself to the cold weather. 99

aggravate

Aggravate means to make worse or more severe.

66 If you scratch a mosquito bite, you'll only aggravate the itch. 99

editorial

An **editorial** is a newspaper article that presents the opinion of the publisher, an editor, or a journalist.

66 The editorial criticized the city's plan to build a stadium. 99

fatigue

Fatigue means bodily or mental tiredness.

66 After hiking for many hours, the group felt great fatigue. 99

array

Array means a grouping or organization of items.

> The dessert table had a large array of cakes and pies.

burrow

Burrow means to make a hole or tunnel in, into, or under something.

> A worm burrows its way underground.

dictator

A **dictator** is a government leader with absolute power.

> The dictator ruled the country with an iron fist.

neglect

Neglect means a failure to pay attention to or take care of properly.

> The wall was crumbling after long years of neglect.

plod

Plod means to trudge or walk heavily and slowly.

> The old mule plodded along the dusty trail.

thrust

A **thrust** is a strong forward push.

> The rocket's engine gave it enough thrust to soar into space.

from Digging for China
by Richard Wilbur

"Far enough down is China," somebody said.
"Dig deep enough and you might see the sky
As clear as at the bottom of a well.
Except it would be real—a different sky.
Then you could **burrow** down until you came
To China! Oh, it's nothing like New Jersey.
There's people, trees, and houses, and all that,
But much, much different. Nothing looks the same."

There Isn't Time!
by Eleanor Farjeon

There isn't time, there isn't time
To do the things I want to do,
With all the mountain-tops to climb,
And all the woods to wander through,
And all the seas to sail upon,
And everywhere there is to go,
And all the people, every one
Who lives upon the earth to know.
There's only time, there's only time
To know a few, and do a few,
And then sit down and make a rhyme
About the rest I want to do.

To Dark Eyes Dreaming

by Zilpha Keatley Snyder

Dreams go fast and far
    these days,
They go by rocket **thrust**,
They go **arrayed**
    in lights
        or in the dust of stars.
Dreams, these days,
    go fast and far.
Dreams are young, these days,
    or very old,
They can be black
    or blue or gold.
They need no special charts,
    nor any fuel.
It seems, only one rule applies,
    to all our dreams—
They will not fly except in open sky.
    A fenced-in dream
        will die.

Comprehension

✔ **TARGET SKILL** **Author's Motive** The reason an author writes is called the author's motive. Authors of stories often write to entertain or to share their own feelings about life. Sometimes they write to teach a lesson about life. Figuring out the author's motive can help you better understand a story.

Here is an excerpt from "The Imprisonment Ends." A young girl and her family have been held for months as political prisoners in a Latin American country. When they are at last freed, members of their family come to greet them. The girl and her family are gathered around a cot on which their sick father is lying.

Though the story is fiction, it tells about something that has really happened to people at certain times. In many countries with repressive governments, people are often imprisoned for voicing unpopular opinions.

The girl responds in an unusual way to the arrival of her relatives. Noting her responses and how she describes them can help you understand how the awful experience of imprisonment might affect a person.

At noon, when we were around his cot, we heard car doors slamming and a tumult of voices, some of which we recognized. Mama and Ricardo leaped to their feet and rushed out of the room. I stood by the door, hiding.

How many times had I dreamed of the moment they would come and my father would say, "See, we are going home at last!" Now that the moment had arrived, I did not want to see any of them. . . .

Uncle Alberto and Aunt Lila were the first to come into the house. I saw them through the half-open doorway. . . .

My cousin Lucía was behind them. . . . With her clear pink complexion, her shiny hair falling to her shoulders, Lucía looked healthy and beautiful. . . .

"Was it awful, Marta?" Lucía asked.

The answers I had so often rehearsed did not come.

This author's motive is not only to entertain but also to help readers understand an experience similar to one she has undergone in her own life. This experience is important enough that the author wants to ensure that it does not go unnoticed by the world.

You can use this graphic organizer to keep track of story clues related to the main character and the plot. Thinking about the clues can help you understand the author's motive.

Clues	Clues	Clues	Clues
I stood by the door, hiding.	How many times had I dreamed of the moment they would come. . .	Now that the moment had arrived, I did not want to see any of them.	The answers I had so often rehearsed did not come.

Author's Motive

The author writes to entertain but also to help readers understand how a traumatic event can isolate someone who experienced it from people who have not been put through it.

✔ TARGET STRATEGY **Analyze/Evaluate** As you read stories, think about how the author's motive affects the story. Ask yourself the following questions:

• What is the author's motive for writing this story?

• How does that motive affect the writing?

• Are the descriptions of events and characters realistic?

• What experience does the author want me to understand?

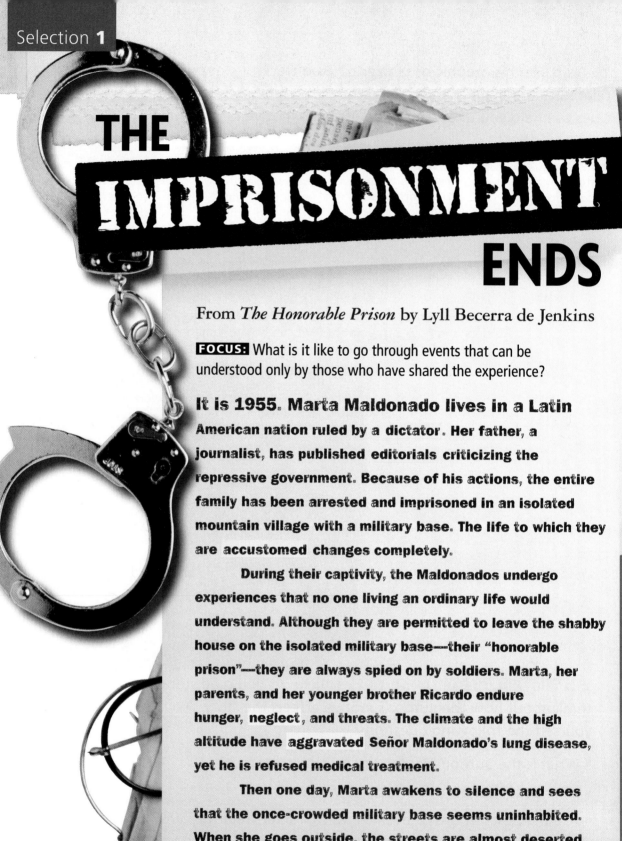

THE IMPRISONMENT ENDS

From *The Honorable Prison* by Lyll Becerra de Jenkins

FOCUS: What is it like to go through events that can be understood only by those who have shared the experience?

It is 1955. Marta Maldonado lives in a Latin American nation ruled by a dictator. Her father, a journalist, has published editorials criticizing the repressive government. Because of his actions, the entire family has been arrested and imprisoned in an isolated mountain village with a military base. The life to which they are accustomed changes completely.

During their captivity, the Maldonados undergo experiences that no one living an ordinary life would understand. Although they are permitted to leave the shabby house on the isolated military base—their "honorable prison"—they are always spied on by soldiers. Marta, her parents, and her younger brother Ricardo endure hunger, neglect, and threats. The climate and the high altitude have aggravated Señor Maldonado's lung disease, yet he is refused medical treatment.

Then one day, Marta awakens to silence and sees that the once-crowded military base seems uninhabited. When she goes outside, the streets are almost deserted. She encounters a peasant plodding along. He informs her that there has been fighting in the capital city.

• •

And then clearly I hear the horses' hooves beating against the pavement of the main road, resounding like a thousand castanets. I stop midway up the hill. Horsemen are waving their hats, yelling "*¡Al fin!*" and that scream, "At last!" seems to erupt from every corner of the earth.

"*¡Viva la libertad!*"

"*¡Vivaaaa!*"

Overcome by **fatigue** and exhilaration, I sit by the door of the house, but only for an instant. The pounding of my heart repeats at last, at last, at last!

• •

Marta realizes that the government has probably been overthrown, and she and her brother rush to Mama, who is sitting by Papa's bedside. Mama receives the news by crying in exhaustion, but Papa remains unconscious and does not respond.

The mayor, who has never displayed any courage by helping the Maldonados before, now visits the family. He calls Señor Maldonado a "powerful voice in the event the country is celebrating today." Since the mayor has a telephone, Mrs. Maldonado demands that he phone for a doctor and an ambulance, and Ricardo supplies the phone numbers of relatives.

• •

They came, as my father had predicted, our relatives and his friends.

At noon, when we were around his cot, we heard car doors slamming and a tumult of voices, some of which we recognized. Mama and Ricardo leaped to their feet and rushed out of the room. I stood by the door, hiding.

How many times had I dreamed of the moment they would come and my father would say, "See, we are going home at last!" Now that the moment had arrived, I did not want to see any of them.

"Margarita, is it you, my dear, my dear!" Uncle Alberto was exclaiming in the entrance hall. There were sniffles. "Ricardito, let me embrace you!"

Uncle Alberto and Aunt Lila were the first to come into the house. I saw them through the half-open doorway. Tall, well-dressed, they looked handsomer than I remembered. Their presence lit the corridor in spite of their solemn faces and dark clothes. I was startled by the contrast with my mother's cadaverous appearance, to which I had grown accustomed. Now, close to her older brother, my mother was an old woman. He and Aunt Lila held Mama by the arms, guiding her cautiously, as though she were disabled.

My cousin Lucía was behind them, one arm around Ricardo. With her clear pink complexion, her shiny hair falling to her shoulders, Lucia looked healthy and beautiful. She was wearing a bright red woolen dress and gold jewelry.

"Was it awful, Marta?" Lucia asked.

The answers I had so often rehearsed did not come.

"It was terrible for us, Marta! You can't imagine how awful it got to be at the end. So many were killed, and there were bombs and burnings everywhere. We had to send the help to do the shopping. We didn't dare go out. Why, not even to the post office, you know. The only safe place was the country club. Mama and I and our friends spent most of our days there, and Papa would pick us up before the curfew."

· ·

My father's name was on everybody's lips. "Miguel was the first who alerted the country to the **torture** of political prisoners" and "We are **indebted** to Miguel!" and "A journalist obsessed by justice and truth, that's who he is, Miguel Maldonado." Someone called him a hero.

I recalled something my father said one evening in our home in the city, after discovering that he was losing friends because of his editorials against the dictator. He said, "Many are calling me a **traitor**. You see, one is either a hero or a traitor. Nothing in between pleases my countrymen."

The hammock was swaying with the comings and goings of the visitors. Suddenly, the ugly house was becoming dear. It was filled with my father's presence, the echo of his words. "They will come, my friends ... and who knows, maybe Uncle Alberto will also be here to drive us to the city. Everyone will say his short speech. It will be a little ridiculous and tiresome ... but we'll survive our small glory."

Risking nothing, they had come at last, indeed. They are here, I thought with bitterness, to **partake** in the momentary glory of "my brother-in-law," "my uncle," "my friend." They know how to play the national sport. How many of them, I wondered, like the mayor, are perennial members of the winning team?

My father was in a coma, yet I felt he was more alive than the ones moving about, patting each other's backs, repeating their empty phrases. I leaned against the hammock. How strange that, of all the emotions overwhelming me all at that moment, I was not feeling my father's absence. His presence was powerful, and I knew at that instant that it would always be with me.

This novel is partly autobiographical: the author, Lyll Becerra de Jenkins, grew up in Latin America, and her father was a prominent judge and an outspoken journalist who publicly criticized his country's repressive government.

STOP AND THINK

1. Why was Marta unimpressed by the people who were praising her father?

2. What emotions besides fear might be felt by someone who endures a difficult experience?

Your Turn

Use Your Words:

accompany	indebted
amusing	parka
axle	partake
canvas	puncture
coma	ripple
emerge	stall
ensure	talcum
entries	terrain
floe	torture
galley	traitor

- Read the words on the list.
- Read the dialogue. Find the words.

MORE ACTIVITIES

1. Take a Survey
Graphic Organizer

If you could enter a race, what kind of race would it be? Ask 12 of your classmates to vote on which race they would enter: running, swimming, or biking. Tally their responses. Make a graph showing your results. Share your results with the rest of the class.

Which Race Would You Enter?	
Race	**Votes**
Running	
Swimming	
Biking	

2. Make a Drawing
Listening and Speaking

Have you ever entered a race and won? Draw a picture of yourself winning a race. Show the picture to your partner. Talk about it with your partner. Describe how you won.

3. Write a Letter
Writing

Suppose you and a parent were in a car race. The car breaks down and you have to walk the rest of the way. Write a letter to a friend telling about your experience. Share your letter with your class.

4. It's Amusing!

Vocabulary

Amusing means "entertaining or funny." With a partner, think of other words that mean the same or almost the same as *amusing*. Make a list of the words and share them with your class.

5. You Are the Poet

Writing

Think of all the words that rhyme with *race*. Write them down. Write a short poem about a race. Share the poem with your partner. Talk about ways the poem can be improved.

6. Make a List

Vocabulary

Think about all the words that have to do with races. The words can relate to running races, bike races, swimming races, or any other race you can think of. With a partner make a list of the words. Share the list with your class.

Running race	Bike race	Swimming race	(other)	(other)

Driving WESTWARD

From *Coast to Coast with Alice* by Patricia Rusch Hyatt

FOCUS: How would it feel to be one of the first people to do something entirely new?

In 1909, cars were still a new invention. It was still rare to see one on the road. The United States had no real highways yet. Road maps didn't even exist. That's when 21-year-old Alice Ramsey got into her Maxwell and set out from New Jersey. She hoped to be the first woman to drive all the way across the country. Alice was accompanied by her friend Minna Jahns, age 16. Her older sisters-in-law, Nettie and Maggie, were also along for the ride. This selection uses historical details. It imagines what Minna's journal might have said. J. D. Murphy, mentioned in the entries, was a reporter following the story.

The Trip Starts   New York State

Our Maxwell touring car is a shiny beauty, and Alice has it perfectly fixed up for the trip. Most Maxwells are painted Speedster Red. But this one is a DR model, so it is painted bright green. DR stands for doctor. It must cost much more than the standard red auto, which I know is $550, because the DR is a more powerful machine, built to drive over hilly country and sandy roads that a doctor must travel to reach sick people. Alice says the steering is a bit stiff, but that's good for starting out.

Early cars were very different from today's cars.

The Maxwell people have exchanged the regular 14-gallon gas tank for one that holds 20 gallons. We have a rack for two extra tires on the right side of the car. And, of course, we have a tire repair kit. There's also a picnic hamper full of food like cornflakes and canned tomatoes, and a box camera. Last week Alice showed all three of us how to take pictures.

The Maxwell's gas tank is just under my seat, and one of my jobs is to keep track of our fuel level with a ruled stick. Someone should invent a device that tells you when the tank is getting empty. Nettie's been asking me to measure almost every hour. I feel like talking back, but I don't want to spoil everything the first day out. Alice whispered to me that Nettie gets nervous, and in a while I'll be able to prove to her that the fuel goes down slowly and doesn't vanish in a poof like a magician's rabbit.

On the auto's left running board is a carbide generator to make the gas fumes that power our headlamps. Yes, we are going to be able to drive after sunset! That's something Lewis and Clark couldn't do when they explored the West about a hundred years ago. To turn on our headlamps, I drop special carbide pellets into the generator; then Alice and I jump down, and I open the front glass over the two headlamps. Alice strikes the match and holds it to each gas escape tube until the flame is steady. Then I snap the glass partway shut, and we're ready to go. We will have to drive somewhat slower at night, but our top speed in the daytime should hit 40 miles an hour!

June 23, 1909
Fixing a Flat   Rochelle, Illinois
    To cross Illinois, we've been joined by J. D. Murphy again and three motorcars full of photographers and car salesmen. Everybody wants to be a part of our trip. The driving has been pretty tame so far, except for the rain, but the locals keep telling us the roads get worse as we move farther west.

Alice and I went shopping this morning for strong towing rope, a block and tackle (to hook and lift the car out of ditches if we need to), and short shovels. Then the four of us climbed aboard and led the parade of news people west over farm roads that crossed cornfields divided by small creeks. I counted 12 scarecrows, and then the Maxwell started to wobble. It was a flat tire!

Maggie asked Alice if she wanted to use the tank of compressed air. But Alice said no because we may need to save that air for flat tires in the desert or in the rain. So I brought Alice the tire repair kit from the spare tire drum, and Nettie brought the pliers and tire irons from the toolbox. The reporters stood around and watched.

Alice cranked our little jack to raise the wheel off the ground. She loosened the tire rings with the irons, pulled out the flat tube, and declared, "This is just like Mother takes the insides out of a turkey before stuffing it for Thanksgiving dinner."

She showed how to feel the inside of the tube for the hole that caused the flat. Then I roughed up the rubber so the cement would stick. Once the cement was tacky on both the tire and the patch, Alice held them together until the patch was set firm.

Of course, I already knew how to fix a flat. Alice was giving the lesson for the reporters, who were scribbling on their notepads.

Before she replaced the tube in its **canvas** tire, Alice felt carefully all around the inside of the tire to make sure there were no nails or tacks to cause another **puncture**. She dusted the tube with **talcum** powder, carefully stuffed it back in place, and replaced the tire rings.

Then Alice turned to the press boys and told them the tire was ready for a pump. And they all took a turn.

The car crosses several more states. In Iowa, the other three women get out and prepare to continue to Omaha, Nebraska, by train. The car needs to be as light as possible for its drive up Danger Hill. Only J. D. Murphy will accompany Alice in the car, to act as her witness. His news story will prove that Alice made it up the hill.

June 29, 1909

Still Waiting in Omaha

Omaha, Nebraska

More News—Alice and J. D. arrived this very afternoon. While Alice left to wash her hair, J. D. told us about climbing Danger Hill. He said after they turned the corner and started up, smooth as you please, they saw another motorcar in trouble about two-thirds of the way up. That car's motor was coughing and spitting. The driver got out several times with a shovel to knock mud off the wheels. His car **stalled** again and again, but luckily his brakes held.

Alice shouted up the hill to the other driver that she had a rope and could pull him up....The driver said yes, please help, so Alice pressed her pedal hard and drove up until she was just past the stalled car.

Alice told the other driver to put his motor in low gear so her engine wouldn't be pulling dead weight. She tied her rear **axle** to the front hook of the other motorcar. It was slippery going, but tire chains kept both cars on Danger Hill road all the way to the top.

I'm sorry I missed watching that tow.

When the car's axle breaks, Alice orders a new one by telephone. Amusingly, it has to be sent from the manufacturer by train.

July 11, 1909

Ranchland Fences   Overton, Nebraska

Alice and a local mechanic had our axle installed by 9 P.M.
last night. Today we've been bumping along cattle and horse trails,
following the telegraph wires west, since there are no real roads and
we have no map. "After all," Alice says, "these poles and wires
MUST lead us to the next town."

The grass out here **ripples** like an ocean blowing around us.
We have been crossing miles and miles of sheep and cattle ranches.
This was the old Overland stage route of years ago.

I have a new job: opening and closing the fence gates as we
drive through the fields.

Alice and her friends arrive safely in California on
August 6. Alice and the car return east by train.
Her former passengers remain in San Francisco for a
few days to see the sights. Then
they also take the train home.
Alice, the first woman to drive
coast to coast, has made her mark
on history.

■ ■ ■ ■ **STOP AND THINK**

1. What does Alice do that shows
   that she is the right person to be
   on this adventure?

2. What might a person like Alice
   look forward to doing nowadays?

THE BOAT CALLED FISH

From *The Lamp, the Ice, and the Boat Called Fish*
by Jacqueline Briggs Martin; pictures by Beth Krommes

In the early decades of the twentieth century, there
were still unexplored territories in the world—mostly
areas that were hard to reach because of terrain or
extreme climate. This selection is based on accounts of
a 1913 Arctic expedition.

FOCUS: In an extreme environment, what skills might be the most
important ones to ensure survival?

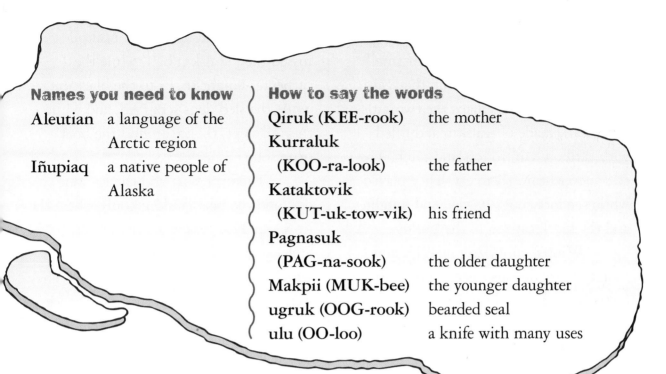

The boat was built in the 1880s to carry salmon and was named *Karluk,* Aleutian for "fish." After a while it carried crews to hunt bowhead whales. Then the hunting stopped, and the *Karluk* had no work—until the summer of 1913, when it sailed north from British Columbia toward the Arctic Circle.

There were no fishing crews and no whalers on board, but scientists of the Canadian Arctic Expedition, traveling up the coast of Alaska to study the plants and people in the high north. The leader of the group was an explorer named Stefansson. He wanted to find new islands in the icy ocean. There were also a cook, a captain, a crew, one black cat, and forty sled dogs.

When the boat reached Point Barrow, Stefansson invited an Iñupiaq family to join the expedition. Stefansson knew the group would need fur clothes and boots of caribou and sealskin to survive the Arctic cold. They would need fresh meat from seals and *ugruk*—bearded seal. Qiruk, the mother, could look at a man, cut a fur skin with her round-bladed *ulu,* and sew a pair of pants that would fit him exactly. She could make boots that would keep his feet from freezing. Kurraluk, the father, and his friend Kataktovik were good hunters. They had the patience to wait by seal holes for hours. Qiruk and Kurraluk brought their two daughters. Pagnasuk was eight years old and little Makpii was two.

219

The crew built a place on the deck for the family to live. Inside their small room they had a seal oil lamp that gave warmth and light. Perhaps the two girls had a ball, made of sealskin and filled with caribou hair, to toss and catch. The crew never heard them cry. They played while the forty dogs howled and fought and the black cat ran in the galley.

Winter came early in 1913, and soon the captain was steering the ship between huge chunks of ice—some as big as houses.

In mid-August the boat was stopped by a large sheet of ice, up to a foot thick and dotted with water holes. As the weather grew colder the water thickened with gray needles of new ice.

While Pagnasuk and Makpii tossed their sealskin ball, while the carpenter taught tricks to the black cat, while the sled dogs scrapped, and while they all slept, the ice around the boat froze solid.

Then the boat and the ice were one, and the boat could go only where the ice went. That was when the leader, Stefansson, and five others left the boat with sleds and dogs to hunt caribou. They were on land when a storm blew the ice-locked boat out to sea. Stefansson sent a report to the government in Ottawa that the *Karluk* would probably be sunk by ice but he was sure its passengers would survive. Then Stefansson was off to look for new land.

That was when the boat's captain, Robert Bartlett, became the leader. That was when Qiruk sewed every day. No one could tell what would happen. Would the boat sink? Would they have enough food? Would they be able to stay warm in the cold, dark winter? As long as the ice was solid the boat was safe. If the ice should crack, then wind or water would be strong enough to push a piece of ice through its wooden sides and the boat would sink.

During that time, Qiruk, whom the crew now called "Auntie," sewed boots, pants, and parkas for the people on the boat. Kurraluk and Kataktovik went seal-hunting out on the ice. These preparations would help the crew to survive.

For three months the boat continued to drift in its icy trap—wherever the wind and water took it. The crew and the scientists used boxes and barrels to build the walls of a house on a large ice **floe** not far from the ship. That ice was thirty feet thick and half as big as a football field—"able to stand a good deal of knocking," the captain wrote later.

In December, while the ice shifted, groaned, and scraped around him, Kurraluk worked in the Arctic twilight and built a house of snow next to the box house. Mr. Hadley, the ship's carpenter, made three long sledges, or sleds. They all knew that if the ship did sink, they would have to haul their clothes and food supplies to land.

LOOK IT UP

For more about the Far North: Inuit, *Karluk* expedition, North Pole exploration, Artic exploration

They kept themselves busy and even had holidays. When Christmas came, the captain, the Iñupiat, the scientists, and the crew feasted on oysters and bear steak, cake and biscuits. The captain gave Auntie a comb, a looking glass, and a new dress. He gave Makpii and Pagnasuk new dresses, too. And he gave Kurraluk and Kataktovik new hunting knives. They ran races and had a tug of war, and everyone was jolly. No one talked about when the boat might sink.

On New Year's Day they went out on the ice to play soccer. Qiruk was goaltender.

The air was so cold the captain could not blow his whistle.

Nine days later, at the end of the day, when Pagnasuk and her sister may have been sitting by the seal oil lamp, listening to their father tell stories of a ten-legged polar bear, they heard a loud splitting sound. A large, sharp point of ice was breaking through the side of their boat!

"All hands abandon ship!" the captain called. He sent Qiruk and the two girls to the box house to start a fire in the stove so all would have a warm shelter. The others carried supplies off the ship and onto the ice floe. The carpenter took the black cat to the box house in a basket. They could not see where they were going in the dark night and blowing snow. The ship's doctor fell into the sea and had to be pulled to safety.

Everyone stood outside to watch the *Karluk* as it disappeared underwater. By the next morning the ice was solid. The *Karluk* was locked under the sea. The thirteen crew members, the captain, the six scientists, the Iñupiaq family, their friend Kataktovik, the dogs, and the cat were left on an island of blue ice in the cold, dark Arctic.

The members of the expedition were stranded for months in the Arctic, with the greatest threats to survival being starvation and exposure to the icy weather. The hunting and food preservation skills of the Iñupiaq family helped ensure that many members of the expedition lived. During that time, Kataktovik and Captain Bartlett separated from the others and journeyed hundreds of miles on foot to find help. Through their courageous efforts, a ship finally picked up the survivors. Without Qiruk, Kurraluk, Kataktovik, and Bartlett, no one from the boat called "Fish" would have emerged from the Arctic alive.

STOP AND THINK

1. Why were the clothes made by Qiruk more useful than the sailors' original clothes?

2. If you knew you were going into an environment of extreme cold, how would you prepare?

UNIT

9 ADVENTURE BECKONS

LOOK AT THE UNIVERSE

What is a telescope?

A telescope is...

☐ a tool for viewing celestial objects.

☐ what Galileo used to make revolutionary discoveries about our solar system.

☐ an instrument for capturing electromagnetic radiation.

☐ a tool that works best if placed beyond Earth's atmosphere.

Who were the fathers of modern rocketry?

The fathers of modern rocketry were...

☐ a Russian math teacher, a German math teacher, and an American scientist.

☐ men who liked to read science fiction.

☐ men who figured out that rockets should have multiple stages.

☐ researchers whose ideas were often ridiculed.

Why was the Apollo 13 mission notable?

The Apollo 13 mission was notable because…

- ☐ its three astronauts faced an emergency in outer space.

- ☐ the astronauts endured difficult and dangerous conditions.

- ☐ the crippled spacecraft had to circle the Moon before returning to Earth.

- ☐ the ship and crew made it back to Earth safely.

Who is Sunita Williams?

Sunita Williams is…

- ☐ a graduate of the U.S. Naval Academy.

- ☐ an experienced helicopter pilot who became an astronaut.

- ☐ an astronaut who set several records while working at the International Space Station.

- ☐ an astronaut who has studied the effects of living in space for extended periods.

What do NASA's rovers do?

NASA's rovers…

- ☐ search for evidence of ancient water on Mars.

- ☐ move slowly around the planet, taking pictures.

- ☐ analyze Martian rocks and soils.

- ☐ communicate their findings with scientists on Earth.

Science Words

characterize

detect

dimension

dwarf

electromagnetic

galaxy

instrument

particular

transport

visible

characterize

To **characterize** is to be a distinctive feature of something.

66 Successful students are characterized by their study habits. 99

detect

To **detect** is to discover something or find that something is present.

66 Their dog detected a squirrel in the attic. 99

dimension

A **dimension** is a measure of space, especially length, width, or height; time is often called the fourth dimension.

66 She read a science fiction story in which people traveled into another dimension. 99

dwarf

A **dwarf** is a relatively small star.

66 White dwarfs are one of the densest kinds of matter in the universe. 99

electromagnetic

Electromagnetic is used to describe the force governing waves of different kinds of radiation.

66 Astronauts encounter more electromagnetic radiation in space than on Earth. 99

galaxy

A **galaxy** is a very big group of stars.

66 We live in the Milky Way Galaxy. 99

instrument

An **instrument** is a tool, usually designed for precision work.

66 The surveyor moved his instruments to a new location and took another reading. 99

particular

Particular means relating to one thing or person.

66 I was stumped by that particular math problem. 99

transport

To **transport** is to move something from one place to another.

66 They needed a truck to transport their magazine collection to the recycling station. 99

visible

Visible is used to describe something that can be seen.

66 A ship was visible on the horizon. 99

WHAT ARE PLANETS LIKE?

Venus and Saturn are mysterious because they are surrounded by thick clouds and gases. But in recent decades scientists have learned a great deal about these planets by sending space probes to them.

VENUS: A Rocky Planet

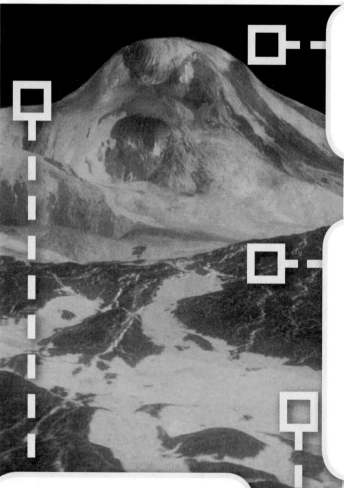

Strong winds—almost 250 miles per hour—push the clouds around. (However, Venus's winds aren't so impressive when compared to Saturn's.)

Venus, whose size and mass are like Earth's, has no moons. The planet's hard, rocky surface is **characterized** by plains, mountains, valleys, and thousands of volcanoes. More than 20 spacecraft have visited Venus since the first probe made a fly-by in 1962.

The atmosphere on Venus is thick, made mostly of carbon dioxide. Droplets of sulfuric acid make it poisonous to humans.

Surface temperatures are as high as 870°F, which is hot enough to melt lead.

Perhaps Saturn's most notable feature is its rings, which humans have been marveling at since the seventeenth century. The rings are made largely of ice chunks and rock bits.

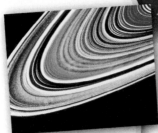

By 2006, scientists had counted 52 moons, and new ones are sure to be discovered.

Saturn is huge—about 764 Earths would fit inside the planet. The body of Saturn is not solid. It is made up of gases and pieces of rock and ice, so you couldn't walk around on it. Five spacecraft have visited Saturn.

The atmosphere is mostly hydrogen and helium. The temperature at the upper layer of Saturn's clouds is about −226°F. Deep inside, the planet generates intense heat.

Saturn's winds blow in opposite directions, east or west, creating bands of color. High in the atmosphere, these winds have been clocked at 615 miles per hour.

Comprehension

✔ **TARGET SKILL** Compare and Contrast

Many selections include information that can be compared or contrasted. When you **compare** things, people, or ideas, you show how they are the same. When you **contrast** them, you show how they are different. **Clue words** help tell you that things, people, or ideas are being compared or contrasted.

The following sentences, taken from the selection "Rocket Science," contain clue words that give hints about people and ideas being compared and contrasted.

Konstantin Tsiolkovsky was born in 1857 in Russia and lived most of his life in a log cabin. He taught high school math. . . . In 1903, he published a scientific article in which he argued that liquid fuels were the best power source for a rocket. He also wrote that rockets should be built in multiple sections, or stages. . . .

Twenty years later, in Germany, another high school math teacher came up with the same ideas for a paper he wrote. . . . Hermann Oberth's professors thought his paper was too much like science fiction and rejected his work. He later earned his degree anyway, and in 1929 went on to launch his first liquid fuel rocket.

> The clue word *another* tells you that one more person will be described. Look for ways that this person is similar to and different from Konstantin Tsiolkovsky.

> The clue word *same* lets you know how the two people were alike.

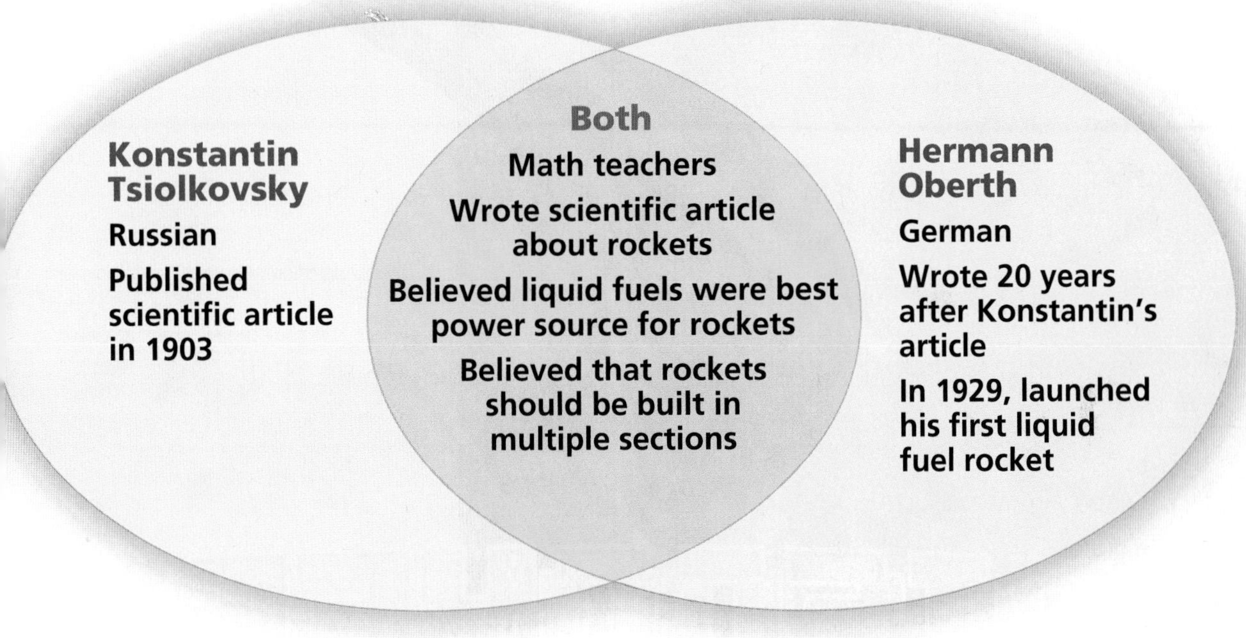

Konstantin Tsiolkovsky

Russian

Published scientific article in 1903

Both

Math teachers

Wrote scientific article about rockets

Believed liquid fuels were best power source for rockets

Believed that rockets should be built in multiple sections

Hermann Oberth

German

Wrote 20 years after Konstantin's article

In 1929, launched his first liquid fuel rocket

The left part of the Venn diagram gives information that shows how Tsiolkovsky was different from Oberth. The right part of the diagram gives information that shows how Oberth was different from Tsiolkovsky. The center area shows how the two men were similar.

✔ TARGET STRATEGY Ask Questions As you read, ask yourself questions that help you compare and contrast people, things, and ideas in the selection. For example, are there similarities in the selection? Are there differences? These kinds of questions will help you better understand the information presented in the selection.

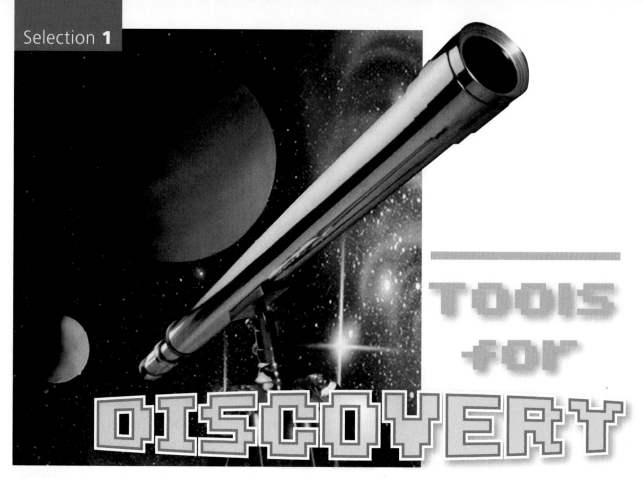

TOOLS for DISCOVERY

FOCUS: How do telescopes help us understand Earth?

No instrument has changed astronomy more than the telescope, which allows us to view distant celestial objects—and even peer back in the fourth dimension, time. Galileo, the great natural philosopher and mathematician, was the first to train a telescope on the skies.

The Earliest Telescopes

In 1609, Galileo was the chair of mathematics at the University of Padua, in what is now Italy. He had spent much of his career investigating motion, and he was known for devising experiments that helped people better understand the natural world. Also, he was not afraid to challenge conventional wisdom.

Sometime in the spring, Galileo received a startling piece of news. Someone in the Netherlands had invented an optical device that showed distant objects as if they were close by. Galileo was

234

intrigued. He set about experimenting with lenses from local eyeglass makers. Using a process of trial and error, he constructed a simple telescope. It had a magnification, or "power," of three—objects looked three times closer than they were. But he wasn't satisfied. He learned how to grind lenses and then built better and better telescopes. By the fall, he had made a telescope with a power of eight. By December, he was studying the Moon through an instrument that magnified objects twenty times.

Galileo's discoveries were breathtaking and revolutionary. The Moon's surface was not smooth—as everyone thought—but rough and mountainous. Far more stars were in the sky than could be seen without a telescope. Jupiter had four moons orbiting it. Sometimes Saturn had a strange appearance, which turned out to be caused by a ring that encircled it. And Venus, the "morning star," moved through a series of phases that were like the phases of the Moon. Findings such as these showed Galileo that Earth was not the center of the universe. Instead, Earth was one of several planets that revolved around the Sun. The scientific revolution took a great step forward.

Electromagnetic radiation

Galileo's telescopes used **visible** light—what the human eye has evolved to see. Over the next three centuries, these "optical telescopes" were greatly improved, and astronomy made great advances. Visible light, however, is only part of the **electromagnetic** radiation that fills the universe. Stars, **galaxies**, black holes, white **dwarfs**, and other bodies in outer space also send out radiation that we can't see. This invisible radiation includes infrared and ultraviolet light, X-rays, gamma rays, radio waves, and microwaves. Optical telescopes cannot **detect** these kinds of radiation.

REREAD

Compare + Contrast

How are X-rays like visible light? How are they different from visible light?

Opening the Radio Window

Karl Jansky started working at the Bell Telephone Laboratories in New Jersey in 1928. Telephone communication was often disrupted by several kinds of interference, and Jansky's job was to figure out where the interference was coming from. He built a directional antenna and started investigating. Within a few years, he had identified all the sources of interference except one. Much to his surprise, he realized that this **particular** interference came from the stars. He concluded in 1932 that the radio waves originated somewhere near the heart of the Milky Way, our home galaxy.

The public was astonished to learn that Earth was constantly being bombarded by cosmic radio waves. A radio engineer in Wheaton, Illinois, decided to **extend** Jansky's investigation. Grote Reber built a bowl-shaped radio receiver in his backyard. Thirty-one feet across, it was the world's first radio telescope—and the first non-optical telescope of any kind. By the end of World War II, Reber had published the first radio map of the sky. The map showed something remarkable. Certain parts of the sky produced strong radio signals even though they had no visible stars. Objects that couldn't be seen were the source of the signals.

Space Telescopes

Since Jansky's and Reber's pioneering work with radio waves, other kinds of telescopes have been built to capture different parts of the electromagnetic spectrum. But they are all limited by Earth's atmosphere, which absorbs or blocks much of the radiation. To get clearer images, many telescopes are located high on mountaintops. An even better solution is to place telescopes on satellites above the atmosphere.

In 1977, the U.S. Congress approved a $36 million budget to build the most sophisticated telescope ever put in space. The telescope would orbit about 370 miles above Earth, giving scientists their clearest views of the universe yet. The new space telescope would be named after Edwin Hubble, the American astronomer who discovered that the universe is expanding.

On April 25, 1990, the space shuttle *Discovery* **transported** the Hubble Space Telescope into orbit. Its instruments could collect visible light, ultraviolet rays, and infrared rays, recording them in a camera that produced images ten times clearer than the best telescope on Earth. Another camera was able to find objects in space that were 50 times fainter than anything that could be detected from Earth. A few weeks later, however, scientists at NASA were dismayed to discover a serious problem. Images coming from the main telescope were fuzzy. The primary mirror of the telescope, scientists learned, was the wrong shape. Since the satellite was flying about 17,000 mph, high above Earth, replacing the mirror was impossible. Luckily, it could be fixed.

Three years later, the shuttle *Endeavor* took a crew of astronauts to repair Hubble. During several space walks, they installed "spectacles" on the telescope. The spectacles are a device with ten small mirrors that correct the paths of light going from the primary mirror to the recording instruments. The mission was a success. Less than a month later, NASA could show the world some incredibly sharp images taken by Hubble.

REREAD

Compare ➕ Contrast

What changed about the images coming from Hubble after the astronauts repaired it?

STOP AND THINK

1. What are some of the kinds of electromagnetic radiation that modern telescopes capture?

2. If you were going to use a telescope, what objects in space would you look at?

Your Turn

Use Your Words:

analyze	obedient
crippled	rage
design	reject
entranced	retire
extend	scramble
far-fetched	solar
flare	spirit
literally	streaming
mitigate	vent
multiple	violate

- Read the words in the list.
- Read the dialogue. Find the words.

I'm entranced by this view of Earth.

It may have seemed like a far-fetched idea, but here we are on the Moon.

I'm eager to analyze some of these lunar rocks.

You need courage, determination, and spirit to get here. Many who volunteered were rejected.

MORE ACTIVITIES

1. You Are the Author
Writing

Imagine that you are part of the lunar mission in the picture. What is your job? What do you miss from Earth? What do you hope to accomplish? Write a paragraph telling your impressions so far.

2. Tell Me About It
Speaking and Listening

Suppose you are a friend of Galileo. He has constructed better and better telescopes, and is starting to make some amazing discoveries. The Moon is mountainous. Jupiter has moons. There are many more stars in the sky than anyone believed. Think of five questions you might ask Galileo. Have your partner play the role of Galileo. Ask the questions. Then switch roles.

3. Write an E-mail
Writing

You made it! All your life you've dreamed of becoming an astronaut, and finally you've arrived at the International Space Station, where you'll spend the next six months. Write

an e-mail to a family member or a friend about your experience in space.

4. Analyze It
Vocabulary

To <u>analyze</u> is to study something. Work with your partner to think of different things you might analyze. Make a list of the words and share them with your class.

5. Make a Venn Diagram
Graphic Organizer

Galileo made a telescope in 1609. The Hubble Space Telescope was launched in 1990. How are they alike? How are they different? Write the characteristics of each telescope in its circle. Write the characteristics they share in the overlapping part of the diagram.

Galileo's Telescope   Hubble Space Telescope

6. Play "What Am I?"
Speaking and Listening

Choose a person or object from the picture. Have a partner ask five yes-or-no questions to figure out which person or object you chose. Then switch roles with your partner.

HOW TO USE A TELESCOPE

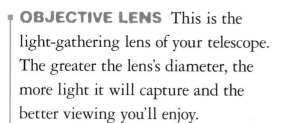

FOCUS: What are key parts of a telescope?

OBJECTIVE LENS This is the light-gathering lens of your telescope. The greater the lens's diameter, the more light it will capture and the better viewing you'll enjoy.

OPTICAL TUBE Here is where light rays coming through the objective lens are focused.

FOCUSING KNOB This knob allows you to focus on objects at different distances.

DIAGONAL MIRROR This mirror allows you to look through the telescope while standing in a comfortable upright position.

EYEPIECE This is what you look through. Your telescope comes with several eyepieces. The 25 mm eyepiece is good to begin with, letting you look at clusters of stars, nebulae, and galaxies. The 25 mm eyepiece will give you a power of 28.

ALTITUDE ADJUSTMENT KNOB Use this knob to move the barrel of the telescope up and downs. (To move the telescope laterally, simply rotate it on the head of the tripod.)

TRIPOD Keeping your telescope steady is crucial for good viewing of celestial objects. Any slight vibration will be greatly magnified in the eyepiece.

Telescope Tips

▶ Never point your telescope near the Sun. Looking at the Sun through a telescope—even for a fraction of a second—can damage your eye permanently. A telescope is best used at night.

▶ Earth's atmosphere will distort images in the telescope, so try to focus on objects high in the sky, rather than close to the horizon. You'll be looking through less atmosphere, and therefore the images will be sharper.

▶ If you want to figure out the magnification, or power, you're using, divide the focal length of the telescope by the focal length of the eyepiece. This telescope has a focal length of 700 mm. Suppose you are using a 9 mm eyepiece to look at the Moon.

$$700 \text{ mm} \div 9 \text{ mm} = 78 \text{ (nearest whole number)}$$

So the power is 78, which means the Moon is magnified 78 times.

▶ Don't assume that a greater power means better viewing. You will see much more detail if the image is steady, clear, and bright. In many circumstances, the best images are seen at lower powers. At higher powers, you will see dimmer images, and it will be more difficult to keep them steady.

▶ Try to set up your telescope away from parking lots, roads, and large buildings. These structures get hot during the day and then release heat at night. The heat rises into the atmosphere, creating disturbances that will hurt the images in your telescope.

▶ Avoid setting up your telescope on wooden decks. For one thing, you'll be near a heat-absorbing building. For another, every time somebody takes a step, the image in your telescope will vibrate.

▶ Your eyes will need about 30 minutes to adjust to the dark. For that first half-hour, work on the settings of your telescope and look at bright, near-sky objects. When your eyes are fully adjusted, you can turn to fainter, deep-sky objects. And don't use any bright flashlights or lanterns, because then you'll have to wait another 30 minutes!

■ ■ ■ STOP AND THINK

1. Why is it often better to use a lower power eyepiece than a greater power eyepiece?

2. What objects have you ever seen in the night sky?

ROCKET SCIENCE

FOCUS: How has rocket science advanced in the last hundred years?

Three men born in three different countries—all teachers, all fans of science fiction books—are considered the fathers of modern rocketry. Although they never met, and were unaware of the others' research, they each came up with the same two key ideas about rockets.

Not Just Math Teachers

Konstantin Tsiolkovsky was born in 1857 in Russia and lived most of his life in a log cabin. He taught high school math. From boyhood, he dreamed of going into space. He loved the novels by Jules Verne about travel to the Moon. In 1903, he published a scientific article in which he argued that liquid fuels were the best power source for a rocket. He also wrote that rockets should be built in **multiple** sections, or stages. As fuel was burned up in one stage, that section could be dropped off to reduce the weight of the remaining rocket.

Twenty years later, in Germany, another high school math teacher came up with the same ideas for a paper he wrote to earn his doctorate degree. Unfortunately, Hermann Oberth's professors thought his paper was too much like science fiction and **rejected** his work. He later earned his degree anyway, and in 1929 went on to launch his first liquid fuel rocket.

A Rocket from a Windmill

But the honor of launching the first true rocket goes to an American scientist, Robert Goddard. Like the other two men, Goddard had figured out that liquid fuel, not solid fuel, was the best way to power a rocket. He also realized that rockets should have multiple stages. After nearly thirty years of failed experiments,

Goddard got a rocket off the ground on March 16, 1926. It didn't look like much. Goddard was a college professor and didn't have a lot of money. He built his rocket with parts from a used windmill that he bought from a farmer. But it worked.

Like Tsiolkovsy and Oberth, Goddard was **entranced** with science fiction. Like them, he was ridiculed for his work. In 1920, editors at a New York newspaper called Goddard's ideas about sending a rocket to the Moon so **far-fetched** that they **violated** the laws of science. Goddard's response? "Every vision is a joke until the first man accomplishes it; then it becomes commonplace."

The Space Race

Rocketry advanced rapidly after Goddard's historic launch. His rocket rose only 41 feet in the air. During World War II, the Germans built V-2 rockets as weapons and launched them against the English. The V-2 could travel hundreds of miles. After the war, several German rocket scientists, including Oberth, came to the United States to work for their former enemy. At the same time, scientists in the Soviet Union were also starting a space program. In 1957, they launched *Sputnik*, the first satellite to go beyond Earth's atmosphere into space.

The launch of *Sputnik* sparked a "space race" between the United States and the Soviet Union. Both countries

began programs of intensive scientific research. Dogs, chimpanzees, and finally people were sent into orbit. Many satellites were launched. On July 16, 1969, an estimated 450 million people watched television images of the first human to walk on the surface of the Moon, U. S. astronaut Neil Armstrong.

Since the last Moon mission in 1972, nobody has gone more than a few hundred miles from Earth.

STOP AND THINK

1. What were the key ideas of the founders of modern rocket science?

2. What space mission would you like to take part in?

SLINGSHOT AROUND THE MOON

FOCUS: What do astronauts on a spacecraft do in an emergency?

Explosion in Space

On April 11, 1970, eight months after Neil Armstrong became the first person to set foot on the Moon, the United States launched another lunar mission, Apollo 13. Astronauts James Lovell, John Swigert, and Fred Haise took off from Florida. For the first couple of days, the mission went smoothly. In fact, one member of Mission Control in Houston, Texas, complained of boredom. Then the astronauts heard a loud bang and felt a vibration. Warning lights started to blink.

What had happened? Almost 200,000 miles away from Earth, one of *Apollo 13*'s oxygen tanks had exploded. What Lovell was watching out the window was oxygen escaping from the second, and last, tank. Oxygen was vital to the astronauts' survival. It was used for breathing and also to make the electrical power that ran everything aboard the ship, including the scrubbers that recycled and cleaned their air. Without power, they would die in space.

Freezing in a Lunar Lifeboat

Fifteen minutes before power ran out in the command module, Mission Control told the crew to head into the lunar module—the smaller craft in which they would have landed on the Moon. The lunar module would become their "lifeboat" until their return to

Earth. However, it had been **designed** to hold two people for two days, not three people for four days. The astronauts didn't have enough food, water, or power. To conserve power, they had to shut down most of the electrical systems. But those electrical systems kept the ship warm; without them, the temperature plummeted to 38°F. It was so cold that the astronauts barely slept. "The sun **streaming** in the windows didn't much help," Lovell recalled later. "We were cold as frogs in a frozen pool."

Radio transmission at 10:08 P.M. Monday, April 13, 1970

Astronaut Swigert: **Okay, Houston, we've had a problem here.**

Mission Control: **This is Houston. Say again please.**

Astronaut Lovell: **Houston, we've had a problem...We are, we are venting something out into the, into space ...It's a gas of some sort.**

The three men on *Apollo 13* and hundreds of engineers at Mission Control **scrambled** to figure out how to get the spacecraft back to Earth as swiftly as possible. It would circle the Moon once and use lunar gravity to sling it back toward Earth. Mission Control did some calculations and gave the crew its numbers. About five hours after the explosion, the astronauts fired *Apollo 13*'s rockets for 35 seconds. Nearing the Moon, they fired the rockets again, this time for five minutes, so that the ship would gain speed. *Apollo 13* rounded the dark side of the Moon and began the long journey home.

On April 17, six days after launching, the **crippled** spacecraft splashed safely into the Pacific Ocean.

■■■ **STOP AND THINK**

1. What was the gas venting from the spacecraft needed for?

2. How do you think you would have reacted if you were on *Apollo 13*?

Sunita Williams, ASTRONAUT

FOCUS: What is the life of an astronaut like?

Helicopter Pilot

Sunita Williams, who describes herself as a "smart aleck," was a good student and a competitive swimmer when she was growing up in Massachusetts. But she wasn't first in her class in high school. She wasn't first in her class at the U.S. Naval Academy, either. She was "just OK," she says. So when it came time for the Navy to hand out job assignments, Suni, as her family and friends call her, didn't get the position she wanted. She had hoped to be a diver or a jet pilot, but the Navy said no. She was trained to fly helicopters instead.

Suni flew a lot of helicopters. After completing her training in 1989, she was assigned to a helicopter squadron in Virginia. She flew in the Mediterranean, Red Sea, and Persian Gulf regions. And in 1992, she was in charge of a helicopter crew that went to Florida to provide relief operations after Hurricane Andrew. Later, she completed test pilot school at the Naval Academy and began flying test flights for many kinds of helicopters. She became a flight instructor and safety officer, and was assigned to the USS *Saipan*, a ship stationed in Virginia.

Not surprisingly, Suni thought she would fly helicopters for the rest of her career. One day, however, she heard an astronaut say that flying a lunar lander was a lot like flying a helicopter. That sparked something inside her. Suni had

REREAD

Compare + Contrast

What two items are being compared?

dreamed of going to the Moon ever since she was five years old. So she applied to NASA's astronaut program. While aboard the *Saipan*, she received word that she'd been selected. At the time, Suni had flown almost 3,000 hours in more than 30 kinds of helicopters.

Three Space Records

Suni began her astronaut training in 1998. She attended scientific and technical lectures, received instructions for flying in the space shuttle and working in the International Space Station (ISS), and prepared herself physically. She even had to learn wilderness survival techniques.

On December 9, 2006, Suni Williams finally launched into space, part of the shuttle *Discovery*'s crew. Two days later, the shuttle docked at the space station. Suni's mission at the space station was to research how people might live and work safely in weightlessness. Before leaving Earth, Suni explained, "Our goal, now that we're going back to the Moon and going to Mars... is how people are going to live out in space for extended periods of time. Over a six-month period we're definitely going to lose bone and muscle mass. So a big part of the experiments that we're doing onboard is how to **mitigate** that... We do that using the treadmill, the bike, and also there's a weight lifting machine that we use to work out and make sure our

bones and muscles are exercised." Did she ever exercise! While her sister Dina ran the Boston Marathon back on Earth, Suni ran along with her in space, going all 26.2 miles on the treadmill. It took her four hours and 24 minutes to finish, with her fellow crew members cheering her on.

Astronauts are allowed to take a few personal items with them on flights. Suni, whose father was born in India, carried a few samosas on board.

Although she hasn't made it to the Moon yet, Suni has already set three records for female astronauts. She spent 195 days on the International Space Station, more than any other woman. She also went on four space walks. And during those space walks, she spent more time working outside the station than any other female astronaut—over twenty-nine hours.

STOP AND THINK

1. What was the purpose of Suni's research on the International Space Station?

2. How would you describe Suni Williams?

LOOK IT UP

For related information: robots in space, rover *Opportunity*, rover *Spirit*, Mars SandBot, NASA robots

ROVER TALES

FOCUS: What is the life of a NASA robot like?

t isn't easy being a robot, especially when you're sent to work on a cold, rocky planet millions of miles away. **Solar flares** and dust storms that can **rage** for months are just some of the things we have to put up with. And I should mention that robots never seem to get to **retire**. NASA scientists promised that we'd have to work for three months. Yet here we are, more than three years after landing, still on the job.

Who are we? NASA calls us "rovers." If I do say so myself, we are top-of-the-line hardware. I'm *Spirit*, and my companion is *Opportunity*. It took us seven months to make the dangerous journey from Earth to Mars. During the trip, we

went through some of the worst solar flares on record. Our computers had to be shut down. Electromagnetic radiation from the Sun could have scrambled our memories permanently.

We finally touched down on Mars in January 2004. *Opportunity* landed in a huge crater, prompting one guy back on Earth to claim that they had hit an "interplanetary hole in one." Those scientists think they are so funny. I landed on what is called Meridiani Planum. It's a flat region with mineral deposits that might show a watery past.

You see, it's all about water. There isn't a drop of water on Mars's surface now, I can assure you. Parched, I'd call it.

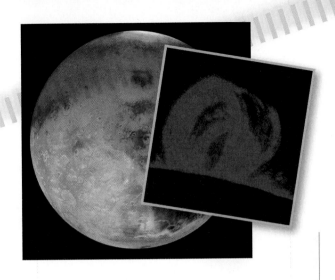

The NASA scientists want to know how, long ago, water might have influenced the planet's environment. That leads straight to the question we're trying to answer: Could surface water have allowed some form of life to develop on Mars?

While our pals in NASA are toiling over their computer screens, *Opportunity* and I have been hard at work, rolling over the Martian landscape wherever they tell us to go. Basically, we're like field geologists. We have panoramic cameras to take photos of the terrain. Scientists study those photos and decide which structures and rocks look promising. We also have spectrometers, which are tools for **analyzing** the elements that make up rocks and soils. Really fine soil—dust actually—we collect with magnets. A "microscopic imager" is great for taking close-up pictures of Martian dirt. Our RATs, or "rock abrasion tools," are for scraping away the old, dusty surfaces of rocks so that we can examine the fresh material underneath. We get our power from the Sun; solar arrays charge our computers and equipment whenever the Sun is out.

On a typical work day, I might travel over about 40 meters of Martian landscape. I'll use one of my robotic arms to move my tools around. The arm has an "elbow" and a "wrist" much like your human arm, and I can use it to put a tool against a rock or patch of soil. Then I examine and analyze the rock or soil and send the data back to Earth.

If it weren't for us, those earth-bound geologists would still be arguing about whether Mars ever had any water. (Yes, we found evidence of ancient Martian water.) And those desk scientists like to take credit. One day, while **obediently** following their instructions, *Opportunity* got stuck in the sand. It took the NASA brainiacs a few weeks of test-driving model rovers back on Earth to figure out how to rescue *Opportunity*. Lead scientist Steve Squyres wrote, "All the action so far has been on Earth, doing testing with the two rovers we have on this planet. It's been nasty work ... shovel-and-wheelbarrow stuff, moving around **literally** tons of fine-grained soil ..."

That's nasty work? He should try our job on Mars.

■ ■ ■ STOP AND THINK

1. What are the rovers looking for?
2. Why does NASA call these robots "rovers"?

SPACE TOURISM:
PRO and CON

FOCUS: Should non-astronauts be allowed to take space trips?

WHAT A RIDE!

Imagine yourself in space gear, strapped into your seat, getting slammed back as the rocket takes off. Eight minutes later, you are at the edge of outer space. Your spacecraft cruises smoothly along, while you gaze out a window at the glowing curved horizon of Earth and the star-studded blackness of space. When the captain says you can unfasten your safety belt, you float around the cabin, weightless!

Until a few years ago, the only people who could fly in space were astronauts who had gone through long, difficult schooling and physical training. Now a few non-astronauts have traveled into space, and they rave about the experience. Dennis Tito, a former space scientist, was the first space tourist. In 2001, he spent eight days in space, six of them on the International Space Station. Since then, other non-astronauts have also traveled to the space station.

A number of companies are working on building spacecraft that will carry passengers into suborbital flight. Several spaceports are being built around the world, including one in New Mexico. A British company has already ordered five new spacecraft that will take tourists into space and back. The cost of a ticket? $200,000. At least 100 people have already bought tickets. As prices eventually fall, many more people will want to experience this fabulous journey and get an awe-inspiring view of Earth from space.

TOO DANGEROUS!

A ride in space would indeed be thrilling. A number of Americans are apparently eager to try it, and businesses are already gearing up for the space tourism industry. However, there's a lot that the promoters of space tourism *aren't* saying. We, as possible consumers of commercial space travel, need to look at the full picture.

There are serious safety concerns involved for non-astronauts. Being in space can have negative effects on the human body, and these effects will undoubtedly be worse for people who don't get the rigorous physical training of astronauts. People with undiscovered health issues may become ill or even die. What happens if someone gets sick or has a heart attack on the way up? Does the ship turn back? How much medical care can or should be provided onboard?

Another issue that is rarely discussed is radiation. Electromagnetic radiation from outer space continuously flows through our bodies, but Earth's atmosphere filters out much of it. In space, people are exposed to far more radiation. How can companies ensure that their passengers will be safe—and won't become ill from the radiation months or years after a flight?

Until questions such as these have been answered, no one should consider space travel safe for non-astronauts.

A NEW KIND OF SPACE TRAVEL?

In January 2008, the British company Virgin Galactic unveiled models of its new spacecraft, *SpaceShipTwo*. The ship is designed to take tourists into space. Customers will experience weightlessness, see Earth as a sphere, and peer at the stars without atmospheric distortion. But *SpaceShipTwo* won't blast off from Earth like a rocket or shuttle. Instead, it will be carried into the sky by a special airplane. The plane, called *WhiteKnight*, has two bodies and four engines. When it reaches the correct altitude, *WhiteKnight* will release *SpaceShipTwo*. The spaceship's pilot will then fire a rocket engine, and the craft will shoot to an altitude of 62 miles or more—the lower reaches of outer space. At the end of the flight, the pilot will adjust the ship's wings, and the craft will glide back to Earth.

LOOK IT UP

For more on space tourism: Blue Origin, commercial astronaut, space hotel

STOP AND THINK

1. What are the main arguments of the writers?

2. How would you respond to their arguments?

UNIT

10 GENERATIONS

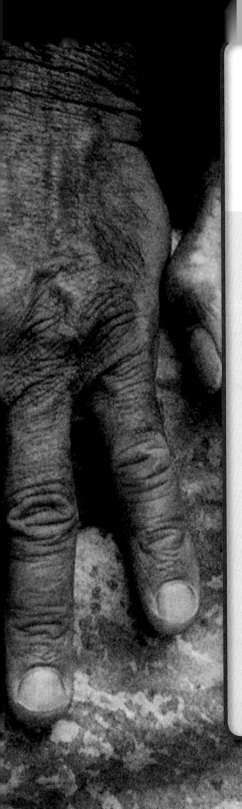

WHAT CAN GENERATIONS LEARN FROM EACH OTHER?

READINGS

What can be a traditional expectation?

A traditional expectation can be that...

☐ you grow up to become a lawyer.

☐ you follow in your father's or mother's footsteps.

☐ girls get married and have children.

☐ boys play sports.

How can a person break away from traditional expectations?

A person can break away from traditional expectations by...

☐ following his or her dreams.

☐ creating a new path.

☐ ignoring other people's prejudices and criticisms.

☐ being open minded.

What does a grandparent know?

A grandparent knows...

☐ the importance of time.

☐ why families stay together.

☐ the value of traditions.

☐ the country and culture we came from.

What might an education include?

An education might include...

☐ going to school.

☐ listening to the stories of our grandparents.

☐ reading books on our own.

☐ learning how to respond to prejudice.

What is a family?

A family is...

☐ the people whom we go home to each day.

☐ everyone who shows up for holidays.

☐ the people who care about us the most.

☐ where we learn important lessons about life.

Literature Words

anthology

distress

endow

ignorant

parchment

prejudice

priority

reminisce

suite

vial

anthology

An **anthology** is a collection of literary or musical pieces.

❝ I found some good poems in an anthology of modern literature. ❞

distress

Distress is strain or suffering, either physical or mental.

❝ The death of her grandfather caused her great distress. ❞

prejudice

A **prejudice** is a negative opinion about a group or race, formed without reason.

❝ The recordings showed that the mayor held a prejudice against foreigners. ❞

priorty

A **priority** is something that comes first in importance.

❝ The coach said our priority should be to learn how to play the game correctly. ❞

endow

To **endow** is to give money that will provide an income to a person or institution.

66 Mrs. Peters promised to help endow the new animal shelter. **99**

ignorant

Ignorant means without knowledge or education.

66 Long ago, ignorant people thought diseases were caused by bad deeds done by the person who was sick. **99**

parchment

Parchment is a tough kind of paper.

66 Our diplomas were printed on parchment. **99**

reminisce

To **reminisce** is to think or talk about past events or experiences.

66 Mr. Jones wanted to reminisce about his childhood. **99**

suite

A **suite** is a group of rooms that are occupied together.

66 The members of the board held their meeting in a hotel suite. **99**

vial

A **vial** a is small bottle or container, often for medicine.

66 The glass vial was locked away in the medicine cabinet. **99**

RiVER
By Shuntaro Tanikawa

Mother,
Why is the river laughing?

Why, because the sun is tickling the river.

Mother,
Why is the river singing?

Because the skylark praised the river's voice.

Mother,
Why is the river cold?

It remembers being once loved by the snow.

Mother,
How old is the river?

It's the same age as the forever young springtime.

Mother,
Why does the river never rest?

Well, you see it's because the mother sea
is waiting for the river to come home.

Translated from the Japanese by Harold Wright

Quintrain

Once… I heard a bird,
an absorbed, ecstatic bird,
eloquently telling
its child:
"Fly away,
soar high:
a few bread crumbs
will suffice you,
but the sky
you need…
the whole sky."

Sa'id Aql

*Translated by
Mansour Ajami*

GRANIZO
by Leroy Quintana

To have been gone so long
But to have forgotten hail,
its name in Spanish, *granizo*,
until a storm, as I drove
toward a place named Golondrinas,
eight miles from the main highway
because I was enchanted by the name
I was home again,
if only for a while, after eighteen years
I remembered grandfather, his cornfield
Somehow granizo belongs to him
He named it each summer
as he sat and watched, defined its terror
An old enemy, the way only water,
if it isn't gentle rain, can be

259

Comprehension

Puerto Rico

Así es la Vida

✔ **TARGET SKILL** **Evidence** Writers do not always provide all the information readers need. For example, a story may be narrated by a character who understands less about a situation than readers need to understand. To understand a story more fully, you can use your own knowledge from experience as well as evidence, or clues, from the story to make inferences. You can make inferences about a story's setting, characters, and themes. As you read, pay close attention to what characters do and say.

Here are some excerpts from "An Hour with Abuelo." Arturo is visiting his grandfather, or *abuelo*, in a nursing home. Arturo is an impatient teenager who is ambitious and won't let anything hold him back. Abuelo is reading from a book he has written about his life in Puerto Rico. A *campo* is a ranch or large farm.

These details show that Abuelo's mother grew up in a city but went to live in the country. From this evidence, you can infer that she valued and probably missed some things from her old life.

Abuelo reads: "I loved words from the beginning of my life. In the *campo* where I was born one of seven sons, there were few books. My mother read them to us over and over...[the books] that she had read as a child and brought with her from the city of Mayagüez; that was before she married my father, a coffee bean farmer, and she taught us words from the newspaper that a boy on a horse brought every week to her. She taught each of us how to write on a slate with chalks that she ordered by mail every year. We used those chalks until they were so small that you lost them between your fingers."

These details show the mother's determination. They also show how hard it was to obtain educational materials. She couldn't get a newspaper or even chalks whenever she felt like it.

Abuelo is showing that opportunities for education didn't come easily, and so nothing was wasted. How Abuelo has dealt with adversity in his life is one of the themes of the story.

You can use this graphic organizer to keep track of evidence from the story and inferences you make.

Clues	Inference
In the *campo* where I was born, there were few books. ...the books Mother had read as a child and brought with her from the city of Mayagüez.	Abuelo's mother came from a city to live in the country. She wanted to pass on her own educational values to her children.
My mother read them to us over and over... ...and she taught us words from the newspaper.... ...the newspaper that a boy on a horse brought every week to her... She taught each of us to write on a slate with chalks that she ordered by mail every year.	Though educational materials were scarce, the mother used everything at her disposal to educate her children. Getting even the simplest items was difficult, and they could only be obtained at certain times.
We used those chalks until they were so small that you lost them between your fingers.	Educational opportunities didn't come easily to Abuelo's family, and they weren't wasted.

✔ **TARGET STRATEGY** **Infer** You can use clues from a story and knowledge from your own experience to make inferences about the story's characters, setting, and theme. As you read, ask yourself questions such as the following:

• Where and when is this part of the story taking place?

• What is the character doing?

• Why is the character doing these things?

• How does the characters actions or feelings relate to the theme of the story?

As you read, list the details that help you make inferences.

ONLY DAUGHTER

by Sandra Cisneros

FOCUS: How do our achievements sometimes surprise our relatives?

Sandra Cisneros grew up as the only daughter in a family of seven children of Mexican American parents living in Chicago. Her traditional-minded working-class father was not exactly a bookworm, and indeed did not read in English at all. His Spanish-language reading preferences consisted of things such as magazines and *fotonovelas*, dramatic Spanish-language picture stories that are like soap operas on paper. So it's somewhat ironic that since childhood, Cisneros aspired toward something that no one in her family, least of all her father, expected of her: she wanted to have a career as an author. How could she overcome her father's distress that she was pursuing a career instead of marrying young, and how could she get her father to see the value in the profession she had chosen?

Once, several years ago, when I was just starting my writing career, I was asked to write my own contributor's note for an **anthology** I was part of. I wrote: "I am the only daughter in a family of six sons. *That* explains everything."

Well, I've thought about that ever since, and yes, it explains a lot to me, but for the reader's sake I should have written: "I am the only daughter in a *Mexican* family of six sons." Or even: "I am the only daughter of a Mexican father and a Mexican American mother." Or: "I am the only daughter of a working-class family of nine." All of these had everything to do with who I am today.

I was/am the only daughter and *only* a daughter. Being an only daughter in a family of six sons forced me by circumstance to spend a lot of time by myself because my brothers felt it beneath them to play with a girl in public. But that aloneness, that loneliness, was good for a would-be writer—it allowed me time to think and think, to imagine, to read and prepare myself. Being only a daughter for my father meant my destiny would lead me to become someone's wife. That's what he believed. But when I was in the fifth grade and shared my plans for college with him, I was sure he understood. I remember my father saying, *"Que bueno, mi'ja,* that's good." That meant a lot to me, especially since my brothers thought the idea hilarious. What I didn't realize was that my father thought college was good for girls—good for finding a husband. After four years of college and two more in graduate school, and still no husband, my father shakes his head even now and says I wasted all that education.

In retrospect, I'm lucky my father believed daughters were meant for husbands. It meant it didn't matter if I majored in something silly like English. After all, I'd find a nice professional eventually, right? This allowed me the liberty to putter about embroidering my little poems and stories without my father interrupting with so much as a "What's that you're writing?"

But the truth is, I wanted him to interrupt. I wanted my father to understand what it was I was scribbling, to introduce me as "My only daughter, the writer." Not as, "This is only my daughter. She teaches." *Es maestra*—teacher. Not even *profesora*.

In a sense, everything I have ever written has been for him, to win his approval even though I know my father can't read English words, even though my father's only reading includes the brown-ink *Esto* sports magazines from Mexico City. Or the *fotonovelas*, the little picture paperbacks with tragedy and trauma erupting from the characters' mouths in bubbles.

My father represents, then, the public majority. A public who is disinterested in reading, and yet one for whom I am writing about and for, and privately trying to woo.

When we were growing up in Chicago, we moved a lot because of my father. He suffered bouts of nostalgia. Then we'd have to let go of our flat, store the furniture with mother's relatives, load the station wagon with baggage and bologna sandwiches and head south. To Mexico City.

We came back, of course. To yet another Chicago flat, another Chicago neighborhood, another Catholic school. Each time, my father would seek out the parish priest, and complain or boast: "I have seven sons."

He meant *siete hijos*, seven children, but he translated it as "sons." "I have seven sons." To anyone who would listen. The Sears Roebuck employee who sold us the washing machine. The short-order cook where my father ate his ham-and-eggs breakfasts. "I have seven sons." As if he deserved a medal from the state.

My papa. He didn't mean anything by the mistranslation, I'm sure. But somehow I could feel myself being erased. I'd tug my father's sleeve and whisper: "Not seven sons. Six! and *one daughter.*"

When my oldest brother graduated from medical school, he fulfilled my father's dream that we study hard and use this—our heads, instead of these—our hands. Even now my father's hands are thick and yellow, stubbed by a history of hammer and nails and twine and coils and springs. "Use this," my father said, tapping his head, "and not these," showing us those hands. He always looked tired when he said it.

Wasn't college an investment? And hadn't I spent all those years in college? And if I didn't marry, what was it all for? Why would anyone go to college and then choose to be poor? Especially someone who had always been poor.

Last year, after ten years of writing professionally, the financial rewards started to trickle in. My second National **Endowment** for the Arts fellowship. A guest professorship at the University of

California, Berkeley. My book, which sold to a major New York publishing house.

At Christmas, I flew home to Chicago. The house was throbbing, same as always: hot tamales and sweet tamales hissing in my mother's pressure cooker, and everybody—mother, six brothers, wives, babies, aunts, cousins—talking too loud and at the same time. Like in a Fellini film, because that's just how we are.

I went upstairs to my father's room. One of my stories had just been translated into Spanish and published in an anthology of Chicano writing and I wanted to show it to him. Ever since he recovered from a stroke two years ago, my father likes to spend his leisure hours horizontally. And that's how I found him, watching a Pedro Infante movie on Galavisión and eating rice pudding.

There was a glass filled with milk on the bedside table. There were several **vials** of pills and balled Kleenex. And on the floor, one black sock. Pedro Infante

was about to burst into song, and my father was laughing.

I'm not sure if it was because my story was translated into Spanish, or because it was published in Mexico, or perhaps because the story dealt with Tepeyac, the *colonia* my father was raised in, and the house he grew up in, but at any rate, my father punched the mute button on his remote control and read my story.

I sat on the bed next to my father and waited. He read it very slowly. As if he were reading each line over and over. He laughed at all the right places and read lines he liked out loud. He pointed and asked questions: "Is this So-and-so?" "Yes," I said. He kept reading.

When he was finally finished, after what seemed like hours, my father looked up and asked: "Where can we get more copies of this for the relatives?"

Of all the wonderful things that happened to me last year, that was the most wonderful.

STOP AND THINK

1. How did Cisneros's story make her father see her in a new way?

2. Why is it so satisfying to gain the respect of one's family?

Your Turn

Use Your Words:

abomination	offensive
bawl	progeny
comprehensible	prosperous
conversation	ravenous
conviction	recreation
fodder	recruit
instill	relent
inter	trudge
intimate	typhoid
notion	vigor

- Read the words on the list.
- Read the dialogue. Find the words.

The idea is to instill a sense of history in the next generation.

It was easy to recruit people to participate in these conversations.

Talking in a small, intimate group like this is much more effective than hearing a speech.

A civil rights activist was interred in my town. Mourners packed the cemetery.

Every topic is fodder for conversation—even the way my parents trudged to a faraway, segregated school.

MORE ACTIVITIES

1. Dialogue
Speaking and Listening

Think about a conversation you had with an older relative about the past. How did you respond? What kinds of questions did you ask? Discuss the conversation with your partner.

2. Family Trip
Writing

Where would you like to go on a family trip? Who would you want to go on the trip? Write a paragraph describing the trip and what you might learn during it.

3. Take a Survey
Graphic Organizer

How far apart are we? Today many families are spread around the country—or even around the globe. The greater the distance, the harder it is to get together for holidays and reunions. Ask 12 classmates how often they see at least one of their grandparents. Use tally marks to record the results. Share the results with your class.

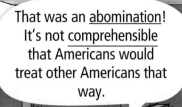

That was an <u>abomination</u>! It's not <u>comprehensible</u> that Americans would treat other Americans that way.

In the sixties we fought against the war with all the <u>vigor</u> we could muster. We brought up our <u>progeny</u> with the same sense of <u>conviction</u>.

I did two tours in Vietnam. When I came home, I had the <u>notion</u> that people would treat me like I had <u>typhoid</u>. But it wasn't like that at all.

My family saw a documentary about the treatment of Japanese Americans during World War II. It made my mother <u>bawl</u>.

So what do you kids do for <u>recreation</u>?

My Japanese grandparents started a business and became <u>prosperous</u>. But then they were sent to an internment camp.

We go for pizza. You guys want to come with us?

That would be super. We're <u>ravenous</u>!

In World War II I took part in the D-Day <u>offensive</u>. We refused to <u>relent</u>.

About how often do you see at least one grandparent?	Number of Students
Every Day	
Once a Week	
Once a Month	
Every Year	
Every Few Years	
Never	

4. Let's Reminisce!
Writing

What do your parents or grandparents reminisce about? Do you think one day you'll reminisce about the same kinds of things? Write a list of the things you might reminisce about when you're older. Share the list with your class.

5. Conduct an Interview
Speaking and Listening

Suppose you are interviewing a grandparent for your school newspaper. Have your partner play the role of "grandparent." Ask your partner five questions about his or her life. Then reverse roles.

BY
JUDITH
ORTIZ
COFER

An Hour with Abuelo

FOCUS: What can we learn from our grandparents and other older people?

Arturo is eager to get ahead in the world and is impatient with anything that holds him back, so a trip to Brooklyn to spend time with Abuelo is not high on his list of priorities. During the visit, Abuelo reads Arturo a story in which he reminisces about his earlier life, including a confrontation with prejudice while serving in the army. Abuelo was never able to overcome the prejudice of the army sergeant long ago, but perhaps he overcomes a few assumptions that his grandson makes about him in the present.

"Just one hour, *una hora,* is all I'm asking of you, son." My grandfather is in a nursing home in Brooklyn, and my mother wants me to spend some time with him, since the doctors say that he doesn't have too long to go now. *I* don't have much time left of my summer vacation, and there's a stack of books next to my bed I've got to read if I'm going to get into the AP English class I want. I'm going stupid in some of my classes, and Mr. Williams, the principal at Central, says that if I passed some reading tests, he'd let me move up.

Besides, I hate the place, the old people's home, especially the way it smells like industrial-strength ammonia and other stuff I won't mention, since it turns my stomach. And really the abuelo always has a lot of relatives visiting him, so I've gotten out of going out there except at Christmas, when a whole vanload of grandchildren are herded over there to give him gifts and a hug. We all make it quick and spend the rest of the time in the recreation area, where they play checkers and stuff with some of the old people's games, and I catch up on back issues of *Modern Maturity.* I'm not picky, I'll read almost anything.

Anyway, after my mother nags me for about a week, I let her drive me to Golden Years. She drops me off in front. She wants me to go in alone and have a "good time" talking to Abuelo. I tell her to be back in one hour or I'll take the bus back to Paterson. She squeezes my hand and says, *"Gracias, hijo."* In a choked-up voice like I'm doing her a big favor.

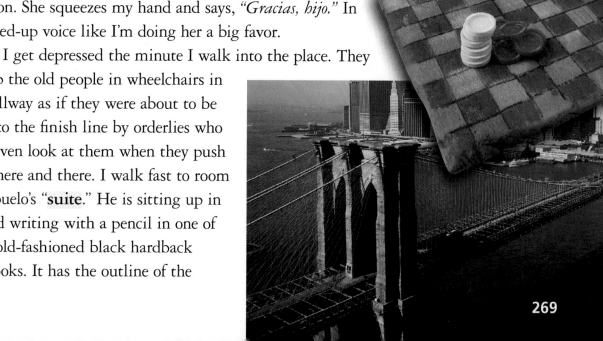

I get depressed the minute I walk into the place. They line up the old people in wheelchairs in the hallway as if they were about to be raced to the finish line by orderlies who don't even look at them when they push them here and there. I walk fast to room 10, Abuelo's "**suite**." He is sitting up in his bed writing with a pencil in one of those old-fashioned black hardback notebooks. It has the outline of the island of Puerto Rico on it. I slide into the hard vinyl chair by his bed. He sort of smiles and the lines on his face get deeper, but he doesn't say anything. Since I'm supposed to talk to him, I say, "What are you doing, Abuelo, writing the story of your life?"

It's supposed to be a joke, but he answers, "Sí, how did you know, Arturo?"

His name is Arturo, too. I was named after him. I don't really know my grandfather. His children, including my mother, came to New York and New Jersey (where I was born) and he stayed on the Island until my grandmother died. Then he got sick, and since nobody could leave their jobs to go take care of him, they brought him to this nursing home in Brooklyn. I see him a couple of times a year, but he's always surrounded by his sons and daughters. My mother tells me that Don Arturo had once been a teacher back in Puerto Rico, but had lost his job after the war. Then he became a farmer. She's always saying in a sad voice, "Ay, bendito! What a waste of a fine mind." Then she usually shrugs her shoulders and says, *"Así es la vida."* That's the way life is. It sometimes makes me mad that the adults I know just accept whatever is thrown at them because "that's the way things are." Not for me. I go after what I want.

Anyway, Abuelo is looking at me like he was trying to see into my head, but he doesn't say anything. Since I like stories, I decide I may as well ask him if he'll read me what he wrote.

I look at my watch: I've already used up twenty minutes of the hour I promised my mother.

Abuelo starts talking in his slow way. He speaks what my mother calls book English. He taught himself from a dictionary, and his words sound stiff, like he's sounding them out in his head before he says them. With his children he speaks Spanish, and that funny book English with us grandchildren. I'm surprised that he's still so sharp, because his body is shrinking like a crumpled-up brown paper sack with some bones in it. But I can see from looking into his eyes that the light is still on in there.

Puerto Rico

Así es la Vida

"It is a short story, Arturo. The story of my life. It will not take very much time to read it."

"I have time, Abuelo." I'm a little embarrassed that he saw me looking at my watch.

"Yes, hijo. You have spoken the truth. La verdad. You have much time."

Abuelo reads: "'I loved words from the beginning of my life. In the *campo* where I was born one of seven sons, there were few books. My mother read them to us over and over: the Bible, the stories of Spanish conquistadors and of pirates that she had read as a child and brought with her from the city of Mayagüez; that was before she married my father, a coffee bean farmer, and she taught us words from the newspaper that a boy on a horse brought every week to her. She taught each of us how to write on a slate with chalks that she ordered by mail every year. We used those chalks until they were so small that you lost them between your fingers.

"'I always wanted to be a writer and a teacher. With my heart and my soul I knew that I wanted to be around books all of my life. And so against the wishes of my father, who wanted all his sons to help him on the land, she sent me to high school in Mayagüez. For four years I boarded with a couple she knew. I paid my rent in labor, and I ate vegetables I grew myself. I wore my clothes until they were thin as **parchment**. But I graduated at the top of my class! My whole family came to see me that day. My mother brought me a wonderful *guayabera,* a white shirt made of the finest cotton and embroidered by her own hands. I was a happy young man.

"'In those days you could teach in a country school with a high school diploma. So I went back to my mountain village and got a job teaching all grades in a little classroom built by the parents of my students.

"'I had books sent to me by the government. I felt like a rich man although the pay was very small. I had books. All the books I wanted! I taught my

students how to read poetry and plays, and how to write them. We made up songs and put on shows for the parents. It was a beautiful time for me.

"'Then the war came, and the American president said that all Puerto Rican men would be drafted. I wrote to our governor and explained that I was the only teacher in the mountain village. I told him that the children would go back to the fields and grow up **ignorant** if I could not teach them their letters. I said that I thought I was a better teacher than a soldier. The governor did not answer my letter. I went into the U.S. Army.

"'I told my sergeant that I could be a teacher in the army. I could teach all the farm boys their letters so that they could read the instructions on the ammunition boxes and not blow themselves up. The sergeant said I was too smart for my own good, and gave me a job cleaning latrines. He said to me there is reading material for you there, scholar. Read the writing on the walls. I spent the war mopping floors and cleaning toilets.

"'When I came back to the Island, things had changed. You had to have a college degree to teach school, even the lower grades. My parents were sick, two of my brothers had been killed in the war, the others had stayed in Nueva York. I was the only one left to help the old people. I became a farmer. I married a good woman who gave me many good children. I taught them all how to read and write before they started school.'"

Abuelo then puts the notebook down on his lap and closes his eyes.

"*Así es la vida* is the title of my book," he says in a whisper, almost to himself. Maybe he's forgotten that I'm there.

For a long time he doesn't say anything else. I think that he's sleeping, but then I see that he's watching me through half-closed lids, maybe waiting for my opinion of his writing. I'm trying to think of something nice to say. I liked it and all, but not the title. And I think that he could've been a teacher if he had wanted to bad enough. Nobody is going to stop me from doing what I want with my life. I'm not going to let *la vida* get in my way. I want to discuss this with him, but the words are not coming into my head in Spanish just yet. I'm about to ask him why he didn't keep fighting to make his dream come true, when an old lady in hot-pink running shoes sort of appears at the door.

She is wearing a pink jogging outfit too. The world's oldest marathoner, I say to myself. She calls out to my grandfather in a flirty voice, "Yoo-hoo, Arturo, remember what day this is? It's poetry-reading day in the rec room! You promised us you'd read your new one today."

I see my abuelo perking up almost immediately. He points to his wheelchair, which is hanging like a huge metal bat in the open closet. He makes it obvious that he wants me to get it. I put it together, and with Mrs. Pink Running Shoes's help, we get him in it. Then he says in a strong deep voice I hardly recognize, "Arturo, get that notebook for me, please."

I hand him another map-of-the-island notebook—this one is red. On it in big letters it says, *POEMAS DE ARTURO.*

I start to push him toward the rec room, but he shakes his finger at me.

"Arturo, look at your watch now. I believe your time is over." He gave me a wicked smile.

Then, with her pushing the wheelchair—maybe a little too fast—they roll down the hall. He is already reading from his notebook, and she's making bird noises. I look at my watch and the hour *is* up, to the minute. I can't help but think that my abuelo has been timing *me*. It cracks me up. I walk slowly down the hall toward the exit sign. I want my mother to have to wait a little. I don't want her to think that I'm in a hurry or anything.

STOP AND THINK

1. How does Arturo show that he doesn't really understand Abuelo's experiences?

2. What have you learned from a much older person?

Passing Learning Along:

IN NORTH AND SOUTH

FOCUS: How can one generation change another generation's chances for a better life?

One way for one generation to help and influence another is by teaching. During some eras, however, whole groups of people were kept out of the educational process. This situation changed because determined teachers and students made great efforts, and sometimes took great risks, to bring about reform.

Connecticut, early 1830s

In 1831, Prudence Crandall was asked to open a private girls' school in the **prosperous** Connecticut town of Canterbury—for white children only.

Things went uneventfully until a few years later, when a young African American, Sarah Harris, asked to attend the school. Though the states of the North had phased out slavery within their borders, they had not done away with prejudice.

Prudence Crandall knew that admitting Sarah Harris would be a problem in Canterbury. Though most people in the area believed in the abolition of slavery, many weren't ready to live in a multiracial society. Instead, they wanted freed African Americans to return to Africa. Crandall, on the other hand, was a Quaker. This religious group believed in racial equality.

LOOK IT UP

For related information:
Prudence Crandall,
Susie King Taylor

Later, Prudence Crandall wrote about her decision: "I said in my heart, here are my **convictions**. What shall I do? Shall I be inactive and permit prejudice, the mother of **abominations**, to remain undisturbed?" She reasoned that she did not have great wealth to donate to the cause of racial justice. All she had was the ability to teach. Since that was the way she could help African Americans, it was her moral duty to take action now.

Townspeople were furious when Sarah Harris was admitted to the school. White parents threatened to pull their daughters out if Sarah was not expelled. Prudence Crandall, with the support of antislavery activists such as William Lloyd Garrison, then took a huge step. She changed the school to an all-black school and **recruited** students from all over the North.

Prudence Crandall

An announcement appeared in Garrison's Abolitionist newspaper *The Liberator.* In it, Crandall said that her school was now open to "young Ladies and little Misses of color," and that students would be learning "Reading, Writing, Arithmetic, English Grammar, Geography, History, Natural and Moral Philosophy, Chemistry, Astronomy, Drawing and Painting, Music on the Piano, together with the French language." In other words, she would be teaching the same demanding curriculum she had presented to her white students.

When the townspeople realized what was happening, they took action. Shopkeepers refused to sell food to the school. People harassed the students on the street and threw rocks at the school building. The more powerful citizens of Canterbury were even able to get Connecticut to pass a so-called Black Law. This measure prevented out-of-state African Americans from coming to Connecticut to get an education. This was the law used to arrest Prudence Crandall in June of 1833, because many of her students came from outside of Connecticut. Crandall was even briefly jailed.

The case against Crandall was dismissed on technical grounds in 1834. She resumed teaching. Shortly afterward, a mob broke into the school. Crandall felt that she could no longer endanger her young students, and she closed the school down for good.

Prudence Crandall's bold experiment did not succeed, but her deed inspired other reformers. Crandall herself continued to teach school, first in Illinois and later in Kansas. Fifty years later, the state of Connecticut apologized to her and awarded her a small pension.

Sea Islands, South Carolina, early 1860s

In many states in the pre-Civil War South, the most basic literacy was forbidden by law to enslaved African Americans. The reason is obvious: literate people can inform themselves by reading. Reading was more dangerous to cotton plantation owners than fire, drought, or the boll weevil, a **ravenous** beetle that devoured cotton crops. The result was that some enslaved people learned to read in secret, but most were illiterate.

One enslaved child who was able to learn reading was Susie King. She lived with her grandmother in the Georgia city of Savannah. Her grandmother sent her to a free black woman, Mrs. Woodhouse, to learn reading. To avoid trouble, the children taught by Mrs. Woodhouse went "with our books wrapped in paper to prevent the police or white persons from seeing them. We went in, one at a time, through the gate, into the yard to the kitchen, which was the schoolroom... The neighbors would see us going in sometimes, but they supposed we were there learning trades...." Later, young Susie learned more from other people.

Within a year of the start of the Civil War, the Union Navy had taken back Confederate territory on the Sea Islands off the coast of South Carolina. White residents of the islands escaped to the mainland, leaving thousands of previously enslaved African Americans on their own. Many Northern reform organizations, as well as at least one Union government official, Secretary of the Treasury Salmon Chase, made arrangements to help these African Americans become educated and self-sufficient.

When Susie King and some relatives escaped Savannah and sailed to the Sea Islands, a Union officer discovered that fourteen-year-old Susie was literate. In a short time, she was urged to become a teacher of younger children on St. Simon's Island. Susie King later wrote: "I had about forty children to teach, beside a number of adults who came to me nights, all of them so eager to learn to read, to read above anything else." Later in the war, Susie King became one of the first African American battlefield nurses.

Meanwhile, trained teachers were traveling down to the Sea Islands from the North. One of them was Charlotte Forten, an African American woman from a well-to-do Pennsylvania family. In October 1862, Charlotte Forten sailed from New York to the island of Port Royal, South Carolina, and then to the island of St. Helena, where she would be stationed. Charlotte Forten wrote an article about her experiences that was published in *The Atlantic Monthly*, a popular magazine, in 1864. In it she said, "I never before saw children so eager to learn, although I had had several years' experience in New England schools. Coming to school is a constant delight and **recreation** to them. They come here as other children go to play."

What became of the young people who were taught by educators such as Prudence Crandall, Susie King, and Charlotte Forten? Perhaps they became teachers or scholars or started businesses. Perhaps their children, grandchildren, or great-grandchildren became scientists, nurses, doctors, pilots, or government officials. Here is just one example of how education passes down through the generations. In Baltimore, Maryland, William Marshall, the son of a formerly enslaved person, **instilled** in his children a love of learning and the desire to use education as a path upward. One of William Marshall's sons, Thurgood Marshall, later became a lawyer. Thurgood Marshall also became the first African American to be appointed to the U.S. Supreme Court.

STOP AND THINK

1. How does the writer of this selection show the effects that teaching can have?

2. If you could become an expert in a skill or an area of knowledge so you could teach others, what skill or area would you choose?

From The Horned Toad

by Gerald Haslam

FOCUS: What can cause the very young and the very old to form deep bonds?

The boy in this story, set in California in the 1940s, is based on the author himself. He grew up in a family with both Latino and non-Latino members. The child narrator's fierce great-grandmother from the Mexican side of the family has come to live with him and his parents. Grandma doesn't seem thrilled to have ended up here. At first she goes on the **offensive**, calling the narrator's father *ese gringo* (that white man) and telling the narrator that horned toads like the one he has found in a nearby lot will spit blood from their eyes. The narrator wonders what kind of person has come to live with the family.

Spanish Terms Used in the Story

el malcriado	badly brought up, a child who talks back
¡Venga aqui!	Come here!
¿Qué deseas tomar?	What would you like to eat?
dulce	sweets or candy
¿Mande?	I beg your pardon?
Para su dulce	for your candy
muy inteligente	very intelligent
"Ola senor sangre de ojos. Que tal?"	Hello, Mr. blood-in-the-eyes. What's up?

That spring, when I discovered the lone horned toad near the back of the lot, it had been rough on my family. Earlier, there had been quiet, unpleasant tension between Mom and Daddy. He was a silent man, not given to emotional displays. It was difficult for him to show affection and I guess the openness of Mom's family made him uneasy. Daddy had no kin in California and rarely mentioned any in Texas. He couldn't seem to understand my mother's large, **intimate** family, their constant noisy concern for one another, and I think he was a little jealous of the time she gave everyone, maybe even me.

I heard her talking on the phone to my various aunts and uncles, usually in Spanish. Even though I couldn't understand, I could sense the stress. I had been afraid they were going to divorce, since she only used Spanish to hide things from me. I'd confronted her with my suspicion, but she comforted me, saying no, that was not the problem. They were merely deciding when it would be our turn to care for Grandma. I didn't understand, although I was relieved.

In truth, we had more room, and my dad made more money in the oil patch than almost anyone else in the family. Since my mother was the closest to Grandma, our place was the logical one for her, but Ese Gringo didn't see it that way, I guess, at least not at first. Finally, after much debate, he **relented**.

In any case, one windy afternoon, my Uncle Manuel and Aunt Toni drove up and deposited four-and-a-half-feet of bewigged, bejeweled Spanish spitfire: a square, pale face topped by a tightly curled black wig that hid a bald head— her hair having been lost to **typhoid** nearly sixty years before—her small white hands veined with rivers of blue. She walked with a prancing bounce that made her appear half her age, and she barked orders in Spanish from the moment she emerged from Manuel and Toni's car. Later, just before they left, I heard Uncle Manuel tell my dad, "Good luck, Charlie. That old lady's dynamite." Daddy only grunted.

She had been with us only two days when I tried to impress her with my horned toad. In fact, nothing I did seemed to impress her, and she referred to me as *el malcriado*, causing my mother to shake her head. Mom explained to me that Grandma was just old and lonely for Grandpa and uncomfortable in town.

I later learned that my great-grandmother—whom we simply called "Grandma"— had been moving from house to house within the family, trying to find a place she'd accept. She hated the city, and most of the aunts and uncles lived in Los Angeles. Our house in Oildale was much closer to the open country where she'd dwelled all her life. She had wanted to come to our place right away because she had raised my mother from a baby when my own grandmother died. But the old lady seemed unimpressed with Daddy, whom she called *"ese gringo."*

Mom told me that Grandma had lived over half a century in the country, away from the noise, away from clutter, away from people. She refused to accompany my mother on shopping trips, or anywhere else. She even refused to climb into a car, and I wondered how Uncle Manuel had managed to load her up in order to bring her to us.

She disliked sidewalks and roads, dancing across them when she had to, then appearing to wipe her feet on earth or grass. Things too civilized simply did not please her. A brother of hers had been killed in the great San Francisco earthquake and that had been the end of her tolerance for cities. Until my great-grandfather died, they lived on a small rancho near Arroyo Cantua, north of Coalinga. Grandpa, who had come north from Sonora as a youth to work as a *vaquero*, had bred horses and cattle, and cowboyed for other ranchers, scraping together enough of a living to raise eleven children.

He had been, until the time of his death, a lean, dark-skinned man with wide shoulders, a large nose, and a sweeping, handle-bar moustache that was white when I knew him. His Indian blood darkened all his **progeny** so that not even I was as fair-skinned as my great-grandmother, Ese Gringo for a father or not.

As it turned out, I didn't really understand very much about Grandma at all. She was old, of course, yet in many ways my parents treated her as though she were younger than me, walking her to the bathroom at night and bringing her presents from the store. In other ways, she was granted adult privileges.

She held court on our front porch, often gazing toward the desert hills east of us or across the street at kids playing on the lot. Occasionally, she would rise, cross the yard and sidewalk and street, skip over them, sometimes stumbling on the curb, and wipe her feet on the lot's sandy soil, then she would slowly circle the boundary between the open middle and the brushy sides, searching for something, it appeared. I never figured out what.

One afternoon I returned from school and saw Grandma perched on the porch as usual, so I started to walk around the house to avoid her sharp, mostly **incomprehensible**, tongue. She had already spotted me. "*¡Venga aqui!*" she ordered, and I understood.

I approached the porch and noticed that Grandma was **vigorously** chewing something. She held a small white bag in one hand. Saying "*¿Qué deseas tomar?*" she withdrew a large orange gumdrop from the bag and began chewing it in her toothless mouth, smacking loudly as she did so. I stood below her for a moment, trying to remember the word for candy. Then it came to me. "*Dulce*," I said.

Still chewing, Grandma replied, "*¿Mande?*"

Knowing she wanted a complete sentence, I again struggled, then came up with "*Deseo dulce.*"

She measured me for a moment, before answering in nearly perfect English, "Oh, so you wan' some candy. Go to the store an' buy some."

I don't know if it was the shock of hearing her speak English for the first time, or the way she denied me a piece of candy, but I suddenly felt tears warm my cheeks and I sprinted into the house and found Mom, who stood at the kitchen sink. "Grandma just talked English," I burst out between light sobs.

"What's wrong?" she asked as she reached out to stroke my head.

"Grandma can talk English," I repeated.

"Of course she can," Mom answered. "What's wrong?"

I wasn't sure what was wrong, but after considering, I told Mom that Grandma had teased me. No sooner had I said that than the old woman appeared at the door and hiked her skirt. Attached to one of her petticoats by safety pins were several small sacks, the white cloth kind that closed with yellow drawstrings. She carefully unhooked one and opened it, withdrawing a dollar, then handed the money to me. "*Para su dulce*," she said. Then, to my mother, she asked, "Why does he **bawl** like a motherless calf?"

"It's nothing," Mother replied.

"Do not weep, little one," the old lady comforted me. She smiled and patted my head. To my mother she said as though just realizing it, "Your baby?"

Somehow that day changed everything. I wasn't afraid of my great-grandmother any longer and, once I began spending time with her on the porch, I realized that my father had also begun directing increased attention to the old woman. Almost every evening Ese Gringo was with Grandma. They talked out there, but I never did hear a real two-way **conversation** between them. Usually Grandma rattled on and Daddy nodded. She'd chuckle and pat his hand and he might grin, even grunt a word or two, before she'd begin talking again. Once I saw my mother standing by the front window watching them together, a smile playing across her face.

No more did I sneak around the house to avoid Grandma after school. Instead, she waited for me and discussed my efforts in class gravely, telling Mother that I was a bright boy, "*muy inteligente*."...

Frequently, I would accompany Grandma to the lot where she would explain that no **fodder** could grow there. Poor pasture or not, the lot was at least unpaved, and Grandma greeted even the tiniest new cactus or flowering weed with joy. "Look how beautiful," she would croon. "In all this ugliness, it lives." Oildale was my home and it didn't look especially ugly to me, so I could only grin and wonder.

Because she liked the lot and things that grew there, I showed her the horned toad when I captured it a second time. I was determined to keep it, although I did not discuss my plans with anyone. I also wanted to hear more about bloody eyes, so I thrust the small animal nearly into her face one afternoon. She did not flinch. *"Ola señor sangre de ojos,"* she said with a mischievous grin. *"¿Qué tal?"* It took me a moment to catch on.

"You were kidding before," I accused.

"Of course," she acknowledged.

"But why?"

"Because the little beast belongs with his own kind in his own place, not in your pocket. Give him his freedom, my son."

I had other plans for the horned toad, but I was clever enough not to cross Grandma. "Yes, Ma'am," I replied. That night I placed the toad in a flower bed cornered by a brick wall Ese Gringo had built the previous summer. It was a spot rich with insects for the toad to eat, and

the little wall, only a foot high, must have seemed massive to so squat an animal.

Nonetheless, the next morning, when I searched for the horned toad it was gone. I had no time to explore the yard for it, so I **trudged** off to school, my belly troubled. How could it have escaped? Classes meant little to me that day. I thought only of my lost pet—I had changed his name to Juan, the same as my great-grandfather—and where I might find him.

I shortened my conversation with Grandma that afternoon so I could search for Juan. "What do you seek?" the old woman asked me as I poked through flower beds beneath the porch. "Praying mantises," I improvised, and she merely nodded, surveying me. But I had eyes only for my lost pet, and I continued pushing through branches and brushing leaves aside. No luck.

Finally, I gave in and turned toward the lot. I found my horned toad nearly across the street, crushed. It had been heading for the miniature desert and had almost made it when an automobile's tire had run over it. One **notion** immediately swept me: if I had left it on its lot, it would still be alive. I stood rooted there in the street, tears slicking my cheeks, and a car honked its horn as it passed, the driver shouting at me.

Grandma joined me, and stroked my back. "The poor little beast," was all she said, then she bent slowly and scooped up what remained of the horned toad and led me out of the street. "We must return him to his own place," she explained, and we trooped, my eyes still clouded, toward the back of the vacant lot. Carefully, I dug a hole with a piece of wood. Grandma placed Juan in it and covered him. We said an Our Father and a Hail Mary, then Grandma walked me back to the house. "Your little Juan is safe with God, my

son," she comforted. We kept the horned toad's death a secret, and we visited his small grave frequently.

Grandma fell just before school ended and summer vacation began. As was her habit, she had walked alone to the vacant lot but this time, on her way back, she tripped over the curb and broke her hip. That following week, when Daddy brought her home from the hospital, she seemed to have shrunken. She sat hunched in a wheelchair on the porch, gazing with faded eyes toward the hills or at the lot, speaking rarely. She still sat every evening with Daddy and even I could tell how concerned he was about her. It got to where he'd look in on her before leaving for work every morning and again at night before turning in. And if Daddy was home, Grandma always wanted him to push her chair when she needed moving, calling "Sharlie!" until he arrived.

I was tugged from sleep on the night she died by voices drumming through the walls into darkness. I couldn't understand them, but was immediately frightened by the uncommon sounds of words in the night. I struggled from bed and walked into the living room just as Daddy closed the front door and a car pulled away.

Mom was sobbing softly on the couch and Daddy walked to her, stroked her head, then noticed me. "Come here, son," he gently ordered.

I walked to him and, uncharacteristically, he put his arm around me. "What's wrong?" I asked, near tears myself. Mom looked up, but before she could speak, Daddy said, "Grandma died." Then he sighed heavily and stood there with his arms around his weeping wife and son.

The next day my Uncle Manuel and Uncle Arnulfo, plus Aunt Chintia, arrived and over food they discussed with my mother where Grandma should be

interred. They argued that it would be too expensive to transport her body home and, besides, they could more easily visit her grave if she was buried in Bakersfield. "They have such nice, manicured grounds at Greenlawn," Aunt Chintia pointed out. Just when it seemed they had agreed, I could remain silent no longer. "But Grandma has to go home," I burst out. "She has to! It's the only thing she really wanted. We can't leave her in the city."

Uncle Arnulfo, who was on the edge, snapped to Mother that I belonged with the other children, not interrupting adult conversation. Mother quietly agreed, but I refused. My father walked into the room then. "What's wrong?" he asked.

"They're going to bury Grandma in Bakersfield, Daddy. Don't let 'em, please."

"Well, son . . ."

"When my horny toad got killed and she helped me to bury it, she said we had to return him to his place."

"Your horny toad?" Mother asked.

"He got squished and me and Grandma buried him in the lot. She said we had to take him back to his place. Honest she did."

No one spoke for a moment, then my father, Ese Gringo, who stood against the sink, responded: "That's right . . ." he paused, then added, "We'll bury her." I saw a weary smile cross my mother's face. "If she wanted to go back to the ranch then that's where we have to take her," Daddy said.

I hugged him and he, right in front of everyone, hugged back.

No one argued. It seemed, suddenly, as though they had all wanted to do exactly what I had begged for.

Grown-ups baffled me. Late that week the entire family, hundreds it seemed, gathered at the little Catholic church in Coalinga for mass, then drove out to Arroyo Cantua and buried Grandma next to Grandpa. She rests there today.

My mother, father, and I drove back to Oildale that afternoon across the scorching westside desert, through sand and tumbleweeds and heat shivers. Quiet and sad, we knew we had done our best. Mom, who usually sat next to the door in the front seat, snuggled close to Daddy, and I heard her whisper to him, "Thank you, Charlie," as she kissed his cheek.

Daddy squeezed her, hesitated as if to clear his throat, then answered, "When you're family, you take care of your own."

STOP AND THINK

1. What does the narrator come to understand about his great-grandmother?

2. What are some things that children and the elderly often have in common?

287

BILL LABOV

Central Middle School

But Mr. Valley, you always say that a person is not guilty until FOUND guilty.

Yes, that's true. So we'll have a trial. Jenny is the accused. Nessa is a witness. I'm the D.A. And the class will be the jury.

Jenny Jackson, I accuse you of passing a note to Nessa Lara.

I am not guilty, so I plead not guilty.

A boat was about to break apart and overturn.

Help! Save my little boy!

It was like our team was near the edge of a big stream, with water tearing along.

Streamline Sal is great in the water.

Sal! They need you!

Don't panic.

If it weren't for you, I would have lost my boy.

It was like Mrs. Neal was saying: "We must all treat each other with respect. We must not be mean to one another."

Get out of my way, kid. Beat it if you know what's good for you.

Mountain Mel does that thing with his shoulders.

Mel, please speak to Dean.

Where did Dean go?

I don't know, but he's nowhere near here.

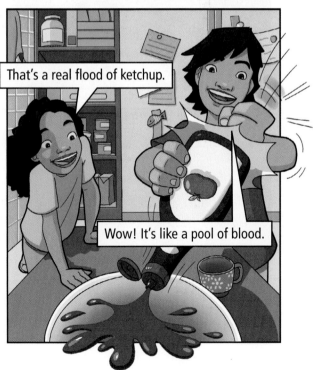

Call on Me

Ghosts in the Basement

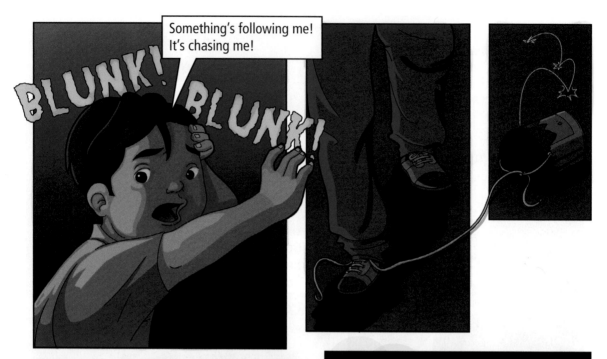

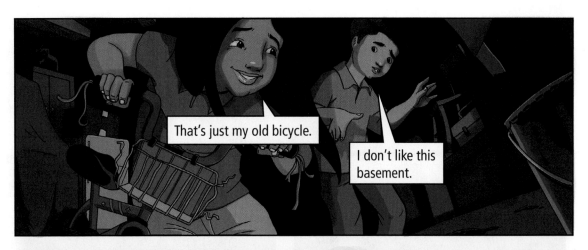

BRENDA! IT'S A GHOST! AND I JUST KILLED IT!

Don't screech! That's no ghost. You just hit an old wasps' nest with your stick.

It's not wasps! It's a ghost's nest!

The Writing on My Wrist

It started when I stayed up all night to watch the late show. My mom got me up at ten to eight. I was half an hour late to school.

I was a wreck. I kept awake in History, but I fell asleep in English.

Then I heard my name called. Mrs. Wren was saying something.

Spell what, Mrs. Wren?

Spell **WRAP**, Shana, as in "**Wrap** up the package."

WRAP was the first word on our spelling list. I knew the answer.

W-R-A-P, wrap.

Very good, Shana.

It was Kelsey. SHE wrote on my wrist when I was asleep.

I hate that girl!

She is always getting in my face. She pokes me with her knee when no one is looking. She passes notes about me to my best friends.

I could wring her neck! I am going to tell her off once and for all!

NICE JOB, KELSEY.

I struck her out three times. Then she had to hit one!

YAY, SHANA, YAY!

YAY, KELSEY, YAY!

We ran the last two legs on the relay race. I gave her a two-second start.

One day I said to myself, "Everything I do is to beat HER. Why am I so mad at her?"

Hey, we're tight.

Today she's my best friend.

Let me tell you what happened to me today,
When I thought every single thing was going my way.

It was late in the day, and we were all uptight.
We had math class coming with Miss Arthurlene Bright.

I have to tell you that this
lady was rough.
She laid down the rules,
and she took no stuff.

If you don't want suspension, you don't want detention,
You'd best do your work and just pay attention.

This day math never got started.
Miss Bright and her class were soon to be parted.

Now listen up, class. Try to understand.
I have to go downstairs and see Mr. Grand.

Now I want no tricks, no stunts,
no acrobatics.

All you're going to do is
do your mathematics.

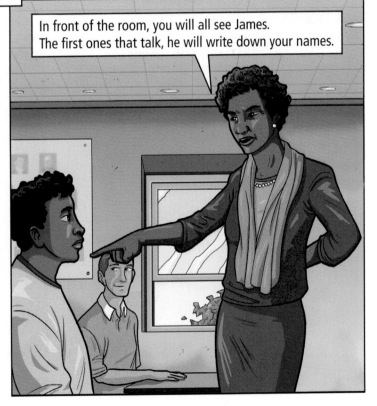

In front of the room, you will all see James.
The first ones that talk, he will write down your names.

I thought, "Wow! This is my shining hour. I have got the glory, I have got the power."

I stood there for a while looking real mean, Running my eyes over the classroom scene.

You can tell that James wants an **A** plus. He thinks he's much better than the rest of us.

Now it seems I just heard somebody talk. Let me have that big stick of chalk.

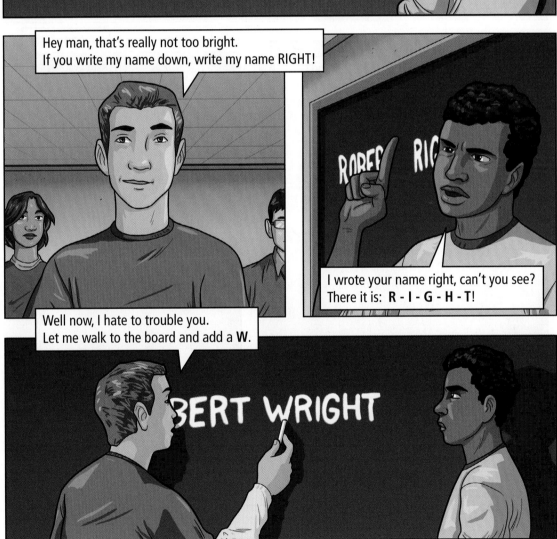

Just then the door opened for Miss Arthurlene Bright.
Everyone in class was frozen with fright.

Well, look here, what do I find?
That Robert Wright is one of a kind.

He writes his name down without any fuss.

And for that, Robert, you deserve an **A** plus.

But James, here you are standing around,
When you should be busy writing names down.

Next time you'd better pay more attention.
Today you have earned two hours' detention.

Now four o'clock comes and I'm going nowhere.
I have one thing to say: life is not fair.

But learn from my case and this I will tell,
It will do you no harm to learn how to spell.

Moving In

Advice from Mr. Fred

GLOSSARY

GLOSSARY

A

able (ā′bəl) – having power or resources to accomplish something

abomination (ə bŏm′ə nā′shən) – something that causes disgust

abstain (ăb stān′) – to hold back from casting a vote

accompany (ə kŭm′pə nē) – to go with or be present with

accustom (ə kŭs′təm) – to become used to

advance (ăd văns′) – to move or put forward; to make progress

aggravate (ăg′rə vāt) – to make worse or more serious

agriculture (ăg′rĭ kŭl′chər) – the science or practice of cultivating the soil, producing crops, and raising livestock

ally (ăl′ī) – a person, group, or nation that sides with another

altar (ôl′tər) – a structure where religious ceremonies take place

alter (ôl′tər) – to change or make different

alternative (ôl tûr′nə tĭv) – one of two choices

amusing (ə myōō′zĭng) – causing to laugh or smile

analyze (ăn′ə līz′) – to separate something into its parts in order to identify it or study it

ancestor (ăn′sĕs tər) – a person from whom one is descended, more distant than a grandparent

anthology (ăn thŏl′ə jē) – a collection of literary pieces such as poems, short stories, or plays

appreciate (ə prē′shē āt′) – to be grateful for or to value greatly

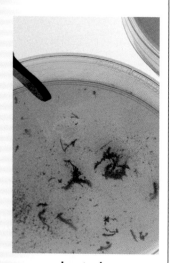

agriculture

bacteria

aquatic (ə kwăt′ĭk) – living, growing, or taking place in, on, or near water

aroma (ə rō′mə) – a pleasant odor or fragrance

array (ə rā′) – an orderly arrangement or display

axle (ăk′səl) – the bar or rod on which a wheel or wheels turn

B

bacteria (băk tîr′ē ə) – one-celled organisms

balance (băl′əns) – a steady and stable state

base (bās) – the supporting part, bottom, or foundation on which something rests

bawl (bôl) – to cry or wail loudly

branch (brănch) – an offshoot or division of the main portion

brittle (brĭt′l) – likely to break, snap, or crack; not flexible

burden (bûr′dn) – to weigh down, load, or overload

burrow (bûr′ō) – to dig a hole or tunnel

C

canvas (kăn′vəs) – a strong, coarse cloth used for making things like sails or tents

capacity (kə păs′ĭ tē) – the amount that can be contained in something

cast (kăst) – to indicate or give one's vote

ceremony (sĕr′ə mō′nē) – a set of formal activities, especially those used on religious or public occasions

chance (chăns) – a risk or gamble; the unpredictable way things happen

ă pat / ā pay / âr care / ä father / ĕ pet / ē bee / ĭ pit / ī pie / îr pier / ŏ pot / ō toe / ô paw / oi noise / ōō took / ōō boot / ou out / ŭ cut /

characterize (kăr′ək tə rīz′) – to be a distinctive quality, trait, or mark of

cherish (chĕr′ĭsh) – to hold dear

churn (chûrn) – to stir or swirl violently

circulate (sûr′kyə lāt) – to move around from place to place

civilized (sĭv′ə līzd) – having a highly developed society and culture

clot (klŏt) – a small, thick clump

coma (kō′mə) – a state of deep unconsciousness, often caused by injury or disease

compete (kəm pēt′) – to strive against another or others to attain a goal or advantage

comprehend (kŏm prĭ hĕnd′) – to understand, to grasp mentally

comprehensible (kŏm′prĭ hĕn′sə bəl) – able to be understood

conclude (kən klōōd′) – to bring or come to an end

conflicted (kən flĭk′tĭd) – feeling uneasy by having opposing opinions, ideas, or urges

consequence (kŏn′sĭ kwĕns) – something that is the effect or result of an earlier occurrence

constantly (kŏn′stənt lē) – all the time; continually

convention (kən vĕn′shən) – a practice or custom that is generally accepted or agreed upon

conversation (kŏn′vər sā′shən) – an informal talk between people

conviction (kən vĭk′shən) – a strong belief

craft (krăft) – skilled artistry and technique in creating or doing something

cripple (krĭp′əl) – to disable or seriously weaken or damage

crucial (krōō′shəl) – extremely important or significant

culture (kŭl′chər) – a society's products of work and thought, including arts, beliefs, and patterns of behavior

current (kûr′ənt) – belonging to the present; happening now

D

debt (dĕt) – something owed, such as money, goods, or services

decade (dĕk′ād) – a period of ten years

declaration (dĕk′lə rā′shən) – a formal or firm statement, either written or oral

decline (dĭ klīn′) – a gradual decrease or downward slope

decompose (dē kəm pōz′) – to rot, decay, or disintegrate

dejected (dĭ jĕk′tĭd) – being in low spirits or depressed

delegate (dĕl′ĭ gĭt) – a person who represents others and acts according to their instructions

democracy (dĭ mŏk′rə sē) – government by the people, usually through representatives whom they elect

depend (dĭ pĕnd′) – to rely upon or be unable to do without

deplete (dĭ plēt′) – to use up

descend (dĭ sĕnd′) – to come down or go down

design (dĭ zīn′) – to plan or create for a specific purpose

detect (dĭ tĕkt′) – to discover the existence or presence of

dictator (dĭk′tā tər) – a ruler who has complete and absolute authority; a tyrant

dimension (dĭ mĕn′shən) – a measurement of extent in space, such as length or width

craft

design

ûr firm / hw which / th thin / *th* this / zh vision /
ə about, item, edible, gallop, circus

electromagnetic

flare

disguise (dĭs gīz′) – to change appearance in order to hide the identity of

displace (dĭs plās′) – to move from the usual place

distress (dĭ strĕs′) – strain, anxiety, or suffering

document (dŏk′yə mənt) – a paper giving information about something; or to produce such a paper

drastic (drăs′tĭk) – strong or extreme

draw (drô) – to take out from a source

dwarf (dwôrf) – a small star

E

echo (ĕk′ō) – a repeated sound caused by the reflection of sound waves

editorial (ĕd′ĭ tôr′ē əl) – a newspaper, magazine, radio, or television statement that expresses the opinion of the editor, publisher, or station

electromagnetic (ĭ lĕk′trō măg nĕt′ĭk) – having magnetism that is produced by an electric current

eloquent (ĕl′ə kwənt) – speaking fluently and powerfully

emerge (ĭ mûrj′) – to come up or out from; to come into view

endowment (ĕn dou′mənt) – money in an account that provides a permanent income to a person or institution

endure (ĕn dŏor′) – to suffer through, or bear pain or difficulty, with patience

ensure (ĕn shŏor′) – to make sure or certain

entitle (ĕn tīt′l) – to give a right to

entrance (ĕn trăns′) – to fill with delight, wonder, or enchantment

entry (ĕn′trē) – an item written into a diary or other record

esophagus (ĭ sŏf′ə gəs) – the tube from the mouth to the stomach

eventual (ĭ vĕn′chŏo əl) – coming at an unspecified time in the future

exploit (ĕk′sploit) – to take the fullest possible advantage of

extend (ĭk stĕnd′) – to make longer in space or time

extinct (ĭk stĭngkt′) – no longer existing or living

extract (ĭk străkt′) – to take or pull out by force or effort, or by chemical or mechanical means

F

far-fetched (fär′fĕcht′) – hard to believe; improbable

fateful (fāt′fəl) – greatly affecting things in the future

fatigue (fə tēg′) – tiredness

flannel (flăn′əl) – a soft, loosely woven fabric

flare (flâr) – a sudden outburst of flame

flicker (flĭk′ər) – to move, shine, or burn unsteadily; to flutter

flimsy (flĭm′zē) – light and thin, not solid or strong

floe (flō) – a sheet of floating ice

fodder (fŏd′ər) – feed for horses and farm animals, especially dried food or hay

foreign (fôr′ĭn) – not in its natural place; coming from outside

found (found) – to set up or establish an organization or institution

frequent (frē′kwənt) – happening or appearing quite often

fugitive (fyŏo′jĭ tĭv) – a person who is running away or escaping from something

function (fŭngk′shən) – the special purpose of something

ă pat / ā pay / âr care / ä father / ĕ pet / ē bee / ĭ pit / ī pie / îr pier /
ŏ pot / ō toe / ô paw / oi noise / ŏo took / ōo boot / ou out / ŭ cut /

fundamental (fŭn'də mĕn'tl)
– being a very important or
essential part of; a foundation

fungi (fŭn'jī) – organisms,
including mushrooms and
molds, that have no leaves,
flowers, or green coloring

G

galaxy (găl'ək sē) – any of the
large independent systems of
stars, gas, and dust in space

galley (găl'ē) – the kitchen on a
ship or aircraft

gasp (găsp) – to struggle for
breath with the mouth open

generate (jĕn'ə rāt) – to produce
or bring into existence

glimpse (glĭmps) – a brief,
incomplete view or look

greedy (grē'dē) – having an
extreme desire to possess
something, often beyond what
one needs

grieve (grēv) – to feel sadness

grim (grĭm) – cheerless; stern

H

hearth (härth) – the floor of a
fireplace and the area in front
of it

heritage (hĕr'ĭ tĭj) – property,
values, or traditions passed on
from earlier generations

hesitate (hĕz'ĭ tāt) – to be slow
to act, speak, or decide

hypothesis (hī pŏth'ĭ sĭs)
– a temporary explanation of
certain facts that can be shown
to be correct or incorrect by
further investigation

I

ignorant (ĭg'nər ənt) – lacking
education or knowledge

image (ĭm'ĭj) – a drawn, reflected,
sculpted, or otherwise visual
copy of someone or something

immediate (ĭ mē'dē ĭt) –
occurring at once

immense (ĭ mĕns') – extremely
large; huge

indebted (ĭn dĕt'ĭd) – having
moral, social, or financial
obligations to another; owing

infinite (ĭn'fə nĭt) – having no
limit or boundaries; endless

install (ĭn stôl') – to set in
position and connect for use

instill (ĭn stĭl') – to give or convey

instrument (ĭn'strə mənt) – a tool
or implement used to do or to
assist work

inter (ĭn tûr') – to bury a body in
a grave or place in a tomb

internal (ĭn tûr'nəl) – of or in the
inside of something

intimate (ĭn'tə mĭt) – marked by
close acquaintance, association,
or familiarity

invalid (ĭn'və lĭd) – someone who
suffers from illness or injury for
a long time

isolate (ī'sə lāt) – to place apart
or alone

K

key (kē) – a crucial element or
piece of information that
provides understanding or
insight into something

L

lack (lăk) – to not have
something; to be without

legend (lĕj'ənd) – a story, which
may or may not be true,
handed down from the past

limitation (lĭm´ĭ tā'shən)
– that which confines or
restricts something; a
shortcoming or defect

literal (lĭt'ər əl) – holding to the
exact or primary meaning of a
word or group of words

fungi

infinite

M

maintain (mān tān′) – to keep in good repair, or to continue

mechanize (měk′ə nīz) – to equip with machines

merchant (mûr′chənt) – someone who buys and sells goods for profit

mineral (mǐn′ər əl) – a solid substance, neither plant nor animal, that occurs naturally in the earth

mitigate (mǐt′ǐgāt) – to make less intense or serious or severe

monarch (mŏn′ərk) – a sole, supreme ruler of a country

motto (mŏt′ō) – a short statement used to express a goal, principle, or ideal

mucus (myo͞o′kəs) – the moist substance that protects the inner surface of hollow organs in the body

multiple (mŭl′tə pəl) – consisting of more than one element

mechanize

N

narrative (năr′ə tǐv) – a spoken or written story or account

native (nā′tǐv) – belonging to a particular place by birth

neglect (nǐ glěkt′) – failure to do, pay attention to, or take care of properly

network (nět′wûrk) – an arrangement of lines or channels that cross or interconnect

notion (nō′shən) – an idea, belief, or opinion

O

obedient (ō bē′dē ənt) – dutifully following orders or instructions

occupy (ŏk′yə pī) – to dwell or reside in, or to have possession of by settling in or conquering

parchment

offensive (ə fěn′sǐv) – an attitude or position of attack

oppose (ə pōz′) – to resist, argue, or fight against

organism (ôr′gə nǐz′əm) – an individual form of life, such as an animal, plant or bacterium

P

parchment (pärch′mənt) – a paperlike material made from animal skins, or a kind of paper resembling this

parka (pär′kə) – a hooded jacket for use in cold weather

partake (pär tāk′) – to participate in or to take a part of, as food

particular (pər tǐk′yə lər) – of or relating to a specific person or thing

patriot (pā′trē ət) – a person who loves, supports, and defends his or her country

pension (pěn′shən) – a sum of money paid regularly from a former employer after retirement

persist (pər sǐst′) – to continue firmly; to continue to exist

persuasive (pər swā′sǐv) – able to convince a person to do or believe something by reasoning, urging, or pleading

photosynthesis (fō′tō sǐn′thǐ sǐs) – the process by which green plants use energy from sunlight to convert carbon dioxide (from the air) and water into carbohydrates, usually releasing oxygen

physical (fǐz′ǐ kəl) – of or related to material things

pierce (pîrs) – to cut into or through as if with a sharp instrument

plod (plŏd) – to move or walk heavily and slowly

ă pat / ā pay / âr care / ä father / ě pet / ē bee / ǐ pit / ī pie / îr pier /
ŏ pot / ō toe / ô paw / oi noise / o͝o took / o͞o boot / ou out / ŭ cut /

plow (plou) – a farm implement used for working the soil and cutting furrows before planting

pluck (plŭk) – using the fingers to pull or pick off or out

port (pôrt) – a harbor or place on a waterway where ships can be loaded and unloaded

prejudice (prĕj′ə dĭs) – a negative judgment or opinion formed beforehand or without knowledge of the facts, especially against another race or religion

presence (prĕz′əns) – being or existing in a place, or having influence by placing troops or representatives there

primitive (prĭm′ĭ tĭv) – simple or crude; at an early stage of development

priority (prī ôr′ĭ tē) – something considered more important than other things or considerations

probe (prōb) – a device that explores and gains information on something unknown

progeny (prŏj′ə nē) – offspring or descendants

proposal (prə pō′zəl) – something put forward to be considered, discussed, or adopted

prosperous (prŏs′pər əs) – successful and well-to-do

puncture (pŭngk′chər) – a small hole made by something sharp and pointed

purify (pyŏŏr′ə fī) – to cleanse or get rid of things that don't belong

R

radiation (rā′ dē ā′shən) – the sending out of energy in the form of rays, waves, or particles

rage (rāj) –furious and violent intensity; a fad or fashion craze

ravenous (răv′ə nəs) – very hungry or greedy

reason (rē′zən) – a motive or cause of something; the ability to think and come to conclusions

rebel (rĕb′əl) – a person who fights against an established government or authority

recover (rĭ kŭv′ər) – to return to or regain a normal condition

recreation (rĕk′rē ā′shən) – a way to refresh and entertain oneself

recruit (rĭ krōōt′) – to enroll or enlist members

reduce (rĭ dōōs′) – to make or become less; to decrease

refine (rĭ fīn′) – to remove impurities or defects from

reject (rĭ jĕkt′) – to refuse to accept or consider or grant

relent (rĭ lĕnt′) – to abandon one's harsh intentions and become more lenient or forgiving

relieve (rĭ lēv′) – to ease by reducing pain, or worry, or a burden

reminisce (rĕm ə nĭs′) – to think or talk about past events and experiences

represent (rĕp rĭ zĕnt′) – to stand in or be a spokesperson for someone or something

reservation (rĕz′ər vā′shən) – an area of land set aside for the use of an American Indian group

respire (rĭ spīr′) – to breathe in and out; to go through the process by which an organism exchanges gases such as oxygen with its environment

resource (rē′sôrs) – an available supply that can be used when needed

port

recreation

ûr firm / hw which / th thin / *th* this / zh vision /
ə about, item, edible, gallop, circus

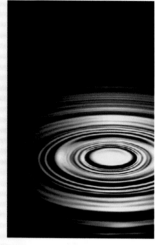

ripple

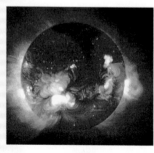

solar

response (rĭ spŏns′) – a reply or reaction

restore (rĭ stôr′) – to bring back to a former, normal, or original condition

retire (rĭ tīr′) – to give up one's regular work because of advancing age

revolt (rĭ vōlt′) – to refuse to accept, or to try to overthrow, authority; or the act of doing so

right (rīt) – something that is due to a person by law, tradition, or fair treatment

ripple (rĭp′əl) – to move like a small wave or series of waves

rival (rī′vəl) – a person or thing competing with another

rustle (rŭs′əl) – a soft crackling sound, like that of paper being crumpled

scarce (skârs) – hard to find or in short supply

scowl (skoul) – to make an angry or disapproving frown

scramble (skrăm′bəl) – to struggle frantically in order to get something or do something

shoal (shōl) – a shallow place or underwater sandbank

shrewd (shro͞od) – having sharp awareness and good sense

shrivel (shrĭv′əl) – to shrink and wrinkle from great heat or cold, or from lack of moisture

shudder (shŭd′ər) – to make a strong shaking movement

significant (sĭg nĭf′ĭ kənt) – having great importance

slight (slīt) – small in size, degree, or amount

sly (slī) – playful and knowing

solar (sō′lər) – of or relating to or proceeding from the Sun

solution (sə lo͞o′shən) – a liquid in which something is dissolved

sow (sō) – to plant or scatter seeds for growing

species (spē′shēz) – a basic category of related organisms that resemble one another and are able to breed among themselves

spectator (spĕk′tā tər) – a person who watches a game, show, or other event

spirit (spĭr′ĭt) – the animating or life force within living beings

stall (stôl) – to stop suddenly due to loss of power

stock (stŏk) – a group or quantity of closely related organisms in a breed or species

stream (strēm) – to flow or pour forth steadily, as a current of water or beam of light

sufficient (sə fĭsh′ənt) – as much as is needed; enough

suite (swēt) – a group of connected rooms that are occupied together

survey (sər vā′) – to look at and take a general view of

swept (swĕpt) – passed or moved smoothly and quickly

symptom (sĭm′təm) – a sign or change that indicates the existence of a disease or condition, especially a change from what is normal

system (sĭs′təm) – a set of connected parts that form a whole or work together

T

talcum (tăl′kəm) – a soft, smooth powder made of the mineral talc, used to keep things dry or moving smoothly

terrain (tə rān′) – the surface features of a stretch of land

thatch (thăch) – a roof made of straw, reeds, or palm leaves

ă pat / ā pay / âr care / ä father / ĕ pet / ē bee / ĭ pit / ī pie / îr pier /
ŏ pot / ō toe / ô paw / oi noise / o͝o took / o͞o boot / ou out / ŭ cut /

thrust (thrŭst) – a strong forward force or push

toil (toil) – to work hard

torture (tôr′chər) – the inflicting of severe and extreme physical or mental pain

trade (trād) – to exchange goods for money or other goods; a business

traitor (trā′tər) – a person who is disloyal to, or betrays, his country

transport (trăns pôrt′) – to carry from one place to another

treaty (trē′tē) – a formal agreement between two or more countries

trudge (trŭj) – to walk with great effort in a heavy footed way

typhoid (tī′foid) – a serious infection caused by bacteria taken into the body through food or drink

U

unity (yōō′nĭ tē) – the condition of being one, or in agreement

upstanding (ŭp stăn′dĭng) – honest; respected

urgent (ûr′jənt) – needing immediate attention or action

V

vast (văst) – very great in area, amount, or size

vent (věnt) – to release or let out through an opening

version (vûr′zhən) – a special form or variation of something

vial (vī′əl) – a small bottle, especially for liquid medicine

vigorously (vĭg′ər əs lē) – strongly, energetically, actively, and forcefully

violate (vī′ə lāt) – to break or act against something such as a law, promise, rule, or treaty

visible (vĭz′ə bəl) – able to be seen, apparent to the eye

volume (vŏl′yōōm) – a book

vow (vou) – a solemn or strong promise, or to make a solemn promise

W

wake (wāk) – the visible track or currents left on water's surface by a boat or ship

waste (wāst) – leftover or useless byproducts of a process such as digestion

weave (wēv) – to make something, such as cloth or rope, by interlacing strands or strips of material

workmanship (wûrk′mən shĭp) – a craftsperson's skill, as shown by the quality of something produced

worship (wûr′shĭp) – to give love and devotion to a sacred being or object through prayers and other rituals

vial

wake

ûr firm / hw which / th thin / *th* this / zh vision / ə about, item, edible, gallop, circus

Acknowledgments

"Lineage" by Margaret Walker from *Poetry from the Masters,* edited by Wade Hudson. Text copyright © 2003 by Wade Hudson. Reprinted by permission of Just Us Books, Inc. All rights reserved.

"Night Chant" from *Racing the Sun* by Paul Pitts. Copyright © 1988 by Paul Pitts. Reprinted by permission of HarperCollins Children's Books, a division of HarperCollins Publishers, Inc. All rights reserved.

"Preparing for the Fiesta" from *The Corn Grows Ripe* by Dorothy Rhoads, illustrated by Jean Charlot. Copyright © 1956 by Dorothy Rhoads and Jean Charlot. Copyright renewed © 1984 by Dorothy Charlot. Reprinted by permission of Puffin Books, a Division of Penguin Young Readers Group, a Member of Penguin Group (USA) Inc., 345 Hudson Street, New York, NY 10014. All rights reserved.

"Untitled" by Shawnetaiye Wynett Duboise. Originally appeared in *When the Rain Sings.* Copyright © 1999 by Shawnetaiye Wynett Duboise. Reprinted by permission of Simon & Schuster Children's Publishing, a division of Simon & Schuster Inc. and the National Museum of the American Indian of the Smithsonian Institution.

"Walkers with the Dawn" by Langston Hughes, illustrated by Benny Andrews. Copyright © 1994 by the Estate of Langston Hughes. Reprinted by permission of Random House Children's Books, a division of Random House, Inc.

"The Train of the Stars" by Abdul-Raheem Saleh al-Raheem. Copyright © 1990 by Abdul-Raheem Saleh al-Raheem. Reprinted by permission of Naomi Shihab Nye.

"Youth" from *The Collected Poems of Langston Hughes* by Langston Hughes, edited by Arnold Ramperstad with David Roessel, Associate Editor. Copyright © 1994 by the Estate of Langston Hughes. Reprinted by permission of Alfred A. Knopf, a division of Random House, Inc.

"Crossing in Darkness" from *Friend on Freedom River* by Gloria Whelan, illustrated by Gijsbert van Frankenhuyzen. Copyright © 2004 by Thomson Gale, a part of Thomson Corporation. Text copyright © 2004 by Gloria Whelan. Illustrations copyright © 2004 by Gijsbert van Frankenhuyzen. Reprinted by permission of Thomson Corporation.

"The Train Ride" from *Peacebound Trains* by Haemi Balgassi, illustrated by Chris K. Soentpiet. Text copyright © 1996 by Haemi Balgassi. Illustrations copyright © 1996 by Chris K. Soentpiet. Reprinted by permission of Houghton Mifflin Harcourt Publishing Company.

Early Thunder by Jean Fritz, illustrated by Lynd Ward. Text copyright © 1967, 1995 by Jean Fritz. All rights reserved. Reprinted by permission of G. P. Putnam's Sons, A Division of Penguin Young Readers Group, a Member of Penguin Group (USA), Inc., 345 Hudson Street, New York, NY 10014. All rights reserved.

"Digging for China" by Richard Wilbur from *A Green Place: Modern Poems* compiled by William Jay Smith. Copyright © 1956 by Richard Wilbur. Reprinted by permission of Houghton Mifflin Harcourt Publishing Company.

"There Isn't Time!" by Eleanor Farjeon, illustrated by Peter Bailey, from *The Oxford Book of Children's Poetry*, edited by Michael Harrison and Christopher Stuart-Clark. Copyright © by Eleanor Farjeon. Illustrations copyright © 2007 by Peter Bailey. Reprinted by permission of David Hingham Associates Limited.

"To Dark Eyes Dreaming" by Zilpha Keatley Snyder. Copyright © 1969 by Zilpha Keatley Snyder. Reprinted by permission of the author.

The Honorable Prison by Lyll Becerra de Jenkins. Copyright © 1988 by Lyll Becerra de Jenkins. Reprinted by permission of Penguin Group (USA) Inc.

Coast to Coast with Alice by Patricia Rush Hyatt. Copyright © 1995 by Carolrhoda Books, Inc. Reprinted by permission of Carolrhoda Books, a division of Lerner Publishing Group, Inc. All rights reserved. No part of this excerpt may be used or reproduced in any manner whatsoever without the prior written permission of Lerner Publishing Group, Inc.

The Lamp, the Ice, and a Boat Called Fish by Jacqueline Briggs Martin, illustrated by Beth Krommes. Text copyright © 2001 by Jaqueline Briggs Martin. Illustrations and illustrator's note copyright © 2001 by Beth Krommes. Reprinted by permission of Houghton Mifflin Harcourt Publishing Company.

"The Horned Toad" by Gerald Haslam. Copyright © 1983 by Gerald Haslam. Reprinted by permission of the author.

"Only Daughter" by Sandra Cisneros, first published in *Glamour,* November 1990. Copyright © 1990 by Sandra Cisneros. Reprinted by permission of Simon & Schuster.

"An Hour with Abuelo" from *An Island Like You* by Judith Ortiz Cofer. Copyright © 1995 by Judith Ortiz Cofer. Reprinted by permission of Puffin Books, a division of Penguin Group (USA) Inc. All rights reserved.

"Quintrain" by Sa'id 'Aql, translated by Mansour Ajami. Copyright © 1998 by Naomi Shihab Nye. All rights reserved. Reprinted by permission of Simon & Schuster Books for Young Readers, an imprint of Simon & Schuster Children's Publishing Division.

"River" by Shuntaro Tanikawa, translated by Harold Wright (North Point). Copyright © 1983 by Harold Wright. Translated by arrangement with Shuntaro Tanikawa. Reprinted by permission of Harold Wright.

"Granizo" by Leroy Quintana. Copyright © 1990 by Leroy Quintana. Reprinted by permission of the author and Chronicle Books, LLC.

xiii (skyline) © Chad Ehlers/Alamy. xiii (seaweed) © Alex L. Fradkin/PhotoDisc. xiii (cow) © Digital Vision. xiii (wheel) © Comstock. xiii (stagecoach) © Dynamic Graphics. xiii (weaving) © Joy Tessman/National Geographic/Getty Images. xiii (terracotta pot) © Stockbyte. xiii (barn) © EyeWire Collection/PhotoDisc. xiv (map) © Bildarchiv Preussischer Kulturbesitz/Art Resource, NY. xiv (tobacco plant) © Bettmann/Corbis. xiv (mission) © Scenics of America/PhotoLink/PhotoDisc. xiv (green circuit) © PhotoLink/PhotoDisc. xiv (red circuit) © PhotoLink/PhotoDisc. xiv (frog) © Artville. xiv (strawberry plant) © Artville. xv (planets) © PhotoDisc. xv (stars) © PhotoDisc. xv (tea party) © Private Collection/The Bridgeman Art Library. xv (lantern) © Stockbyte. xv (flag) © Collection of the New-York Historical Society/The Bridgeman Art Library. xvi (smokestack) © Michael Prince/Corbis. xvi (nest) © CMCD, Inc./PhotoDisc. xvi (ferret) © CMCD, Inc./PhotoDisc. xvi (crab) © AP Photo/California Department of Fish and Game. xvi (Great Wall China) © Ed Freeman/Stone/Getty/Images. xvi (protest) © AP Photo. xvi (typewriter) © C Squared Studios/PhotoDisc. xvii (observatory) © Roger Ressmeyer/Corbis. xvii (rover) © NASA Jet Propulsion Laboratory (NASA-JPL). xvii (television set) © CMCD, Inc./PhotoDisc. xvii (Apollo recovery) © NASA Headquarters - GReatest Images of NASA (NASA-HQ-GRIN). xvii (space shuttle) © Stockbyte. xvii (hands) © Raechel Running/Solus-Veer/Corbis. xvii (seedling) © Shutterstock. xvii (tamales) © Getty Images. 2-3 © Chad Ehlers/Alamy. 4 © PhotoDisc. 5 © HMHCo. 5 (br) © Jack Hollingsworth/PhotoDisc. 6 (tr) © CMCD, Inc./PhotoDisc. 7 (cl) © CMCD, Inc./PhotoDisc. 8 © Ron Goebel. 9 © Ron Goebel. 10-1 © Bettmann/Corbis. 12 © Natalie Fobes/Corbis. 13 (tl) © Alex L. Fradkin/PhotoDisc. 13 (tr) © Stockbyte. 14-5 © Kim Westerskov/Alamy. 15 (br) © Comstock. 17 © James Cavallini/Photo Researchers, Inc. 18-9 © James Cavallini/Photo Researchers, Inc. 20 (bl) © PhotoDisc. 20-1 (b) © Corbis. 22-3 © Sean Justice/Corbis. 24 © Comstock. 25 (tr) © Digital Vision. 25 (br) © Shutterstock. 26-7 © Dynamic Graphics. 28 (c) © Stockbyte. 28 (b) © PhotoDisc. 29 (t) © Comstock. 29 (c) © Glen Allison/PhotoDisc. 29 (b) © S. Meltzer/PhotoLink/PhotoDisc. 32 © Joy Tessman/National Geographic/Getty Images. 33 © Brand X Pictures. 34 (t) © Getty Images. 34 (cr) © EyeWire Collection/PhotoDisc. 34 (bl) © Comstock. 34 (br) © Stockbyte. 35 (sheep) © Neil Beer/PhotoDisc. 35 (bucket) © Getty Images. 35 (car) © Shutterstock. 35 (bl) © Siede Preis/PhotoDisc. 35 (tr) © Shutterstock. 36 © EyeWire Collection/PhotoDisc. 37 © Getty Images. 40 (l) © PhotoDisc. 40 (b) © Corbis. 41 © Barry Lewis/Corbis. 42 © David Muench/Corbis. 43 © PhotoDisc. 45-9 (r) © Getty Images. 50-1 © Bildarchiv Preussischer Kulturbesitz/Art Resource, NY. 52 (c) © EyeWire. 52 (b) © CMCD, Inc./PhotoDisc. 53 (t) © PhotoLink/PhotoDisc. 53 (c) © Comstock. 53 (b) © C. McIntyre/

PhotoLink/PhotoDisc. 56 © Bettmann/Corbis. 57 © PIO Images. 58 © Delaware Art Museum, Wilmington, USA, Howard Pyle Collection/Bridgeman Art Library. 60 © HMHCo. 61 © HMHCo. 64-5 © Delaware Art Museum, Wilmington, USA, Howard Pyle Collection/Bridgeman Art Library. 65 (tr) © Bettmann/Corbis. 66 © PoodlesRock/Corbis. 67 © Bettmann/Corbis. 68-9 © Digital Stock. 70 © EyeWire. 71 © C Squared Studios/PhotoDisc. 72 © Scenics of America/PhotoLink/PhotoDisc. 73 © Giraudon/Art Resource, NY. 74 © HMHCo. 75 © The Print Collector/Alamy. 76 (t) © Comstock. 76 (b) © Comstock. 77 © Getty Images. 78-9 (t) © PhotoLink/PhotoDisc. 78-9 (b) © PhotoLink/PhotoDisc. 80 (c) © C Squared Studios/PhotoDisc. 80 (b) © Getty Images. 81 (t) © C Squared Studios/PhotoDisc. 81 (c) © Shutterstock. 81 (b) © Steve Cole/PhotoDisc. 84 © Siede Preis/PhotoDisc. 84-5 (ivy frame) © C Squared Studios/PhotoDisc. 85 (tl) © Artville. 85 (tr) © Artville. 86 © Jean-Paul Joubert/Photo Researchers, Inc. 88 (alfalfa) © AGStockUSA, Inc./Alamy. 88 (avocado) © Iconotec. 88 (corn field) © EyeWire Collection/PhotoDisc. 88 (corn) © Stockbyte. 88 (cow) © PhotoDisc. 88 (tree) © Shutterstock. 88 (wheat field) © Robert Glusic/PhotoDisc. 88 (wheat sheaf) © Artville. 88 chicken © G.K. & Vikki Hart/PhotoDisc. 89 (burrito) © Artville. 89 (cheese) © Stockbyte. 89 (cooked chicken) © Artville. 89 (flour) © Image Ideas. 89 (guacamole) © Artville. 89 (milk) © Artville. 89 (tortillas) © Kari Marttila/Alamy. 93 © MedicalRF.com/Alamy. 94 © Jean-Paul Joubert/Photo Researchers, Inc. 95 © Nucleus Medical Art, Inc./Alamy. 96-7 © Susumu Nishinaga/Photo Reseachers, Inc. 98 (basket) © Jules Frazier/Photodisc/Getty Images. 98-9 (t) © Bruce Heinemann/PhotoDisc. 99 (corn) © Artville. 100 © Artville. 101 (t) © Image Ideas. 101 (c) © Lester Lefkowitz/Corbis. 102 (t) © Sven Nackstrand/AFP/Getty Images). 102 (bl) © Artville. 102 (bc) © PhotoDisc. 102 (br) © Artville. 103 (t) © PHOTOTAKE Inc./Alamy. 103 (br) © PHOTOTAKE Inc./Alamy. 104 © Randy Allbritton/PhotoDisc. 105 (tr) © Thomas Brummett/PhotoDisc. 105 (c) © C Squared Studios/PhotoDisc. 106-7 © PhotoDisc. 108 (c) © PhotoLink/PhotoDisc. 108 (b) © Digital Vision. 109 (t) © Lawrence Lawry/PhotoDisc. 109 (c) © John Wang/PhotoDisc. 109 (b) © PhotoLink/PhotoDisc. 113 (b) © Brand X Pictures. 113 (t) © PhotoDisc. 117 © PhotoDisc. 118 © PhotoDisc. 120 (br) © PhotoDisc. 136-7 © Private Collection/The Bridgeman Art Library. 138 (c) © HMHCo. 138 (b) © PhotoDisc. 139 (t) © Stockbyte. 139 (c) © EyeWire. 139 (b) © EyeWire. 144 (tr) © Bristol City Museum and Art Gallery, UK/The Bridgeman Art Library. 145 © Library of Congress. 146 (tr) © Bristol City Museum and Art Gallery, UK/The Bridgeman Art Library. 146 (c) © PhotoDisc. 147 Library of Congress. 150-1 (t) © Dmitri Kessel/Time & Life Pictures/Getty Images. 150-1 (b) © Stockbyte. 152 (c) © Stockbyte. 152 (b) © Bettmann/Corbis. 153 (t) Library of Congress. 153 (cr) © PhotoDisc. 154 © Chateau de Versailles, France, Giraudon/The Bridgeman Art Library. 155 © Kunsthistorisches Museum, Vienna, Austria/The Bridgeman Art Library. 156 (bl) © Collection of the New-

York Historical Society/The Bridgeman Art Library. 156 (br) © Collection of the New-York Historical Society/The Bridgeman Art Library. 157 (tl) © Corbis. 157 (tr) © Comstock. 159 © Bettmann/Corbis. 160 © Bettmann/Corbis. 161 © North Wind Picture Archives. 162 © Private Collection/The Bridgeman Art Library. 163 © Schomburg Center for Research in Black Culture, The New York Public Library, New York/Art Resource, NY. 164 © Art Resource, NY. 165 © Massachusetts Historical Society, Boston, MA/The Bridgeman Art Library. 166-167 © Michael Prince/Corbis. 168 (t) © Alamy. 168 (b) © AP Photo/California Department of Fish and Game. 169 (t) © Corbis. 169 (c) © Getty Images. 169 (b) © CMCD, Inc./PhotoDisc. 172 © Shutterstock. 173 © BLOOMImage /Getty Images. 174 © Rick & Nora Bowers/Alamy. 175 © CMCD, Inc./PhotoDisc. 177 © AP Photo/Texas Cooperative Extension, Jerrold Summerlin. 178-9 © AP Photo/California Department of Fish and Game. 178-9 (b) © Siede Preis/PhotoDisc. 182 (t) © Dave Thompson/LifeFile/PhotoDisc. 182 (cr) © HMHCo. 183 © Matthieu Paley/Corbis. 183 (cr) © Artville. 184 (t) © AP Photo/Dolores Ochoa. 184 (b) © HMHCo. 185 © Getty Images. 186 © Corbis. 187 (c) © CMCD, Inc./PhotoDisc. 187 (b) © Brand X Pictures. 188 © David Fleetham/Taxi/Getty Images. 189 © S. Alden/PhotoLink/PhotoDisc. 190 © Robert Glusic/PhotoDisc. 191 © Peter Johnson/Corbis. 192 © CMCD, Inc./PhotoDisc. 193 © Rick & Nora Bowers/Alamy. 194-5 © Ed Freeman/Stone/Getty/Images. 196 (c) © Hans Weisenhoffer/PhotoDisc. 196 (b) © Jack Hollingsworth/PhotoDisc. 197 (t) © Hans Weisenhoffer/PhotoDisc. 197 (c) © Image Farm. 197 (b) © Stockbyte. 200 (t) © CMCD, Inc./PhotoDisc. 200 (cl) © Cartesia/PhotoDisc Imaging. 200 (b) © Comstock. 200-1 (bkgd) © Albert J. Copley/PhotoDisc. 203 © AP Photo. 204 (tl) © CMCD, Inc./PhotoDisc. 204 (pad) © CMCD, Inc./PhotoDisc. 204 (r) © CMCD, Inc./PhotoDisc. 205 (t) © AP Photo. 205 (cr) © Comstock. 206 (bl) © Comstock. 206 (br) © Luis Acosta/AFP/Getty Images. 207 (b) © C Squared Studios/PhotoDisc. 208 © Comstock. 209 (image) © AP Photo/Fernando Llano. 209 (tv set) © CMCD, Inc./PhotoDisc. 212 (cow) © CMCD, Inc./PhotoDisc. 212 (tl) © J. Luke/PhotoLink/PhotoDisc. 213 © Car Culture/Corbis. 213 (br) © Artville. 214 (c) © Robert Glusic/PhotoDisc. 214 (bl) © CMCD, Inc./PhotoDisc. 214 (rope) © Brand X Pictures. 215 (farm) © Scenics of America/PhotoLink/PhotoDisc. 215 (frame) © Image Farm. 216 (telegrams) © Comstock. 216 (fields) © PhotoLink/PhotoDisc. 216 (frame) © Shutterstock. 216 (bl) © Comstock. 217 (frame) © Ryan McVay/PhotoDisc. 217 (horses) © Shutterstock. 224-5 © Roger Ressmeyer/Corbis. 226 (t) © Artville. 226 (b) © Stockbyte. 227 (t) © PhotoDisc. 227 (c) © Shutterstock. 227 (b) © PhotoDisc. 230 © NASA. 230-1 (t, b) © Image Ideas. 231 © NASA. 231 (t) © PhotoDisc. 232 (c) © Bettmann/Corbis. 234 © Brand X Pictures. 235 (c) © PhotoDisc. 235 (b) © Gustavo Tomsich/Corbis. 236 © NASA Jet Propulsion Laboratory (NASA-JPL). 237 (t) © NASA Johnson Space Center - Earth Sciences and Image Analysis (NASA-JSC-ES&IA). 237 (c) © NASA Jet Propulsion Laboratory (NASA-JPL). 237 (b) © PhotoDisc. 240 (t) © PhotoDisc. 240 (b) © Thomas Brummett/PhotoDisc. 241 (t) © PhotoDisc. 241 (c) © PhotoDisc. 241 (saturn) © PhotoDisc. 241 (b) © PhotoDisc. 242 © PhotoDisc. 243 (tr) © PhotoDisc. 243 (c) © Bettmann/Corbis. 244 (tl) © NASA Johnson Space Center (NASA-JSC). 244 (tr) © NASA Johnson Space Center (NASA-JSC). 244 (b) © NASA Johnson Space Center (NASA-JSC). 245 (tr) © PhotoDisc. 245 (c) © NASA Johnson Space Center (NASA-JSC). 245 (b) © NASA Headquarters - GReatest Images of NASA (NASA-HQ-GRIN). 245 (tv set) © CMCD/PhotoDisc. 246 (t) © NASA. 246 (moon) © Shutterstock. 247 © Shutterstock. 248 © NASA Jet Propulsion Laboratory (NASA-JPL. 249 (tl) © PhotoDisc. 249 (tc) © PhotoDisc. 250 (tl) © NASA Glenn Research Center (NASA-GRC). 250 (c) © NTV/Handout/epa/Corbis. 251 © Getty Images. 252-3 © Raechel Running/Solus-Veer/Corbis. 254 (t) © Artville. 254 (c) © Brand X Pictures. 255 (t) © EyeWire Collection/PhotoDisc. 255 (c) © Shutterstock. 255 (b) © CMCD, Inc./PhotoDisc. 258 © Robert Glusic/PhotoDisc. 259 (insets) © Don Farrall, LightWorks Studio/PhotoDisc. 259 (l) © Stockbyte. 259 (r) © Stockbyte. 260 © CMCD, Inc./PhotoDisc. 261 (c) © Siede Preis/PhotoDisc. 261 (br) © Susanna Bennett/Alamy. 262 (l) © Alamy. 262 (b) © EyeWire. 262 (pepper) © PhotoDisc. 262 (rings) © Steve Cole/PhotoDisc. 264 © CMCD, Inc./PhotoDisc. 265 (tr) © Brand X Pictures. 265 (bl) © Getty Images. 268 (t) © Forrest Smyth/Alamy. 268 (b) © Artville. 269 (br) © Scenics of America/PhotoLink/PhotoDisc. 269 (cr) © Comstock. 270 © CMCD, Inc./PhotoDisc. 271 (c) © Siede Preis/PhotoDisc. 271 (br) © Susanna Bennett/Alamy. 272 (cr) © PhotoDisc. 272 (bc) © C Squared Studios/PhotoDisc. 272 (br) © Corbis. 273 © Thomas Brummett/PhotoDisc. 274 © Artville. 274 (t) © HMHCo. 275 (tr) © Bettmann/Corbis. 275 (purple) © HMHCo. 275 (b) © HMHCo. 275 (peg board) © HMHCo. 276 (b) © Comstock. 276 (t) © HMHCo. 277 © Brand X Pictures. 278 (bl) © PhotoDisc. 278 (t) © Robert Fried/Alamy. 279 (b) © CMCD, Inc./PhotoDisc. 280 © Digital Stock. 281 (bl) © Getty Images. 281 (br) © Jeremy Woodhouse/PhotoDisc. 282 © F. Schussler/PhotoLink/PhotoDisc. 283 © Shutterstock. 284 (b) © Siede Preis/PhotoDisc. 284 (br) © Artville. 285 © PhotoDisc. 286 © PhotoDisc. 287 © Digital Stock. Glos 2 (t) © EyeWire/PhotoDisc. Glos 2 (b) © Steve Cole/PhotoDisc. Glos 3 (t) © HMHCo. Glos 3 (b) © Brand X Pictures. Glos 4 (t) © HMHCo. Glos 4 (b) © Juice Drops. Glos 5 (t) © Corbis. Glos 5 (b) © Albert J. Copley/PhotoDisc. Glos 6 (t) © EyeWire Collection/PhotoDisc. Glos 6 (b) © Ed McDonald Photography/HMHCo. Glos 7 (t) © Kim Steele /PhotoDisc. Glos 7 (b) © Shutterstock. Glos 8 (t) © Don Farrall, LightWorks Studio/PhotoDisc. Glos 8 (b) © PhotoDisc. Glos 9 (t) © Nancy R. Cohen/PhotoDisc. Glos 9 (b) © Ryan McVay /PhotoDisc.